THE ARCHAEOLOGY
OF THE
LAND OF ISRAEL

THE ARCHAEOLOGY
OF THE
LAND OF ISRAEL

From the Prehistoric Beginnings
to the End of the First Temple Period

by
YOHANAN AHARONI

Edited by Miriam Aharoni

SCM PRESS LTD

Translated by Anson F. Rainey from the Hebrew

הארכיאולוגיה של ארץ-ישראל

© 1978 "Shikmona" Publishing Company
Limited, Jerusalem
Translation © 1982 Anson F. Rainey

Scripture quotations from the Revised Standard
Version of the Bible are copyrighted 1946, 1952,
© 1971, 1973 by the Division of Christian Education of the National Council of the Churches of
Christ in the U.S.A., and are used by permission.

334 00018 1
First published in Great Britain 1982
by SCM Press Ltd
58 Bloomsbury Street   London   WC1
Printed in the United States of America

CONTENTS

CONTENTS

LIST OF ILLUSTRATIONS

FIGURES

vii

PLATES

PHOTOGRAPHS

TRANSLATOR'S PREFACE

A TRANSLATION of the present work into English needs no apology. The contributions of Yohanan Aharoni to the archaeology of his native land are well known both in Israel and abroad and this summation of his final interpretations will be welcomed by everyone in the field. The book should be extremely useful as an introductory textbook, and will give student and specialist alike an awareness of the achievements that resulted from the work of Aharoni and his closest disciples.

Throughout the book we have usually used the term Eretz-Israel, or the Land of Israel. By this is meant the total area inhabited by the Israelite people, corresponding most closely to the territory governed by David and Solomon. Aharoni has demonstrated its legitimacy as a geographical entity throughout most of the biblical period. Although it is something of an anachronism for the prehistoric and Canaanite eras, the reader will find it no less so than the commonly accepted Palestine. Eretz-Israel is perhaps the only nonpolitical term in use today, except perhaps for Canaan, which does not represent precisely the territory dealt with in the Israelite period.

In other place names, no attempt at uniformity has been made. Sites are generally referred to by the name most commonly found in the archaeological literature. A few places that have both Arabic and Modern Hebrew names will be found cross-referenced in the index. Wherever a site is widely known by its biblical name, that has been preferred, with spelling of the standard Bible versions. Arabic and Modern Hebrew names are given in a standard transcription but with a minimum of diacritical marks. The uninitiated reader may be puzzled by such variants as Tell (from Arabic) and Tel (from Modern Hebrew) or Beth- (Biblical English), Bet- (Modern Hebrew) and Beit (Arabic). However,

xiii

this is not a work on historical geography; the main point is to facilitate further reading about the various sites in the professional literature.

A word of thanks is due to Mrs. Miriam Aharoni for entrusting me with the task of translation. It was a privilege once again to pore over the words, to enter into the thoughts of Yohanan Aharoni. It is my hope that the book will bring him some increased measure of the recognition he has long deserved. His patience and integrity in the quest for truth, and his love of his land and people, are a part of his legacy to us his colleagues, and to me personally.

ANSON F. RAINEY

FOREWORD

SOME years ago Dr. Reuven Hecht suggested to Professor Yohanan Aharoni that he write a book on "The Archaeology of Eretz-Israel." After considering the matter, Professor Aharoni agreed to this proposal.

In its form, the book resembles that of W. F. Albright's *The Archaeology of Palestine*, written about thirty years ago, but in many respects it differs from all others on this subject. The author was privileged to write this book, but he did not live to see it published.

The author presents here the results of the investigations conducted in all the fields of the archaeology of Eretz-Israel until a short time before his death. The book has a brief geographical introduction dealing with the place of Eretz-Israel in the framework of the ancient Near East, sections on prehistory and the protohistoric Chalcolithic period, three chapters on the Bronze (Canaanite) Age and three on the Iron Age (Israelite period).

Since Albright wrote his book, there have been many new discoveries about every period treated, and methods of research have been greatly refined. New concepts have crystallized in the light of excavations in the country conducted by young scholars, many of whom are Aharoni's disciples. Many of the contributions of this new generation of Israeli archaeologists are presented here for the first time to a wider audience.

The main body of the book consists of the chapters on the Israelite period. Here we find new ideas which have not yet been presented in scholarly publications, since this was the age which Aharoni himself was investigating as historian, biblical scholar, and archaeologist. He gave special attention to the period of the formation of the Israelite people in its land, a subject in which he had a very deep personal interest. For the last fifteen years of his life, Aharoni was engaged in researches and excavations in the Negeb at Arad, Masos, and Beer-sheba. In the light of the results, he formulated ideas concerning the nature of the Israelite conquest and the form of its settlement in the Negeb.

Among other things, this book contains Aharoni's concept of the settlement by the Philistines—the date of their penetration into the country and their subsequent territorial expansion.

There is no doubt that certain ideas expressed in this book will arouse controversy among scholars. Many will not agree with Aharoni's ideas, which to some extent conflict with the scholarly "consensus." From the beginning of his career, however, it was always his practice to disregard the majority opinion when he believed in some new idea based on actual finds in the field. He never hesitated to speak and write what he felt was the correct view.

As intimated above, the book was written in rough draft some months before his death, and therefore it became my responsibility to see it through the press.

I wish to thank Prof. Moshe Kochavi, who helped me with advice. I owe a vote of thanks to Dr. Ram Gophna, who was unceasing in his willingness to answer my many questions, to Prof. Ora Negbi for her help, likewise to Dr. A. Kempinski, to Prof. Opher Bar-Yoseph, who read the chapter on prehistory and made some useful suggestions, to Mrs. Ilana Mozel for her help in preparing the plates of stone tools, to Dr. Z. Herzog and Mr. Moshkovitz for their assistance in preparing the materials for the various plans. Thanks are also due to Mr. A. Hay for photography of the ceramic plates. Also to Mrs. Ora Paran for drawing the plans, to Mrs. Rodica Pinhas for the graphic preparation of the plates with stone tools; to Miss G. Bacci for her assistance with the bibliography. To all of them I give my deepest appreciation.

MIRIAM AHARONI

It is a pleasant obligation to acknowledge those individuals and institutions which granted me permission to publish the following photographs: The Institute of Archaeology, Tel Aviv University, Nos. 1, 4, 12–14, 20, 26–44, 46–52; Dr. B. Rothenberg, Nos. 2, 4A, 22A, 23,

25; Prof. J. Perrot, Nos. 3, 5; Mr. P. Bar-Adon, Mr. Y. Schweig, and the Israel Exploration Society, Nos. 6–8; Mrs. N. Lapp and the W. F. Albright Institute of Archaeological Research, No. 11; the Israel Dept. of Antiquities and Museums of the Ministry of Education and Culture and Mr. D. Allon, Nos. 9–10; Prof. A. Biran, No. 22; Dr. Claire Epstein, No. 19; the Israel Exploration Society and the Antiquities Dept., Nos. 17, 24, 54; Dr. R. Gophna and the Israel Museum, No. 21; R. Gophna and the Institute of Archaeology, Tel Aviv University, No. 15; Dr. Y. Beit-Aryeh, No. 16; Mr. S. Dar, No. 18; Mr. A. Mazar, No. 45; Dr. R. Cleave, No. 53.

Photography was done by Y. Aharoni, A. Glick, A. Hay, D. Haris, Z. Radovan, B. Rothenberg, and Y. Schweig.

PREHISTORIC CHRONOLOGY

Years B.C.E.	Geological Epoch	Glacial Stage (European)	Cultural Phase	Culture in Eretz-Israel
3100				
			Chalcolithic	Ghassulian
4300		Atlantic	—————	Wadi Rabba
	Holocene			Horvat Minha
			Pottery Neolithic	
				Yarmukian
6000				
		Boreal	Pre-Pottery Neolithic	Phase B
8300		Pre-Boreal		Phase A
				Natufian
			Epipaleolithic	Geometric Kebaran
18,000				Kebaran
		Würm		Levantine Aurignacian
	Upper Pleistocene		Upper Paleolithic	Phases I-III
40,000		(Last Pluvial)		Emireh, etc.
			Middle Paleolithic	Mousterian Yabrudian
75,000			—————	
		Riss-Würm		Yabrudian Upper Acheulean
125,000		Riss		
	Middle Pleistocene	Mindel-Riss		
		Mindel	Lower Paleolithic	Middle Acheulean
700,000				Lower Acheulean Oldowan
	Lower Pleistocene	Günz-Mindel		
		Günz		
2,000,000				

ARCHAEOLOGICAL PERIODS
OF ERETZ-ISRAEL

Age	Archaeological Period	Years b.c.e. (Approximate)	Description
Stone Age	Paleolithic	2,000,000 to 16,000	Prehistoric era
	Epipaleolithic	16,000 to 8,300	
	Neolithic	8300 to 4000	
Chalcolithic Age		4000 to 3150	Ghassulian and Beer-sheba cultures; beginning of copper use
Early Canaanite (Early Bronze) Age	EC I	3150 to 2850	Urbanization, trade, culture, religion, art
	EC II	2850 to 2650	
	EC III	2650 to 2350	
	EC IV	2350 to 2200	
Middle Canaanite (Middle Bronze) Age	MC I	2200 to 2000	Seminomadic
	MC IIA	2000 to 1800	Fortified cities, beginning of bronze use
	MC IIB	1800 to 1550	
Late Canaanite (Late Bronze) Age	LC I	1550 to 1400	Egyptian rule in Canaan
	LC II	1400 to 1200	Beginning of arrival of tribes of Israel
Israelite (Iron) Age	Isr. IA	1200 to 1150	Arrival of sea people (Philistines)
	Isr. IB	1150 to 1000	The Judges
	Isr. IIA	1000 to 925	United Monarchy
	Isr. IIB	925 to 800	Division into two kingdoms, Israel, Judah
		800 to 721	Israel from Jehu dynasty to destruction of Samaria
	Isr. IIC	721 to 587/6	Judah alone until fall of Jerusalem

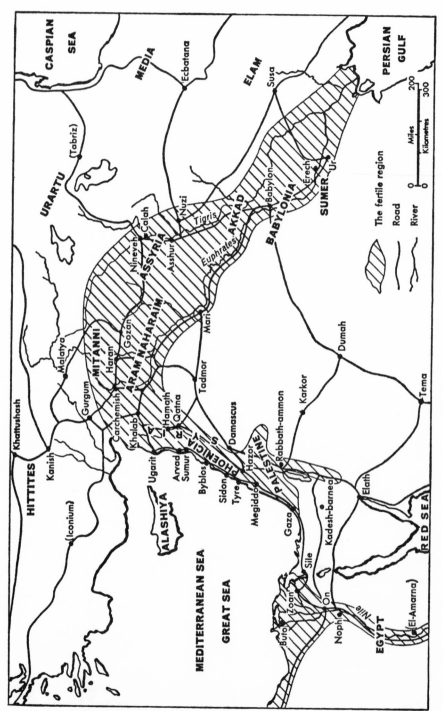

The Fertile Crescent

INTRODUCTION:

ERETZ-ISRAEL AND ITS BOUNDARIES

THERE are three features which determine the general character of Eretz-Israel: it is small, greatly fragmented, and poor in natural resources.

A small country. The land is a narrow strip between the sea on the west and the desert on the east, whose width does not exceed 120 km. across. Its natural border in the north is formed by the mountains of Lebanon and Anti-Lebanon with their snowcapped peaks; in the south, its boundary is the wilderness. The settled area extended during most periods just slightly to the south of the latitude of Beer-sheba. In this region, its length is slightly less than 300 km., and its overall area is around 35,000 sq. km. This area is about the same as that of Switzerland or Denmark and exceeds the area of Belgium or Holland; it is about 12 percent of the area of Italy or 30 percent of the area of Greece, and if it is compared to the neighboring countries, it is about 20 percent of the size of Syria, about 9 percent of Iraq, about 4 percent of Egypt and about 2 percent of the territory of Saudi Arabia. Of course, these calculations take into account the desert areas which were not reckoned with the territory of Eretz-Israel, but this does not change the basic fact that we are dealing with one of the smaller countries of the world.

Its uniqueness stems from the wide deserts that surround it on the east and south. Unlike Egypt, called the gift of the Nile, the Land of Israel is the gift of the sea. The westerly winds bring the blessing of their rains during the winter, and to the extent that they are caught by the mountain ridges, the amount of precipitation increases. The mountains of Transjordan, which reach a height of 1,243 m. in Gilead and 1,727 m. in Edom south of Petra, are the last barrier on the threshold of the desert. At the southern end of the country, the sea-coast turns westward in a broad arc, so that at the estuary of the "Brook of Egypt" (el-ʻArish—the southwestern boundary of Eretz-Israel) the sea is actually on the north. Beer-sheba, el-ʻArish, and Port Said, which is on the northern coast of Egypt, are located approximately at the same latitude. South of Eretz-Israel is the desert.

When Moses stood on Mt. Nebo, "the LORD showed him all the land, Gilead as far as Dan, all Naphtali, the land of Ephraim, and Manasseh, all the land of Judah as far as the Western Sea, the Negeb . . ." (Deut. 34:1–3). While one need not assume that all this land could be seen from that peak, this description reflects accurately the character of the country: from its mountaintops on a clear day one may view most of its territory from Galilee to the Negeb and from the sea to the eastern desert.

A fragmented land. In spite of its small territory, the Land of Israel is full of contrasts and quite difficult to traverse. Except for the narrow coastal plain in the north which broadens toward the south, the general nature of the country is mountainous. Its mountaintops reach above 1000 m. in most parts of the country. This hilly character is further enhanced by the deep rift of the Jordan Valley and the Arabah, which cleaves the entire country from north to south and has its continuation in the Lebanese Beqaʻ, in Syria, and in the Gulf of Elath (Gulf of ʻAqaba) between Sinai and Saudi Arabia. This deep geological rift reaches 200 m. below sea level at the Sea of Galilee and descends to 400 m. around the Dead Sea, the deepest point on the earth's land surface. Therefore, in most parts of the country, there are extreme variations in altitude within very short distances. Around the vicinity of Jerusalem-Hebron, one ascends to about 1000 m. above sea level, of which 500–600 m. is on a steep gradient about 10 to 20 km. wide. From here to the Dead Sea region one goes down about 1000 m. in less than 20 km. as the crow flies, and then ascends to that altitude by an abrupt incline to the heights of Transjordan. These steep ranges of hills form serious barriers to highways, and in many places the hills are cut by vertical canyons hundreds of meters deep.

The sharp topographical contrasts fragment the country into quite different climatic zones in spite of geographical proximity. The westerly wind warms up and withholds its precipitation while it descends into the valleys. From the standpoint of settlement, the humid coastal plain, the hill regions with their Mediterranean climate, and the fiery

Jordan Valley are three disparate worlds. The differences are particularly sharp in the south, where precipitation is lighter. A few kilometers east of Jerusalem and Hebron, there begins the wild, arid Wilderness of Judah where, with the exception of a few oases, there were never permanent settlements. This region served as a convenient refuge for rebels and renegades.

Eretz-Israel is, therefore, a land of many internal contrasts in spite of its small area, and this condition has always encouraged its division into separate ethnic units.

Natural resources. The country is not richly blessed with natural resources. Most of the rocks are limestone created on the sea floor during relatively late geological periods. Only at the southern end of the Arabah does one find deeply formed granites not covered by much later sedimentary deposits. Their sharp peaks resemble in appearance the lofty granite mountains of southern Sinai.

Appreciable segments of southern Transjordan and of the Jabbok region in Gilead are covered by a thick layer of red sandstone called Nubian, a product of a long period of desert conditions. The high, steep mountains of Edom receive their name from these red sandstones which are visible from afar. To the north of the country, we find expanses of grayish-black basalt, the product of ancient volcanic action. This is the dominant rock in northern Transjordan, and the ancient cones of the many volcanoes stand out sharply among the hills of Bashan and Golan. Layers of basalt are also widespread in eastern lower Galilee, and two of its most famous peaks are extinct volcanoes, the Hill of Moreh in the Valley of Jezreel and the Horns of Hattin overlooking the Chinnereth.

Stone of various kinds for construction purposes is, therefore, not lacking in most areas of the country. However, there is very little else in the way of mineral resources. In Transjordan some ancient sources of iron have been discovered and copper mines have been found on both sides of the Arabah between the Dead Sea and the Gulf of Elath. It would appear that these are the mineral resources referred to in the biblical allusion to "a land whose stones are iron, and out of whose hills you can dig copper" (Deut. 8:9).

That passage comes at the end of a description of the agricultural wealth of Eretz-Israel which is the main point: "For the LORD your God is bringing you into a good land, a land of brooks of water, of fountains and springs, flowing forth in valleys and hills, a land of wheat and barley, of vines and fig trees and pomegranates, a land of olive trees and honey" (Deut. 8:7–8). Elsewhere one has the definition, "a land flowing with milk and honey," with the explanation: "for the land which you are entering to take possession of it is not like the land of Egypt from which you have come, where you sowed your seed and watered it with your feet, like a garden of vegetables: but the land which you are going over to possess is a land of hills and valleys, which drinks water by the rain from heaven" (Deut. 11:10–11).

This is a most illuminating description. Agriculture in the country was based mainly on rain-nourished crops without the need for irrigation, in contrast to its mighty neighbors. Egypt and large portions of Mesopotamia are in fact deserts whose productivity is dependent upon utilization of water from the great rivers which pass through them. Eretz-Israel enjoyed the gifts of God—rain and dew—which obviate human activity. But this advantage carries its own disadvantage.

The rainy season is limited to the winter months, and the amount of precipitation differs greatly in various parts of the country. Furthermore, drought years are regular phenomena during which precipitation is inadequate in most of the land, or so sporadic that the crops do not survive. Archaeological researches have shown that these conditions were not basically different during the last four to five thousand years, in the historical periods of Eretz-Israel. This fact is also reflected in the written historical sources: years of drought and famine run like a scarlet thread through its history.

The cultivable areas are also limited and varied. Most of the limestones are hard rock from the Cenomanian, Turonian, and Eocene periods and are not greatly subject to erosion. They do weather into the fertile red soil known as *terra rossa,* so famous in the Mediterranean area. This soil has created the rich alluvial valleys, of which the most important is Jezreel. However, these valleys are limited in area, and segments of the coastal plain were covered with shifting sands and ridges of sandstone *(kurkar).* An extensive area of the Sharon was covered by layers of red sand resulting from the disintegration of relatively late geological strata. Today this is the outstanding district for citrus groves, thanks to irrigation and soil enrichment, but in antiquity it was not possible to exploit this land agriculturally. Most of it was covered by scrub forest until the last century.

In some parts of the hilly region, one also finds Senonian chalk deposits, in particular to the north of Mt. Ephraim and in the Wilderness of Judah. This is a soft rock which easily weathers into a light-colored soil that trickles away and settles very quickly. It is very poor for agriculture. On the other hand, this type of rock creates convenient valleys for passage, and the exposed strips of Senonian chalk along the foot of the hills form the most convenient thoroughfares through the hill country.

The northwestern portion of the Negeb is broad and level and covered with a thin, fertile layer of loess soil deposited by the wind. However, this region is too arid to permit systematic agriculture. The loess also tends to form a characteristic crust with the first rain that prevents the absorption of moisture. This characteristic facilitates the flow of water and the delineation of the broad and deep Negeb wadis ("furrows") in which floodwaters rage for hours or even days during the winter. Such features enhance the dryness of the area, but they also aid in the collection of water in cisterns and in various areas of production.

Most parts of the land are hill-country soils from which the topsoil is rapidly eroded if it is not protected by flora or artificial terraces. Natural forestation covered most of the hill-country areas in antiquity until people cleared them and created cultivable patches by constructing terraces. With the abandonment of villages, the terraces collapsed and the soil was eroded, so that today large segments are no longer of value for anything but reforestation. Remains of these terraces, visible on nearly every slope, testify to the intensity of cultivation in antiquity.

The aridity of Eretz-Israel is also intensified by the karstic nature of the limestone: most of the water seeps through with great speed until it reaches impermeable strata. Only part of this water flows forth in springs, the richest of which are found around the edges of the plains, along the geological faults. Most of the water is collected at a subterranean level which the ancients were unable to utilize.

Therefore, although Eretz-Israel was blessed with water sources and fruitful agricultural areas, they were scattered and limited. This was a small country, fragmented into various regions differing widely from one another, and its economic resources were humble and restricted. Nevertheless, this little country has influenced the history of humanity and the development of civilization far beyond its natural endowments. What were the causes for this?

The factors were two: its special geopolitical situation and the people who linked their own destiny to that land, the people of Israel.

Eretz-Israel is a land bridge between Asia and Africa. On both sides of it, there are the lands of the great rivers, the cradle of human civilization, Mesopotamia—the land of the Tigris and the Euphrates—and Egypt—the land of the Nile. These are broad territories with rich alluvial soils watered by those mighty rivers. The rivers also serve as communication links, as convenient transportation arteries, and as sources for irrigation. In the third millennium b.c.e., in those lands, mighty powers had already arisen controlling extensive territories, and had inaugurated routes of commerce to distant parts. In Mesopotamia and in Egypt, the foundation was laid for many sciences, including the ancient writing systems that formed the basis for all of the later scripts. The Land of Israel is the southwestern arm of the Fertile Crescent that covers a broad arc from the Persian Gulf, encompassing Mesopotamia and Syria, with deserts on the inner side and mountain ranges on the outer side of the curve. Communication between the two main foci of ancient culture had to pass through the Land of Israel.

From this fact the routes crossing the country from north to south derive their great importance. The topographical conditions determined fixed routes with few alternatives. The two most important routes were that along the coast, denoted in the Bible as "the way of the sea" (Isa. 9:1 [Heb., 8:23]), and the road traversing the Transjordanian highlands, known as "the King's Highway" (Num. 20:17; 21:22). "The Way of the Sea" runs the length of the coast, and from the Sharon Plain it enters the Valley of Jezreel, whence it leads northward via several secondary routes. Megiddo, situated near the exit of this main route into the Valley, is a key point on the Way of the Sea. The King's Highway, crossing the Transjordanian plateau, has two secondary routes: one to the east along an easily passable region on the fringe of the desert, and another to the west going up into the central, more densely settled hill region. The latter route was more convenient from the standpoint of water supply and concentration of settlements but the traveler had to cross the deep canyons and wadis dividing the highlands, in particular the Arnon which drains into the Dead Sea.

These routes gave Eretz-Israel its great importance in the framework of the civilized nations of the ancient Near East. They were, at once, a curse and a blessing. They brought wealth, and permitted the occupants of the land to share in the achievements of ancient civilization, but they also brought countless campaigns of aggression leaving destruction and desolation in their wake. Control of these highways was always the ambition of the mighty powers in the region.

But the uniqueness of Eretz-Israel is also connected with the Israelite people that chose it as a homeland. Although a long period preceded their arrival, and for a long time afterward the Israelite people were largely separated from the land, no other name became permanently attached to the land throughout its long history.

The nature of its broken terrain led to social fragmentation and to the appearance of various ethnic groups in its different regions, such as Edom, Moab, and Ammon in Transjordan, or the Philistines on the coastal plain. During the conquest, the people of Israel did not find themselves confronted with one people but in the various narratives we find the Canaanite, the Amorite, the Hittite, the Perizzite, the Jebusite, the Hivite, and others (e.g., Josh. 11:3). Yet in the eyes of the big powers the Land of Israel was part of Syria. The Egyptians called it Retenu, Khurru, and Canaan, while the Mesopotamians referred to it as Amurru, the West Land. These names always included considerable parts of Syria together with Eretz-Israel, and their echoes are also found in the Bible. This is the "Patriarchal region" including all of Syria and Eretz-Israel, "from the river of Egypt to the great river, the river Euphrates" (Gen. 15:18, etc.). A more precise boundary is the "border of the land of Canaan" that extended up to Lebo-Hamath in the Lebanese Beqa' (Num. 34:8). At the greatest expansion by Israel in the reigns of David and Solomon, the boundaries of the kingdom approximated the concepts of the ancient borders that the sons of Israel found before them upon their arrival in the land: two concepts are referred to in the Solomonic narratives. For the dedication of the Temple, Solomon assembled a mighty convocation, "from Lebo-Hamath to the Brook of Egypt" (I Kings 8:65). Moreover, "he had dominion over all the lands beyond the river" (I Kings 4:24 [Heb., 5:4]). "Beyond the River" is the later Assyrian term applied to Syria and Eretz-Israel, i.e., the western side of the Euphrates from the standpoint of the Mesopotamians.

The boundaries of Israelite settlement, by contrast, extended from Mt. Hermon to desert (Josh. 11:17, etc.). This is the classic boundary of Eretz-Israel "from Dan to Beer-sheba" (II Sam. 24:2, etc.); this allusion is to the royal administrative and cultic centers on the frontier to the north and south. The settlement of the Israelite tribes from Dan, at the foot of Hermon, to Beer-sheba on the border of the desert converted the region thus enclosed into the Land of Israel and thence into "the Holy Land" for a large portion of the world's population in much later periods.

Most of the people of Israel were expelled and forced to emigrate from their land nearly two thousand years ago; since then, the Land of Israel has become once more dissected and fragmented, part of the Levant. The Assyrian and Persian "Province Beyond the River" gave way to the Greco-Roman "Syria." The Romans were the first to change the name of Judea to Palestina, from the Philistines who lived on the coast, in order to expunge the name of Israel/Judah.

Geographical position on one hand and the contribution of the people of Israel to human civilization on the other are the factors which have increased the importance of the Land of Israel and made its long history one of the most enthralling chapters in the course of human events.

I

THE PREHISTORIC ERA

THE earliest inscriptions referring to people and events in Eretz-Israel are from the beginning of the second millennium B.C.E. This historic period of about four thousand years was preceded by a long prehistoric era during which people left material traces without any other information about their character, culture, or identity. With regard to Eretz-Israel, the third millennium B.C.E. (the Early Canaanite period) is also a mute period, which has not left any inscriptional material in spite of the rich and powerful cultures flourishing then in the country. The situation may be altered by new discoveries, since, in Mesopotamia and Egypt, this is already the age of the great early kingdoms that emerged into the light of history thanks to the discovery of an abundance of inscriptions of various kinds. In Eretz-Israel it is still a protohistoric period elucidated only indirectly by means of contacts with the neighboring historical cultures.

The ancient archaeological periods are denoted—on the basis of their material remains—the Stone, Chalcolithic (copper and stone), and Bronze (in Israeli archaeology often called Canaanite) Ages. These, like all chronological terms, are quite schematic and are to be used only as aids for reference and not as precise delineations of their respective periods. During the Early Bronze Age, people were still using copper in Eretz-Israel, but even copper implements are rare enough. At the same time, the appearance of the various metals is closely interrelated with the development of technology and civilization. So it is justifiable to use them as definitive of a new age. However, such definition reveals mostly the limitation of our knowledge. In fact, we are familiar with only a small portion of the material complex from any one period. Prehistoric people did not use only stone tools and

9

implements of bone, shell, etc. There is no doubt that they also had available implements of wood, baskets and mats, skins and cloth. They lived not only in caves or buildings made of stone or mud, but certainly also in huts, wooden shacks, tents, and structures made of other perishable materials. Organic materials are not preservable in the climatic conditions of Israel except in the dry caves of the Judean Wilderness, and even there the earliest remains of organic materials found thus far derive from the Chalcolithic period. We must take these limitations into account when dealing with the most ancient periods.

The Stone Age comprises a very large chapter in the history of humanity, and its various stages are measured in thousands and ten thousands of years. The appearance of the first toolmaking people takes place at the beginning of the Quaternary era or the Pleistocene, about two million years ago; new discoveries in Africa seem to be pushing their appearance back much earlier. Modern methods of dating make it possible today to fix more accurately absolute dates for these geological periods, in particular for the last seventy thousand years, the dates for which are established by the disintegration of radioactive carbon 14 in organic materials.

Although the geology, the morphology, and the climate were fundamentally established before this era, extensive changes did not take place in Eretz-Israel as they did during the Ice Age in Europe. Nevertheless, in this country appreciable climatic changes did occur leaving their mark on the development of animals and people. The alterations are generally correlated with the glacial and interglacial periods of Europe. In the Lower Pleistocene, there was a cooling off leading to the creation of vast areas of ice in northern Europe and America. Periods of glacial advance are paralleled by heavy pluvial periods in our region. Thus, for example, the correlation has been proposed between the early pluvial ages and the early periods of glaciation. After the latter came a dry period, the Great Interpluvial, which continued from 300,000 to 200,000 years ago with an appreciable rise in sea level and the inundation of extensive areas of the country's coast because of the melting of the glaciers. The succeeding 80,000 years were again more moist and cooler, the Second Ice Age in Europe. Between 120,-000 and 70,000 years ago, there occurred the Second Interpluvial period of Europe with a warming up and drying off and a rise in sea level. The Third and last Pluvial period took place about 70,000 to 11,000 years ago, and it is subdivided into cold, moist stages with intervening times of warmer climate (stadials and interstadials). With the beginning of the Holocene (the present era), the climate was stabilized, though certain changes have taken place in temperature and precipitation levels. These changes, of course, were not great, but they still had an appreciable influence on the flora and fauna because of the geographical situation of the country on the fringe of the desert. The Land of Israel was suitable and convenient for human habitation throughout all of the Pleistocene era, but the climatic variations led to extensive changes in the ecological environment. In the moist pluvial periods, there were forests and swamps in the country, with an abundance of flora and large animals such as elephants, rhinoceroses, and bears, and swamp animals such as the hippopotamus and the crocodile. In the dry interpluvials, there was a desert flora, and the normal wildlife hunted by people included oxen, horses, mountain goats, and gazelles. These variations made their impact on the development of people, and they encouraged population movements over broad areas. The geographical situation of Eretz-Israel as an intercontinental land bridge led to its being a meeting ground for cultures and races already in the prehistoric eras.

It is customary to divide the Stone Age in our region into three subperiods: the Early, Middle, and Late—i.e., Paleolithic, Epipaleolithic (including the so-called Natufian), and the Neolithic. These periods are not uniform. The earlier ones are longer, and the later are much shorter. The division is based upon humanity's development. The first steps in cultural progress were slow; during hundreds of thousands of years, there were relatively few changes. The great change came with the transition from food-gathering and hunting to food production. Thenceforth, the development of civilization and technology progressed at an accelerated pace. Races of toolmaking people were present in the country for two million years, although the dates for these earlier periods are still largely conjectural. *Homo sapiens* appears here in the latter stage of the Paleolithic, about 40,000 years ago. The end of the Paleolithic is dated today at about 17,000 B.C.E. (only from this point is there any meaning to the concept "Before the Common Era"). The Epipaleolithic continues for about 9,000 years, and the Neolithic for about 4,000—periods which, in length, are not at all comparable to the long Paleolithic. People first lit a campfire about 200,000 years ago; they produced the first handmade material —pottery—about 8000 B.C.E.; another four thousand years passed before the extraction of the first copper; about a thousand years later writing was invented, and another fifteen hundred years were needed before the adoption of the alphabetic script (in the land of Canaan!), a discovery that made writing available to the many. This occurred less than four thousand years ago, only yesterday in relation to the age of human beings on earth.

THE PALEOLITHIC PERIOD

During the entire Paleolithic—more than two million years—people existed by hunting and food-gathering. Their remains have been discovered at open "stations" where they had encamped in times of congenial climate but also especially in caves where they found refuge from the rain and cold. In some of the caves, people lived for extensive periods, leaving after them deep layers of their debris. It is in these caves that the human remains have been examined stratigraphically, a method for determining the late and early, by means of the stratified layers. The fauna of the various periods has been investigated as well as tools of stone and a few of bone, the only implements to survive the ravages of time which bear witness to technological development, to the activities of ancient people, and to a bit of their beliefs and outlook. The distribution of wildlife that was hunted or domesticated can be ascertained by study of the bones found in the prehistoric layers, and of the flora—by means of analysis of the pollen particles, which are better preserved than other organic materials. Remains of human skeletons have also been found from the different periods, beginning with the primitive races and continuing down to the appearance of *Homo sapiens*. The various cultures that have been discovered are generally designated by the name of the place where they were first uncovered or studies about them published. A large number of these names are French because that country has been a pioneer in prehistoric research; nevertheless, some of them, in particular the local specialized cultures, are denoted by certain place-names in Eretz-Israel.

The long Paleolithic period is itself divided into three main subperiods: the Early, Middle, and Late. The spread of culture was greater and development more rapid during the later phases. The earlier stages were longer and the development slower, with fewer local innovations. The same lithic culture with only minor variations was spread across vast areas. People migrated from region to region, bringing with them their culture and customs unchanged for tens of thousands of years. In the Natufian period, differentiation became more marked: technology developed, and invention followed invention while regional cultures passed from the scene before there was time for them to be disseminated across extensive territories.

Lower Paleolithic. The most ancient human remains in this country were found in 1959 at a site called 'Ubeidiyah by an Israeli expedition under the leadership of M. Stekelis. The site is in the northern Jordan Valley, south of Chinnereth on the ground of Kibbutz Afikim. The remains were found in strata associated with the end of the Lower Pleistocene, about 900,000 to 700,000 years ago. This was a moist pluvial period, evidently corresponding to a glacial period in Europe. The occupational deposits were found in strata lying upon a steep folding and faulting incline to the southeast and to the northwest, testifying to the continued sinking of the valley along the length of the geological fault during the later periods.

It would appear that during the moist periods ancient people settled here near the shore of a lake that covered all of the middle Jordan Valley from the vicinity of Chinnereth down to Kibbutz Gesher. The stone tools found were of the simplest types, made from flint, basalt, or dolomite pebbles collected in the vicinity. Most of them are cutting tools, having one side sharpened by breaking off several flakes. Beside them were found roundish implements and a few hand tools. This culture resembles the second phase of the Oldowan culture discovered in Africa; thus it was denoted by Stekelis as a local variant of Olduvai Bed II and finally Early Acheulean. Thus far, this culture is known in northeastern Africa and eastern Asia, and it would appear that already in that early stage, Eretz-Israel was serving as a connecting link between these two widely separated regions.

The worked bones found at this site include types of animals no longer found in the country, e.g., elephants, rhinoceroses, hippopotamuses, alligators, bears, gazelles, and certain types of fish. Most of the bones show signs of breaking and scraping by flint tools to remove the flesh, meaning that the animals served as human food. There was no trace on them of burning, so one would deduce that the production and use of fire were not yet known. The presence of people is also indicated by fragments of a human temple and an incisor, but these fragments were too small to permit any comprehension of their physical build.

The next step was technical control over bifacial stonecutting in the production of implements. Typical are the tools worked on both sides, usually with one edge lengthened and sharpened. The tools are reminiscent of the Acheulean of Europe and belong to the Middle Pleistocene. This culture was discovered beside Jisr Binat-Ya'qub (Gesher Benot Ya'akov), the Bridge of Jacob's Daughters, south of the Huleh. In its lower phase were found a number of hand axes and cleavers of basalt of Middle Acheulean type along with elephant bones. Flints made by a similar technique have also been found on the surface in the Rephaim Valley in Jerusalem. Evidently, the main subsistence of these people was by hunting, which included the larger species of animals in Eretz-Israel and the vicinity at that time (Plate 1).

Chronologically close, though apparently somewhat later, is another culture discovered in the lowest strata of two of the most famous prehistoric caves: Tabun, one of the Carmel caves excavated by D. Garrod (Photo 1), and the cave of Umm Qatafah in the southern Judean Wilderness investigated by Neuville. That culture is called Tayacian and is typified by crude, thick flakes with only a small percentage of stone cores. In any case, the finds of these assemblages are extremely poor. It is conjectured that the cave dwellers were largely engaged in food-gathering rather than hunting. Perhaps these two cultures, as in Europe, existed side by side for a long time with only slight progress, i.e., from the latter part of the First Interpluvial through the Second Pluvial and the Second Interpluvial—a period of more than 200,000 years. Climatic changes, in particular the colder periods, seem to have forced people to look for cover in natural caves, at least during certain seasons of the year. In the Tayacian strata at Umm Qatafah the first hearths were found, with traces of burning, bones, and stones sometimes surrounded by a circle of large stones— the earliest testimony to the use of fire in the Middle East. The Second Pluvial period began, according to the experts, about 200,000 years ago.

The last phase of the earlier Paleolithic is called Yabrudian after a cliff shelter at Yabrud on the eastern slope of Mt. Senir (the Anti-Lebanon) north of Damascus. This same culture has been found in the caves of Zuttiyah and Tabun, in the latter to a thickness of more than seven meters of deposit. It is typified by broad, slanted racloirs (side scrapers) made from thick flakes and mostly small hand axes, an indus-

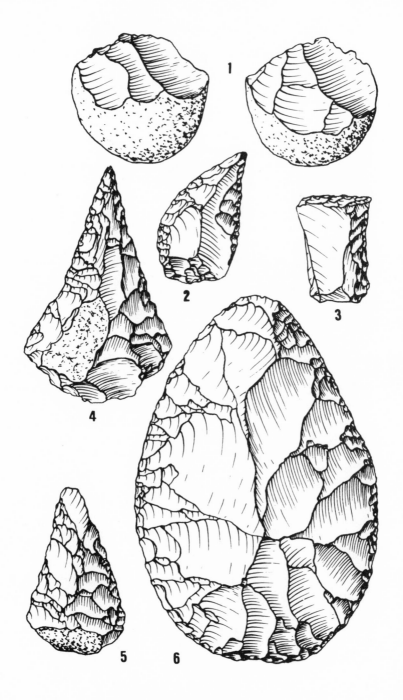

PLATE 1. Lower Paleolithic flint tools

try reminiscent of the Micoquian culture and also the Mousterian of the European Laquina type. Geological and paleontological researches have established the age of the Yabrudian culture from the First Interpluvial to the beginning of the Last Pluvial.

Middle Paleolithic. This period belongs mainly to the last phase of the Last Pluvial, and its age is estimated at about 30,000 years. From this period we have the earliest carbon-14 date at a cave at Ras el-Kalb north of Beirut, the age of which is somewhat more than 52,000 years. The climate in the country was warmer and more humid than in our time, with very thick flora and big forest and swamp animals.

The most typical culture of this period is called Mousterian after the contemporary site in France. Flint implements were worked in a precise and refined manner. Especially widespread are triangular points sharpened at one end, sometimes with retouching around the edges. These blades evidently served as javelin heads or as daggers with wooden handles. Henceforth, implements appear of a more complex nature, whose efficiency and striking ability were much greater than simple hand tools (Plate 2).

In Europe, scholars have succeeded in distinguishing between the Mousterian culture, with implements having a fine retouching, and the Levalloisian, the implements of which are characterized by a simpler retouching with flakes and points made by a special flaking technique. The former were generally found in rock shelters and the latter in open stations. The lithic industries from the Middle Paleolithic represent a mixture of the two industries and therefore they were first designated Levallois-Mousterian. However, today the distinction between the Levallois technique and the Mousterian is generally accepted. Within the complex of Mousterian cultures, one distinguishes between those making greater or lesser use of the Levallois technique.

The oldest tombs discovered in the country are related to this period; they were found in several caves—three in the Carmel (el-Kebarah, et-Tabun, and es-Sukhul), one near Nazareth (Mt. of Precipitation), two in Upper Galilee (ez-Zuttiyah and the 'Amud cave in Nahal 'Amud). The Galilee man found in the Zuttiyah cave is the oldest of all and is dated to the Yabrudian. The eleven skeletons whose remains were found in the Carmel caves and the ten from the cave in the Mt. of Precipitation belong to the Mousterian, while the latter are earlier than those from Carmel. All of them are intentional burials; the dead

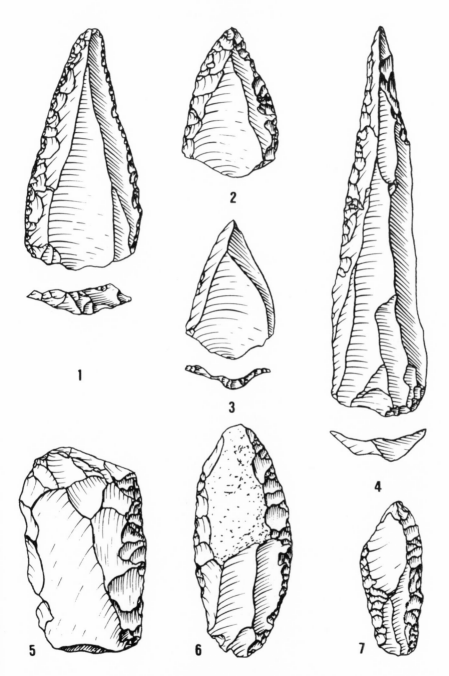

PLATE 2. Middle Paleolithic flint tools

were placed in different postures—on the back, side, or face, but always with the feet contracted. One grasped in his hand the jawbone of a wild boar, evidently provision for the dead. All the skeletons, in spite of the individual differences between them, belong to a special type having intermediate features between the European *Homo neanderthalensis* and *Homo sapiens.* So it has received the cognomen *Palaeoanthropus palaestinensis.* Their height was greater than that of the Neanderthal and the long limbs are of *Homo sapiens* type. The thick eye sockets are neanderthaloid but the skull is longer and the chin more prominent. Their posture was evidently more erect than that of the Neanderthal.

Opinions are still divided on the question of whether *Palaeoanthropus palaestinensis* is an intermediate between *Homo sapiens* and the Neanderthal or a more advanced evolutionary type. Garrod indicates that the first possibility is less likely since the two types have not been discovered in this vicinity from that period, as one would expect in the case of a connection between them. Thus, one must note that the flint implements of the *Palaeoanthropus palaestinensis* testify to a certain mixture of characteristics, and the transition from the Middle to the Upper Paleolithic is more gradual in the Near East than in Europe.

Upper Paleolithic. The lithic industries of this period are notable for perfected blades, points, and even scrapers that remind us of the Aurignacian of Europe. This is the age of the famous prehistoric cave drawings of Europe, the likes of which have yet to be discovered in other regions (Plate 3; Photo 2). In Israel, an early phase of that period has been found in the Amirah cave in Galilee and in et-Tubban in the Judean Wilderness. A good stratification of later skeletons was found at Iraq el-Ahmar in Wadi Hariton and in the Carmel caves, in Kebarah, and in el-Wad (Photo 2). That was a time of climatic changes; after a cold and more moist phase, the climate stabilized into almost its present character. This change finds expression in the gradual disappearance of animals requiring a moist climate and of rich flora, such as the *Dama mesopotamica,* with the gradual increase of animals accustomed to heat and small quantities of dry food, e.g., the gazelle. In the train of the fauna that migrated to more moist regions, people also migrated, and the tribes that remained in the country were forced to adapt to new living conditions. People went over more and more to hunting small animals and to fishing, which was possible only with the gradual

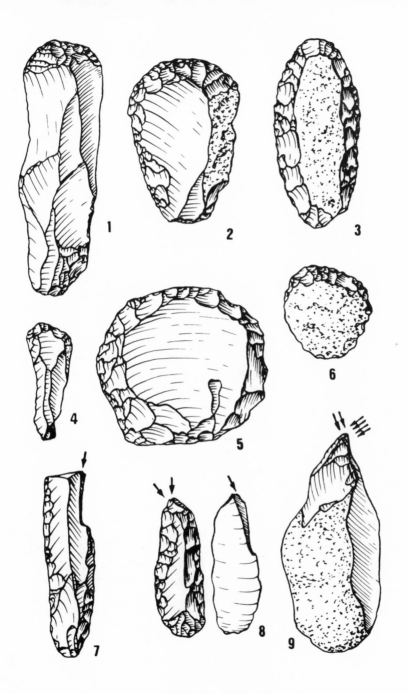

PLATE 3. Upper Paleolithic flint tools

perfection of suitable implements.

It would appear that this was a period of decisive development in the history of humanity. This idea is illustrated not only in the perfected stone and flint tools, but also in human customs that can be perceived through various finds. From this period date the earliest dwellings in the form of huts and tents on floors or definitive surfaces. A few human figurines found in Europe suggest that these people were in need of clothing, and the aesthetic sense for decoration by bone and shell seems to have been aroused. The differences between the various cultures became deeper, and there are less clear connections between the Middle East and more distant regions such as Europe, Asia, and Africa. The human bones from the later phase of the Upper Paleolithic in the caves of the Mt. of Precipitation and Iraq el-Ahmar belong to *Homo sapiens*.

The Epipaleolithic. This period, which some prefer to call the Natufian, was one of the decisive ages in humanity's development. Eretz-Israel and its vicinity seem to have played a major role.

Throughout the world, this was the period at the end of the Ice Age. A general warming had taken place, the glaciers had retreated, and the seas had risen from the melted snows flowing into them. In the Land of Israel, the thick foliage and the many animals related to it retreated. The typical Mediterranean environment with semiarid regions began to develop, the closer one approached the desert. There were long periods of dryness. People were forced to change their living habits and their means of sustenance. It was an important stage on their long road in the fight for survival, strewn with obstacles and difficulties, and with some triumphs over them.

The earlier phases of the Epipaleolithic are called the Kebaran and Geometric Kebaran I (after the cave of Kebarah). They are typified by small hunting settlements, with housing in huts of reeds or curtains containing an assemblage of microliths and occasional grindstones and bone implements (Photo 4). The main Epipaleolithic culture in the country is called the Natufian after a cave in Wadi Natuf (between Jerusalem and Tel Aviv) where the culture was first investigated systematically. The same culture is found in the caves of Galilee, the Carmel, the Judean Wilderness to the east of Jerusalem, and in circular sites in the Negeb. This is the first period in which large open permanent settlements are found in various parts of the country.

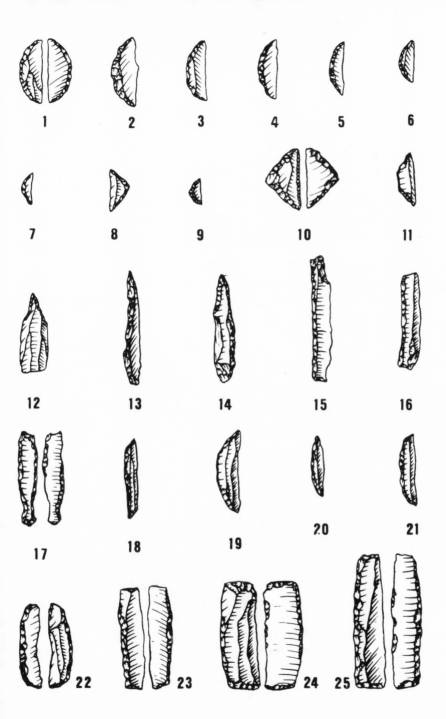

PLATE 4. Epipaleolithic flint tools

The two most impressive examples of Natufian settlements were excavated at Eynan in eastern Galilee (by J. Perrot) and at the mouth of Nahal Oren on the Carmel slopes (by Stekelis). The sites of these settlements are related to their nature. Both of them are located at the foot of rocky cliffs in whose caves the occupants were able to find refuge when necessary. Both are on the edge of rich valleys with an abundance of fresh water, near waters rich in fish: Eynan on the ancient bank of the Huleh, and Nahal Oren in a region of swampy lakes along the Carmel coast not far from the Mediterranean shore.

From the buildings, round stone foundations have been preserved, evidently the bases for huts built mainly of wood and skins.

Among the implements found in these settlements, the most typical are microlithic flints made for attachment to handles of wood and bone for hunting, fishing, and cultivation. All of these prove that Natufian man was at the beginning of one of the great revolutions in human history: the transition from hunting and gathering food to methodical agriculture (Plate 4).

Flints and prehistoric drawings from the parallel cultures in Europe testify that the hunting crafts were assisted by two important discoveries, the bow and the trap. Arrows with heads made of microlithic flint flakes were a strong weapon, swift and long-range, in contrast to sling stones or spears thrown by hand. The pit or other types of traps made possible a much more certain and efficient manner of hunting. In addition, the fishing craft with hooks made of flint flakes and with nets opened for people a wide range of inexhaustible food supply. But the greatest achievement was the beginning of seasonal agriculture as evidenced by sickles and flint hoes. In particular, many stone mortars and pestles indicate the large quantities of grain at people's disposal. This revolutionary economy made possible the maintenance of permanent settlements; it would seem that for the first time in the history of humanity, the economy was regular and fairly dependable. Perhaps certain surpluses were even stored from time to time.

This relative wealth and security is also expressed in the intellectual and religious life revealed in the Natufian culture. This is the first period in the history of the country when real art objects are preserved. Figurines of stone and bone in anthropomorphic and zoomorphic styles have been found, most executed in a realistic manner showing great artistic ability. The majority of them may have had a magic function in the increase of fertility for people and soil; thus, they began a long tradition of the earth mother who reigns in all the cultures of the ancient East. But beside them, there also appear implements decorated with plastic designs, including beads and worked shells which reflect the beginning of the development of a real artistic sense.

Another innovation is the many burials from the Natufian found under dwellings and at the openings of caves. At Eynan a large plastered stone circle was found with graves covered by stone slabs and traces of burning. Also in Nahal Oren were found the remains of burning on top of graves along with large stone mortars having a hole opened in the bottom, evidently a means of communication with the dead. The bodies were laid with legs contracted, and on the heads of the women only were there strings of sea shells. All of this indicates a development in burial customs and unmistakable ritual practices for the dead.

The Natufian culture lasted for less than two thousand years (about 10,000 to 8300 B.C.E.), a short period in comparison to the long Paleolithic. However, it seems that during this age the foundations of human civilization were created: permanent dwellings, food production, and art and ritual.

This is also the beginning of the most ancient town in the world—Jericho. The early phase belongs to the Natufian period, and the flint and bone assemblages of that stratum, including, among other things, a harpoon head and a crescent, have clear affinities with the lower Natufian strata of the Carmel caves. The rich spring and the warm and protected ecological conditions attracted ancient people to settle there and to put down roots of permanent settlement. Carbon-14 dates have established that these strata belong to the period between about 9300 and 8300 B.C.E.

THE NEOLITHIC PERIOD

The last phase of the Stone Age continued in Eretz-Israel for some four thousand years (about 8300 to 4000 B.C.E.). Although the beginning of agriculture evidently goes back to the Natufian, it is only in the Neolithic that people made the decisive step from a food-gathering and hunting economy to one of food production by means of animal domestication and cultivation. This transition bound people more and more to one region and to a particular place; thus, the permanent settlements now were no longer the exception but

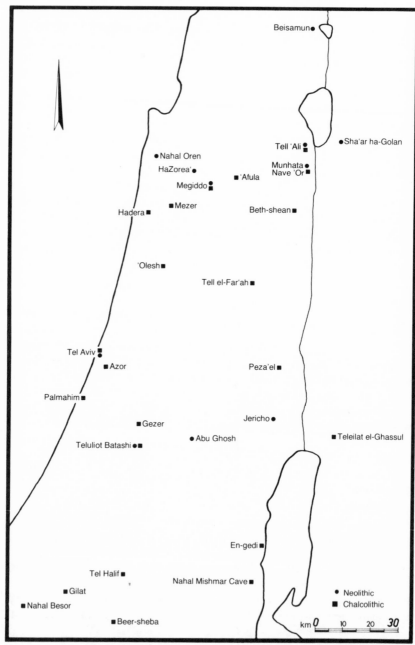

Beisamun●

Tell 'Ali●
■
●Sha'ar ha-Golan

●Nahal Oren
HaZorea'●
Munhata●
Nave 'Or■
●'Afula
Megiddo●
■
■Mezer
Hadera■
Beth-shean■

'Olesh■
Tell el-Far'ah■

Tel Aviv■
●
■Azor
Peza'el■
Palmahim■

■Gezer
Jericho●
Teluliot Batashi●■
●Abu Ghosh
■Teleilat el-Ghassul

En-gedi■

Tel Halif■
Nahal Mishmar Cave■
● Neolithic
■ Chalcolithic
■Gilat
■Nahal Besor
■Beer-sheba
km **0**   10   20   **30**

FIG. 1. Map of Neolithic and Chalcolithic sites

became a widespread phenomenon.

Neolithic settlements, to name only the most outstanding, have been discovered in various parts of the country: on the coastal plain (Nahal Oren), in the Valley of Jezreel (between Jokneam and Megiddo), the Jordan Valley (Munhata, Tell 'Ali, Sha'ar ha-Golan, Jericho), in the hill country and on the fringe of the Judean Wilderness (Wadi Tahun, Abu Ghosh), in Transjordan (Abu Suwan beside Jerash and Beldhah near Petra) and in the Negeb (Nahal Besor).

Discernible differences exist in the material culture of the various regions, and it would appear that people's attachment to a certain region and the limitation of their wanderings led to a development of local cultures. These differences make the relative dating of the various sites difficult so it is not always clear which were earlier or which were contemporary in spite of the differences between them (Plate 5).

There is no essential difference between the Natufian cultures and the Neolithic. Their characteristic flint implements, the hoe (for cultivation), the ax (for cutting trees), and the winged arrowhead (for hunting), and also the microliths for fishing and the mounted implements, are not fundamentally different. But now they are much more widespread. A more basic change is the invention of pottery, which happened in the middle of the Neolithic period (about 5500 B.C.E.). The discovery that clay found in any place changes its characteristics at a certain temperature furnished people with cheap and sturdy containers. Henceforth, pottery vessels replaced in large measure those of wood, skin, and reeds and became the most common household vessels. Concomitantly, the clay vessels become one of the most important means employed by the archaeologist to identify a period and establish its date. Pottery is resistant to the ravages of time in contrast to perishable organic materials. The vessel may be smashed into pieces but these maintain their form and texture, and even their colors and decorations, almost without change. The technology of pottery-making, the forms of the vessels and their decorations, changed from age to age, and thus lend themselves to ever-increasing precision in diagnosis, thanks to the many stratigraphic excavations carried out at various mounds in the country. Everywhere that pottery was used, the vessels appear by the thousands; these broken pots were not in use for long periods of time and had no function after being broken.

Therefore, it is commonly accepted today that the Neolithic cultures be divided into the Pre-Pottery and the Pottery. As with all such divi-

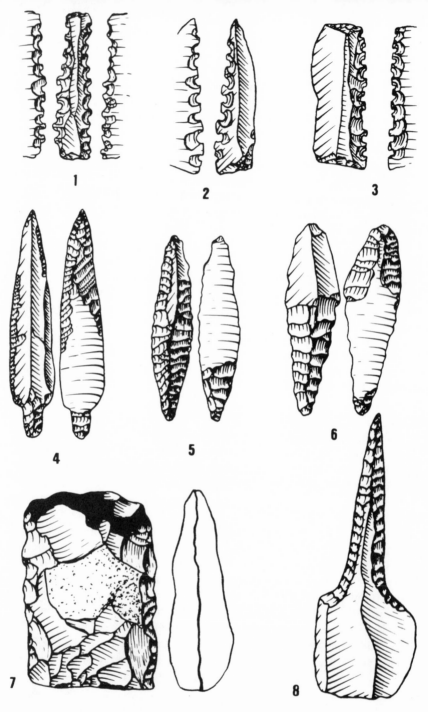

PLATE 5. Neolithic flint tools

sions, there is a certain amount of arbitrariness and artificiality. The appearance of ceramics did not come at the same time in every region with the broad spectrum of local cultures, and in the Pottery phase there were unprogressive peripheral sites that were still at a Pre-Pottery stage.

Jericho is the key site for the Neolithic period. This place still holds the crown as the earliest town in the world, having public buildings and impressive fortifications at about 8000 B.C.E., about four thousand years before the beginning of urbanization in the country and in the entire ancient East. K. Kenyon estimates that in this city there dwelt a population of about two thousand. What were the economic resources and the circumstances of the founding of this large organized town in a period when people were still in the first stages of transition to permanent settlement and agriculture? To a large degree, the plenteous spring and the warm, comfortable climate were contributing factors, and the fertile soil of the valley permitted an abundance of irrigational cultivation unparalleled elsewhere. And thus, there were also found tools and storage vessels, witnesses to intensive cultivation. However, according to one opinion, these circumstances are insufficient to explain the existence of a town so large and well developed. Perhaps its main wealth came from commerce based on the mineral treasures of the nearby Dead Sea: salt, bitumen, and sulfur—three very precious and much-sought-after minerals in antiquity. All of these factors still do not explain the need for the strong fortifications which were erected with great expenditure of effort. Did the nomadic and seminomadic population nearby cast a longing eye on the treasures of its storehouses? Or perhaps there were additional towns within close range that threatened its security, and are as yet undiscovered?

The early strata of Jericho were first excavated by Garstang in 1935–36. Above the stratum of the earliest settlement, typified by microliths (Natufian), he established eight Neolithic strata without pottery (X–XVII) and two strata with ceramics (VIII–IX).

During the excavations by Kenyon in 1952–58, Garstang's conclusions were corrected and refined, so that today her stratigraphic designations are used. After the Natufian settlement, she established two Pre-Pottery phases (Pre-Pottery Neolithic A and B) and, after them, two ceramic phases (Pottery Neolithic A and B).

As previously mentioned, the beginning of the settlement in Jericho belongs to the Natufian culture, and carbon-14 samples have established a date between about 10,000 and 7500 B.C.E. A thick stratum of floors was discovered having humps around their edges that may have supported tents or huts. A clearly isolated structure found there is a raised clay platform plastered and having a pair of sockets. In Kenyon's opinion, it was a cult place, perhaps the remains of a temple set up by the Natufian hunters beside the spring of Jericho.

It would appear that there is a continuity between this earliest phase and the Pre-Pottery A in many details of Natufian culture. To this phase belong the first houses, round structures built from bricks with a flat base and rounded top in the form of a loaf (plano-convex). The houses were slightly sunk into the ground and their walls, which slanted inward, suggested roofs in the form of domes (Photo 4A). Already in the earliest phase of the Pre-Pottery A period, the settlement was surrounded by a stone wall about 3 m. thick; later on, the wall was reinforced by a moat cut in the rock to a width of 9 m. and a depth of two or more meters. Inside of the wall was a round tower built entirely of stone with a diameter of 8.5 m. preserved to the height of 7.75 m. Within was found a closed staircase leading from its base to the top. The connection of this "tower" with the fortifications is not clear, since it is built, as mentioned above, inside of the wall and its function has yet to be properly elucidated. However, its construction is a wonderful organizational and technical achievement by the residents of the ancient city, and that in the eighth millennium B.C.E., some five thousand years before the first pyramids in Egypt (Fig. 2). At Jericho, there is no continuity between the Pre-Pottery A and the Pre-Pottery B, but rather, a new culture established itself there after the site had been destroyed and abandoned for a certain time. The flint implements belong to the Tahunian culture, named after Wadi Tahun near Bethlehem. In the vicinity, there was a group of Pre-Pottery Neolithic sites. It would appear that we have to do with new settlers coming from afar who brought with them a different but well-established cultural tradition. Not only their implements but also their buildings were of a new style. They contained larger, rectangular rooms with rounded corners arranged around courtyards. They were made of elongated bricks stamped with a herringbone pattern made by thumb impressions (Photo 4A). The roofs were evidently flat. The floors and the walls were covered with white plaster, smoothed and polished and often painted.

To this phase also belong the clear evidences of animal domestica-

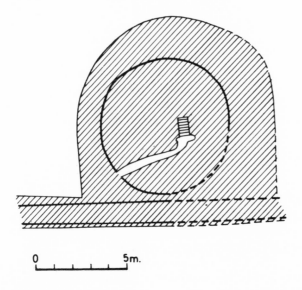

0   5m.

FIG. 2. Jericho. The round tower and the wall

tion, of goats in particular, which assumed by now a prominent place in the economy alongside hunting and cultivation. Likewise, there is evidence of trade with quite distant regions, e.g., shells from the Mediterranean, turquoise certainly brought from Sinai, and even obsidian deriving from Anatolia. Kenyon is of the opinion that this settlement was also surrounded by a stone wall, but the evidence is not sufficiently clear. In any case, that wall (which may have been nothing but a retaining wall for the houses) does not belong to the first phase, and it was destroyed after a while by the pressure of the structures leaning against it. On the other hand, there are impressive indications of the ritual and religious life of these people. Two buildings seem to have served for ritual. One is a rectangular chamber, having in the center of one of its shorter walls a niche with a rounded stone slab. Not far away in the courtyard debris, there was found a basalt pillar which originally may have stood on the stone base in the niche. Is this the first *massebah* (stele) denoting the deity, the same cultic object that enjoyed such a long development down to the Canaanite and Israelite periods? A second building, interpreted as a temple, is a rectangular room with chambers on two sides having rounded walls. Its floor was plastered with burnished clay, and in the center was a rectangular basin, also plastered. Of special interest are the remains of two groups of figurines made from unburnt clay. Each group apparently included representations of a man, woman, and child, somewhat smaller than normal size. They were placed in such a manner as to be seen only from the front, since the back side was flat. The lines of the face and hair were indented and the eyes were made of sea shells, giving them a mysterious air. This is evidently the first example of a temple representing the combination of a deity, a goddess, and a divine child, a triad which also has a long history in the ancient East. Garstang related them to the Pottery Neolithic, but Kenyon's work has shown similar fragments of human images, albeit more schematic, in the last phase of the Pre-Pottery (Fig. 3).

Some unique evidence points to the beliefs and rituals pertaining to the dead. Under the floors there were burials; part of the skeletons were missing the skull except for the lower jaw. These skulls were found in the rooms, themselves covered with clay and molded. The ears, nose, and eyebrows were molded and painted with a natural color, and in the eye sockets, shells were inserted. They now look down from the shelf of the museum, human faces with wonderfully realistic vitality: the patriarchs of Jericho from Pre-Pottery B who went to their reward more than seventy-five hundred years ago. Similar examples have been found at Beisamun in the Huleh Valley (Photo 3).

Remains with great similarity to those of people from Pre-Pottery B at Jericho also have appeared elsewhere in Eretz-Israel, e.g., at Munhata and Tell 'Ali in the northern Jordan Valley and Abu Ghosh beside Jerusalem, in Nahal Oren at the foot of the Carmel, and particularly in Wadi Beiah beside Petra in southern Transjordan.

This is a group of settlers who seem to have come from the north, from Syria or perhaps Anatolia, where one may note a similarity to sites such as Hacilar and Chatal Huyuk. This group spent a long time in the country but finally disappeared, and the people of the Pottery Neolithic culture are not their continuation.

Most of the Pre-Pottery Neolithic sites were abandoned and not resettled. After them, there was a period of cessation before they were reoccupied. This is especially notable at Jericho. Between the Pre-

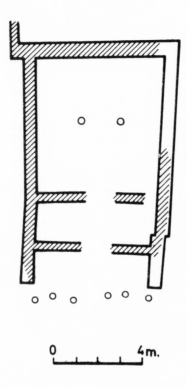

FIG. 3. Jericho. The Neolithic temple

Pottery stratum and the appearance of the pottery level there is a level of destruction, abandonment, and erosion during which the tell was unoccupied for a certain time.

It is clear that pottery manufacture, which appears during some phase of the Neolithic, was not invented in this country. Rather, it was imported by new settlers. The same conclusion is evidenced by the other elements of the material culture, which are totally different from those of the Pre-Pottery Neolithic. The tools of stone and flint are not the same, and now for the first time are found the toothed sickle blades typical of this country down to the Canaanite period. The building tradition has disappeared, and the new settlers dwell once again in shacks and tents, sometimes erected over pits dug in the ground. Only at the end of the period are there rather poor buildings at Jericho constructed of rounded or flat/concave bricks of a different quality.

Therefore, it is clear that in spite of the new technological achievements, the Pottery Neolithic culture in Eretz-Israel was something of a retrogression from its predecessors. It seems that at least during certain phases of the Pre-Pottery period, Eretz-Israel stood on the front line of the progress of civilization in the ancient East; but now it is pushed aside, and the important centers of this period are to be found in Syria, Iraq, and Anatolia.

In various parts of the country, especially the fertile valleys, there have been found sites of the Pottery Neolithic but there is still no certainty as to their relationship or to a general chronology. At Jericho, Kenyon divided the Neolithic ceramics to two groups (A and B) which correspond more or less to Strata IX and VIII of Garstang's excavation. In phase A we have, besides simple and crude vessels, others much more refined with geometric decorations and burnishing with a reddish brown color. Phase B is characterized by a perfection of forms and a greatly improved technology along with plastic decoration, especially a herringbone design instead of the burnishing and painting (Plate 6).

The common denominator of the various Pottery Neolithic sites discovered on the coastal plain, in the Jezreel Valley, and in the northern Jordan Valley, is a special type of dark burnished pottery, sometimes with plastic decoration.

A unique Pottery Neolithic culture was discovered by Stekelis at Sha'ar ha-Golan. This was a settlement planted on the banks of the Yarmuk, hence its title, "Yarmukian culture." It is a model of combined cultivation, fishing, and hunting. The dwellings were huts and tents over dugouts cut into the ground, with flat roofs supported by wooden pillars; one of them served for burial and the other as a workshop for flint tools and art objects.

The flint tools are made in the Pre-Pottery Neolithic tradition of the finished implement. There are also some new types such as the toothed sickle.

The pottery is simple and crude, fired at a low temperature. Most of the vessels have a red slip (apparently to make them more impermeable) and plastic decorations, especially the herringbone pattern (Plate

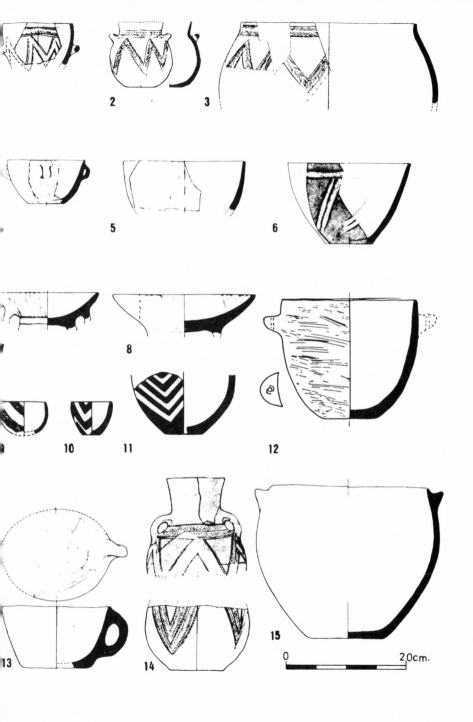

PLATE 6. Neolithic pottery

6:14). The Yarmukian culture is characterized by a rare richness of art objects made from wadi stones and clay, and painted red. Most of them are figurines depicting human forms in a schematic manner, mostly women, and there are also models of the male and female sexual organs. This is another interesting embodiment of the fertility cult that began in the Natufian (Photo 5).

Similar figurines with schematic female forms on rocks are also known from the Pre-Pottery Neolithic of Nahal Oren. As indicated, it is not impossible that some of the Pre-Pottery sites overlap chronologically with ceramic sites, and it is still most difficult to establish the relative dating between various assemblages. In the hill regions and along the edge of the Judean Wilderness, there are practically no Pottery Neolithic sites to be found, so it may be that the Tahunian culture held out longer there.

From the standpoint of building technology and stone tools, the last stage of the Neolithic, i.e., the Pottery, appears to be a retrogression. The increase in sites signifies a considerable progress by people in cultivation and in the transition to permanent settlement. It should be noted that Neolithic sherds also appear in the earliest strata at some of the largest and most important tells in the country, e.g., Megiddo, Beth-shean, Tell el-Far'ah (North). The natural factors which made these places desirable at all times—water sources, rich land, and control over routes—already were commensurate with the human life pattern in that period. Pottery Neolithic sites have also been found on the southern border of Eretz-Israel (Nahal Besor), and in the northern Sinai desert on the routes leading to Egypt. All these proclaim a new era. In about 4000 B.C.E. the long Stone Age came to an end, and a new chapter opened in which human civilization began to develop with great strides, having as its center the Middle East.

II

THE CHALCOLITHIC PERIOD

THE Chalcolithic corresponds to the fourth millennium B.C.E. and represents an intermediary stage between the long prehistoric era and the beginning of clear archaeological periods. In Eretz-Israel, we still derive all of our information from the remains of material culture. However, this is the time when the great centers of culture in the Middle East were taking shape in the land of the Tigris and Euphrates, on one hand, and in the land of the Nile, on the other. The rise of those great, well-organized centers, the cities and the large monarchies, goes along with the invention of the early writing systems and the beginning of their dissemination—cuneiform in Mesopotamia began in the mid-fourth millennium and hieroglyphics in Egypt at the beginning of the third millennium.

We must again be reminded that all archaeological terminology is general and schematic. True, the first copper implements appear in the Chalcolithic period (*chalkos* = copper; *lithos* = stone), and there is most assuredly a close connection between the beginning of the use of metal and the great acceleration of cultural development. However, in Eretz-Israel only copper implements are used, even in the "Early Bronze Age," and they are of limited distribution.

The period under discussion is characterized by a very rapid and significant advance of culture throughout the country in every respect, associated with a higher population density than was ever known before. But this advance began in the shadow of the mighty neighboring civilizations, and was influenced by them. In addition, these cultures clearly were not generated and did not arise in Eretz-Israel; they came in suddenly, already well-defined and developed. Thus, the geopolitical nature of the Land of Israel is now fully prominent for the first time:

a small country with limited natural resources located at a crossroads of trunk lines connecting the early foci of civilization.

The Chalcolithic culture is a large occupation wave of agricultural-ists and shepherds who penetrated mainly into the valleys and the fringes of the country during the first half of the fourth millennium B.C.E. It first became known to us from a site in the southeastern Jordan Valley located opposite Jericho, not far from the Dead Sea. This site consists of five small mounds called Teleilat el-Ghassul from which we have derived the term "Ghassulian culture."

Teleilat el-Ghassul was a large, unfortified village made up of several adjacent mounds. Excavations have been conducted in three of them, and the upper stratum was mainly uncovered there. It consists of rectangular buildings, the walls of which were made of brick, usually on stone foundations. Although the general plan is not very regular, it would seem that the basic unit was a rectangular broad room to which were attached large courtyards in various directions, some ir-regular in accordance with the available open spaces. Short alleys

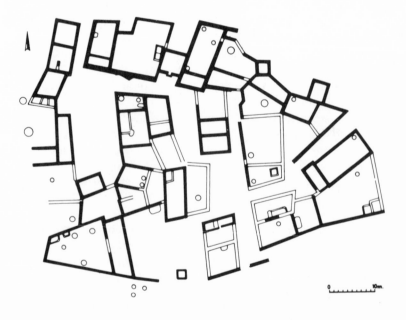

FIG. 4. Teleilat el-Ghassul. Plan of the settlement (Stratum IV)

passed between blocks of buildings. A great many silos were found in them, some with a depth and diameter of about 2 m.; these were for storing grain. The depth of the strata reaches about 4 m., and there were four main occupation levels. The settlement existed for an appreciable period of time, evidently with a continuity of several centuries. Cultivation seems to have held the main place in the economy of the town. To this the silos are witness, since in some of them grains were still preserved, but so too the various working tools, e.g., hoes and flint sickle blades, mortars and grindstones. Date and olive pits were also found. The date palm is one of the most typical trees of the warm climate in the southern Jordan Valley until this very day, but not so the olive, which requires a cooler atmosphere; thus, there is testimony to connections with the hill regions. We do not have any information about the fauna, but it is probable that raising small cattle played a major role in the economy. The large courtyards surely must have served as stockades for cattle as well, and the many fan scrapers present must have been for the preparation of skins. These are flat flint tools in the shape of a fan, having at their extremities the outer crust of the nucleus. Arrowheads are rare, indicating that hunting no longer was a real factor in the local economy (Photo 16).

The wide spectrum of pottery vessels found indicates a well-formulated pottery tradition. They are made by hand, some on mats the imprint of which was impressed on the flat bases; only the upper part of the bowls was smoothed with the aid of a tournette. Plastic decorations and also those with bands of red-brown color were found. Especially typical is a bowl with straight sides and a rim decorated by a red strip. A vessel typical of Ghassulian pottery is the censer, a long, slender, horn-shaped cup, often with color decoration and with small lug handles, the so-called "cornets." Another typical vessel is a large container with handles at each end that evidently served as a butter churn. In the Beer-sheba region, a pottery figurine was found in the form of a woman carrying on her head a vessel like a churn made of skin. The use of copper implements is indicated by axes and awls. One should not draw conclusions from their small numbers since that valuable metal could be melted down and reused even after the implement was broken or worn down (Photo 10; Plate 7:10, 13).

More surprising were the colored wall murals found in the internal plaster of some of the house walls. They include various geometric designs and also some imaginary animals. Particularly impressive is a

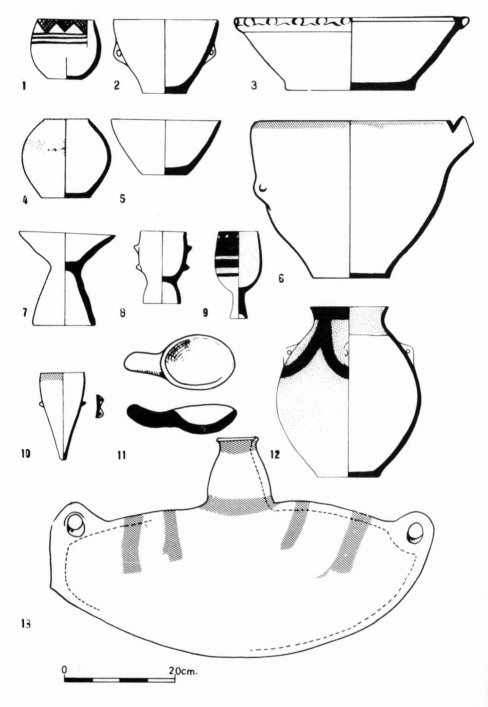

PLATE 7. Chalcolithic pottery

large colored mural with an eight-pointed star in the center, nearly 2 m. in diameter, with two additional stars inside surrounded by circles. Around it were scattered other geometric patterns and strange animals. Especially striking was a mask of a mythological being having large eyes. It would appear that these drawings are associated with an ancient art and mythology; they were renewed from time to time, perhaps in special ceremonies. They bear witness to a well-crystallized tradition and to an appreciable artistic ability. Thus far, they are unique in Eretz-Israel. Almost contemporary wall murals are also known from Mesopotamia and from a slightly earlier period at Chatal Huyuk.

Many sites of nearly the same period have been discovered in the northern Negeb. They were examined at three particular sites near Beer-sheba—Be'er Matar, Be'er Zafad, and Horvat Beter. These are three small sites less than a kilometer from one another on the two banks of Nahal Beer-sheba west of the new city. As indicated by their names, two of them are located by wells that served the Bedouin for water supply. An especially surprising feature in the history of this country is that in the earlier stages of these settlements, the occupants did not live in houses but in underground chambers hewn into the loess soil. During the first phase large rooms were dug with a length of about 7 to 10 m. and a width of about 3 m. The entry to the cave/rooms was through a slanted passageway cut from the side or top of the mound.

This form of dwelling is foreign to Eretz-Israel, and does not conform to local conditions. The underground passages in the depths of the earth are more suitable for extreme climatic conditions with high temperatures during the day and summertime, with lower temperatures at night and in the winter. One may conjecture that these dwellings represent habits from the settlers' original homeland, conditions similar to those of the Ararat and Caucasus region. Perhaps their origin is in those northern caves, which would explain why they chose to settle in the arid Negeb and the Judean Wilderness with their climatic extremes between day and night, summer and winter. These are also regions of caves and as the excavations have shown, their economy was based mainly on small cattle which they had certainly brought with them. The many natural caves in the cliffs of the wilderness seem to have reminded them of conditions in their homeland. There is hardly a livable cave in the Judean Wilderness in which remains of the

Chalcolithic period have not been found, even those which are nearly inaccessible.

The underground chambers are unsuitable for conditions in the land, even in the Negeb. The climatic conditions are not so extreme that the advantage of the mild temperature in the chambers was a factor against their many disadvantages: difficulty of access through the narrow shaft, complete darkness, and insufficient ventilation. Furthermore, the loess soil is not conducive to such quarrying. Of course, it is relatively easy to dig, but this is not stable rock, and within a short time the roofs cracked and caved in, as seen in the excavations. The occupants sought a solution to that problem without relinquishing the principle of the chambers; they went over to a new type of smaller rooms, oval in shape, with a length of no more than 4 m., connected one to another by narrow corridors. Instead of one large room, a dwelling unit was now comprised of four or five smaller, more stable chambers. The entryway to a chain of rooms was through a vertical shaft in the sides of which steps are discernible. Sometimes there was more than one shaft, evidently necessary for purposes of ventilation. When some of these underground compartments also collapsed, they adopted a new system, still without surrendering the basic principle of below-surface dwellings. In craters formed instead of the caved-in chambers, there were now built round or ovoid rooms with walls of sun-dried bricks on stone foundations, leaning outward against the loess soil. These rooms were roofed over with wooden beams crossed at ground level upon which reeds and crushed soil were laid. Thus, one had a house still underground but whose walls and roof were of more sturdy construction.

However, in the end the occupants abandoned the idea of the subterranean house and began building regular structures. This seems to have taken place after a certain occupation gap as evidenced by the thin layers of loess accumulated across the entryways to the older chambers. On the surface, they now built rectangular rooms, the walls of which were made of bricks on stone foundations. This is an instructive picture of adaptation by the settlers to the conditions in this land and its region, which were unfavorable to their previously known building customs.

One of the surprising things about the excavations was that some of the underground buildings contained household vessels arranged as if they were being stored until the occupants returned. In some of the

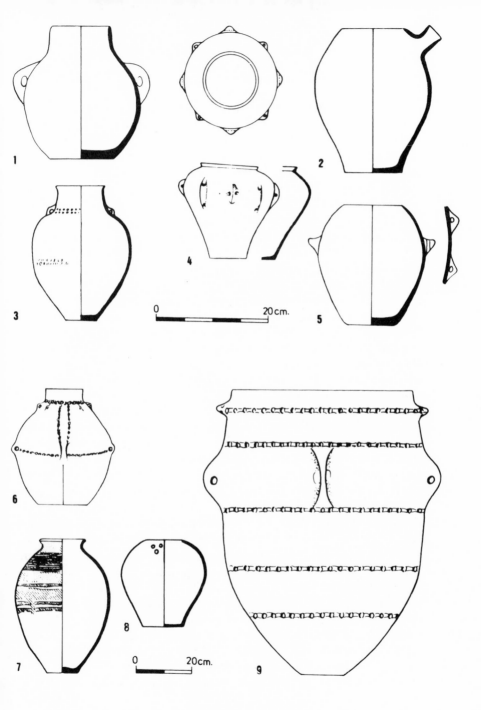

PLATE 8. Chalcolithic pottery

storage pits cut into the floors were found domestic vessels of pottery and basalt lying one inside another, small bowls in larger kraters. It is clear, therefore, that the occupants of the house did not leave the place in haste but only after putting away their utensils in a well-ordered manner. In one of the granaries, they stopped up the shaft entries so that the subterranean houses remained sealed until modern excavation.

From these facts, one can see that the settlers abandoned their site under particular circumstances, either seasonal wanderings or perhaps in a time of severe drought. Their intention was to return at the proper time, but in actuality they failed to do so. It may be that these seasonal migrations were one of the reasons that the settlers chose the underground granaries, which could be hidden and camouflaged during their seasonal absence (Plate 8).

Every one of the settlements at Be'er Matar and Be'er Zafad included about ten units with a large room in the center, possibly a public place not designated for living quarters. Perrot estimates the population of each such settlement at no more than 200 people. It would appear that these were clans, and the number of neighboring settlements may have comprised one tribe. In addition to the main branches of the economy founded on seasonal cultivation of grains and vegetables and on cattle-raising, in each settlement a certain craft specialization was evident, surely preserved in the framework of the family, and transferred from father to son as in the guilds known from later periods. At Be'er Matar a workshop was found for making copper tools, while at Be'er Zafad tools were found of an artist engaged in carving ivory and bone. Indications were also present for the manufacture of stone tools.

The workshop at Be'er Matar for making copper implements is the earliest discovered in this country. Malachite ores were found there, having a composition that points to an origin in the Arabah, along with flint anvils for breaking the ore, fireplaces with metal slag and vessels for pouring and casting the copper. The tools found here and elsewhere include axes, chisels, awls, and mace-heads. There were also various ornaments cast by the *cire perdue* technique.

The people of the Beer-sheba culture achieved their clearest artistic expression in the carving of ivory and bone. The complete incisor of an elephant was found in one of the underground houses at Be'er Zafad; beside it were the artisan's tools: a copper point affixed to a bone handle for carving and a stone slab on which the ivory was worked. One of the ivory figurines was found in the entryway to his house.

Bone and ivory implements include various ornaments such as earrings, pendants, head pins, and ivory plaques. Most impressive are the ivory figurines, including those of bearded men and naked women. All are depicted erect with the arms hanging down and the hands stroking the stomach, but there are many variations in the form. One figurine of a pregnant woman is distinguished by its realistic lines and delicate execution except for the arms which are carved in the routine manner; regrettably, the head is missing. It may be conjectured that this "Venus of Beer-sheba," as Perrot called her, represents the goddess of fertility whose ritual was so widespread in the ancient East.

It is possible that the highly perfected basalt implements served for household ritual on the family level. In several of the dwellings, there were found sets of three basalt vessels, two bowls with flat bases and a bowl on a raised foot with windows carved in it. This bowl/chalice is reminiscent of incense burners from later periods.

In contrast to the inhabitants of the Jordan Valley, the Ghassulians, who lived in permanent settlements and engaged principally in cultivation, the settlers in the Negeb, those of the Beer-sheba culture, remained seminomadic with a livelihood based on cattle and household crafts. The same would appear to apply to the contemporary groups in the Judean Wilderness; they form a geographic link between the Jordan Valley and the Negeb. Cattle pens for small cattle were found near the caves and it is clear that seasonal pasture was the only possible economic activity for that arid region. It is obviously a numerically large population, and the question must be asked whether in that ancient period also, the caves, or some of them, may have served as a last refuge in a time of crisis. At En-gedi, the main oasis of the Judean Wilderness, a temple was found. The building itself is a very clear broad room about 20 m. wide and only 4 m. in depth. Opposite the entrance on the southern side, there was a raised, horseshoe-shaped platform on which a round stone base was found, probably a stand for an image of the deity. Down the middle of the room, there were stone benches, surely places for standing the cult vessels; at both ends of the room were numerous small pits containing remnants of offerings, especially fragments of bowls, cups, and animal bones.

In front of the building was a broad courtyard surrounded by a stone fence; a round installation was in the center, about 3 m. in diameter, a sort of basin or pool, apparently intended for drink offerings (water from the spring) during ritual ceremonies. In the corner of the courtyard, there was a small structure, also a broad room, obviously for use by the temple servitors. Two gates led to the courtyard: on the south, a sort of gatehouse with benches around the inside walls, evidently the

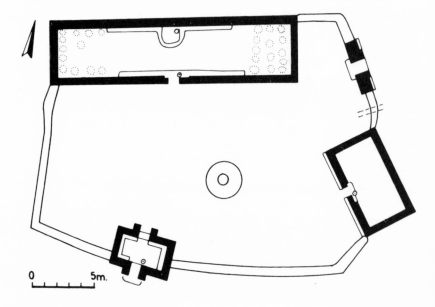

0   5m.

FIG. 5. En-gedi. Chalcolithic temple

main entry facing the spring, and on the east, a simple opening looking out toward Nahal David. This well-designed temple occupying a dominant position above the oasis and the Dead Sea is not associated with an adjacent settlement. Thus far, none has come to light at En-gedi from the Chalcolithic period. Therefore, it seems likely that this was a central temple serving the seminomadic population of the entire region.

In the temple itself, only a few objects were found, among them a fragment of a figurine and an Egyptian alabaster vessel, which means that the temple was abandoned without being wrecked and burned. One of the refuge caves in the Judean Wilderness contained a special treasure discovered by P. Bar-Adon. It was comprised of unique cultic vessels and one must assume that they originally were in use at the En-gedi temple. The "treasure cave" is on a lofty, barely accessible cliff in Nahal Mishmar, about 10 km. southwest of En-gedi. In the depths of the cave the hoard was found wrapped in a mat. It added up to 429 objects, mostly of copper with a few of stone and ivory. Except for a few chisels, these are clearly not objects for everyday use but rather a unique assemblage of undoubtedly cultic artifacts. They include more than two hundred "mace-heads," the majority of copper with a number of stone (Photo 8). They were certainly mounted on wooden sticks; analogous examples have been found elsewhere. Most surprising were eight hollow, decorated "reeds," one with a human face and another with heads of wild goats (Photo 7); ten "diadems" or "crowns" having geometric decorations, raised buttons, openings, and animal forms (Photo 6); and five ivory objects made from hippopotamus tusks in the form of "candlesticks" with a surface full of holes and one larger central hole. It must be noted that the fragment of a similar ivory object showed up at Be'er Matar near Beer-sheba.

All of these objects were surely used in ritual at a temple and it would seem that they were hidden in the nearby cave when the cult place was abandoned. A treasure so rich in exquisite metal implements testifies to the wealth, the mature tradition, and the artistic and technical ability of the Ghassulian culture. The copper objects contain a large percentage of arsenic typical of copper ores from eastern Anatolia and Armenia. The metal and perhaps the objects themselves came from that region and may suggest that population's origin (Photos 6–8).

Burial caves from the Chalcolithic period have been discovered mainly on the coastal plain between Hadera and Gadera. They are famous for the ossuaries found in them. The first such cave was excavated in 1934 by Sukenik at Hadera, and since then many additional examples have been found, the most important being from Azor, Ben-Shemen, and Benei Braq. The caves themselves were hewn out of the ground, and they remind one in form of the dwelling chambers of the Beer-sheba culture. The offering vessels of pottery and basalt found in them belong to the Ghassulian culture.

As to the ossuaries, most were made of pottery but a few are of stone. In them were placed the bones of the deceased as a secondary burial after the flesh had decayed; some were in the form of jars or of animals, but most of the ceramic examples were shaped like houses with a large window on the front face through which the bones were inserted along with the skull. Some of the roofs were slanted and some of the houses stand on pillars, features appropriate to wet, swampy regions. It is conjectured that this form of house was adapted to the Sharon Plain. Inasmuch as the Negeb sites, in particular, testify to a seminomadic society with no local burials, it is possible that those same people moved northward during the summer seeking pasturage for their flocks. The temporary form of burial and the secondary interment of the bones would be typical of nomads and seminomads, although we find this custom in other circumstances, e.g., the Jewish burial caves in the Second Temple period.

Recently, settlements have been found here and there beside the cemeteries. These may be the summer encampments of the seminomadic population. Therefore, it is possible that the house forms of the ossuaries do not derive from Eretz-Israel but rather represent a tradition of a homeland having a higher rainfall.

The decorations of these ossuaries are especially interesting, both of paint and in relief; they are further evidence of the rich and highly sophisticated tradition of the Chalcolithic period. They include geometric patterns, types of "capitals" and human faces having a projecting snout and large eyes reminiscent of the decorations on the copper implements from the Judean Wilderness (Photo 9).

Carbon-14 tests have shown that the Chalcolithic people reached this country in the first half of the fourth millennium B.C.E., and the end of this occupation wave is fixed at about 3150 B.C.E. It would appear that the new settlers, migrating to the country from the north in large numbers, did not find a rival population here. So they were able to establish themselves on undefended sites in areas convenient for habitation and pasturage. They brought with them a new and well-developed technology as reflected in their dwellings, their tools, and their many artistic creations, mainly intended for cultic use. The pottery repertoire is very fine and quite varied; it is uniquely well-fired and outstanding for its decorations in color and relief (Plate 7; Photo 10). Implements and figurines of bone and ivory indicate a sophisticated artistic tradition. The basalt bowls, made by a technique of drilling and grinding, are marvelous for their refinement and beauty, so much so that one is hard pressed to find comparable examples in later periods. The Ghassulian people also brought with them the knowledge of copper-working, and the wonderful treasure of the Judean Wilderness bears witness to the high level of their technical ability in this field. The end of the Chalcolithic Ghassulian culture resembles its beginning by its abruptness, and the riddle of its disappearance is still shrouded in mystery. All of the settlements investigated thus far were abandoned at the same time, apparently during the thirty-second century B.C.E. Most of them were forsaken by their occupants and not destroyed at the hand of an enemy. But it is hard to envisage anything else for small, open settlements which were never meant for defense. Was that a time of extended droughts that forced them to migrate to other areas, or did they have to give way under the pressure of new arrivals? Was their presence in caves of refuge in the Judean Wilderness indicative of that catastrophe? In any case, it would appear that the priests of the En-gedi temple packed up their implements and hid them in the cave when they left their cult site, never to return.

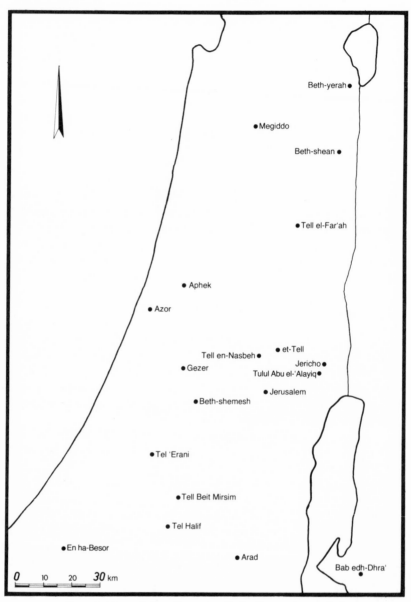

FIG. 6. Map of sites from the Early Canaanite period

III

THE CANAANITE PERIOD

EARLY CANAANITE

THE Early Canaanite is a long and significant period in the history of Eretz-Israel during which the foundations of Canaanite culture were laid. It lasted about one thousand years, from approximately the thirty-second to the twenty-third century B.C.E. These dates are principally based on the chronology of Egypt, according to vessels and inscriptions discovered in excavations linking the two countries in various chronological periods. They are subject to minor changes within a century or so since the absolute chronology of Egypt is still not sufficiently well founded for this era. In Eretz-Israel, this was still a mute period, suitably called protohistoric. In the neighboring lands, especially Mesopotamia and Egypt, it is already a historical era in the full sense of that term, being well known to us from a rich fund of written documents of a political, economic, ritual, and literary nature. Eretz-Israel, located between them, remains in the shadow while the searchlights of history are illuminating its neighbors. Thus far, texts have not been found here except for a few isolated Egyptian examples found on imported items.

During this age, most of the large, important cities of Eretz-Israel were established, and occupation continued in them for a long time until the typical projecting tells were created that are so easily discernible in the landscape even now. Again and again, new towns were built on the ruins of the buildings from previous occupation; city walls, which themselves were usually built one upon another atop the steep slope, were what gave them their artificial shape, protecting the slopes from erosion and decay. The continuity of their occupation and rebuilding during more than twenty-five hundred years, in spite of all the destructions and occupational gaps that occurred, testify that the economic and settlement factors did not undergo a fundamental change throughout that time.

When one examines the location of these sites, a number of factors become evident which explain their choice in terms of fundamental occupational and economic circumstances of a stable nature. Generally, hills convenient for fortification were chosen, located on water sources in the center of agricultural areas and beside major road junctions. It is thus clear that these were fortified urban centers for agricultural districts which supported them along with the income from foreign and local commerce conducted along the important trunk routes. These factors have also come to light in the various excavations. The household utensils and the remains of seeds and grains indicate that the cultivation of crops, including cereals, fruit trees, and vegetables, was one of the main branches of the economy. Various imported objects also testify to strong commercial ties, particularly with Egypt.

These tells are urban centers that are important henceforth in the country down to the age of the Canaanite city-states during the Israelite conquest. Most central settlements were now urban in their essential nature, i.e., a large settlement with a central government, the economy of whose people was based on various occupations; alongside private houses there are now public buildings such as palaces, temples, central granaries, and fortifications. This is a tremendous innovation in the history of the country, which had not known urban settlements thus far, except for Jericho. Therefore, Kenyon proposed to denote the Bronze Age as the "Urban period," a title indicating the principal occupational change of the entire era, especially since copper was still being used in the "Early Bronze Age." This is true in and of itself, but since that designation, like all other definitions, must remain general and schematic, it has not been widely accepted. Beside the urban settlement there were also many villages. Most of the towns were preceded by a village settlement though the elements are not always sufficiently clear. Therefore, it would seem to us that the name "Canaanite" is more suitable. This is the general name for the population of the country during the Israelite conquest, when more extensive historical illumination begins. The royal Canaanite cities were a fixed element throughout the entire Canaanite period of nearly two thousand years.

There is no direct connection between the Chalcolithic Ghassulian culture and the new settlers who penetrated the country from the north in the thirty-second century B.C.E. Of course, the remains of their first settlements are simple; only a few very poor structures have been found, and there is no fundamental difference between these villages and the Chalcolithic settlements. One opinion holds that there was a certain contemporaneity between the new settlers and the last of the Chalcolithic still holding out for a while in the south. It is true that there exists one widely distributed vessel, the hole-mouth jar, that served for storage and cooking, found in both cultures, which may indicate some connection between them. Yet the coevality has not been proved and is not yet based on stratigraphic data but only on the fact that certain groups of the new settlers did not penetrate into the southern region. Even if there is no time gap between them, and if they really did have an encounter at a certain stage, which is still in doubt, the new arrivals brought with them some distinct innovations in their artifacts (as expressed in burial forms, their economy, and their material culture). All of these served to introduce a new era associated with urbanized culture (Plate 9:23). At the beginning of the Early Canaanite I, including the gray burnished phase, apsidal buildings (in which one wall is rounded to form a sort of apse) are found alongside the usual rectangular buildings. It seems evident that this is a building tradition brought to the country by the new occupants which they used for a limited time along with other traditions. Apsidal buildings are not known in either Egypt or Mesopotamia, but they are widespread in the Aegean region, e.g., at Troy. It is true that in the Aegean they are somewhat later, and that that tradition was maintained there for a longer time. It is possible, therefore, that the source of this architecture is northern Anatolia, in the homeland of the gray burnished ware, from which it spread southward into various regions.

The new settlers brought with them a tradition of family burial caves, the "patriarchal tomb," to which people were gathered when their time came. These caves were found outside the settlements, some natural ones being expanded to serve as tombs while others were entirely hewn out by people on the slopes of the cliffs. In these caves were found a large number of skeletons, the first being moved aside when a new interment took place. Most of the funerary gifts were of the usual pottery vessels of that period, generally small and refined, sometimes accompanied by copper weapons or ornaments left with the

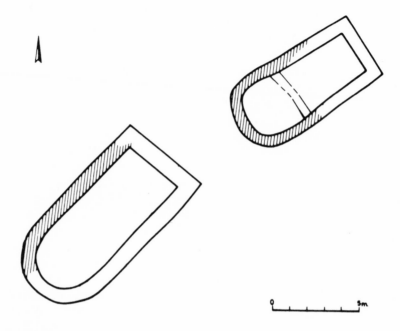

FIG. 7. Apsidal buildings

deceased. Jars for storage and cooking, so ubiquitous in the settlements, were almost entirely missing in the graves. This is a new and
completely different custom from the isolated and secondary burials
practiced thus far, and it testifies to a new population having a distinct
tradition of fixed settlement.

The burial caves from the Early Canaanite discovered thus far are
not numerous in contrast to the large quantity of graves from the later
period. The question arises as to whether this is accidental, or if the
small number is related to their distance from settlements and their
extended period of usage.

Since 1965 excavations have been conducted at Bab edh-Dhra' on
the eastern side of the Dead Sea in the Lisan (Heb. Lashon) area, at
first by Bedouins and later under scientific supervision. A huge ceme-

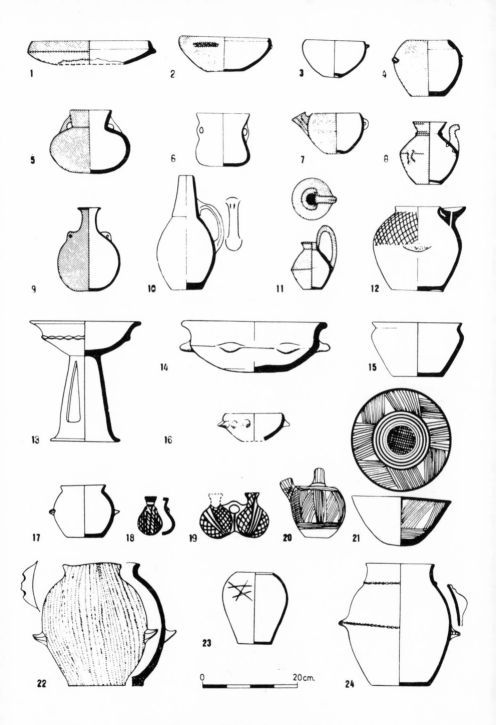

PLATE 9. Pottery of Early Canaanite I

tery has been discovered containing thousands of graves, the largest burial ground of this period known thus far in the Near East. This cemetery contains graves from every phase of the Early Canaanite period, some shaft tombs excavated in the soil of the Lisan and some constructed charnel houses resembling in form the regular dwellings, circular in the earlier and rectangular in the later phase. The cemetery included several hundred such charnel houses, and one of them, excavated stratigraphically, included about 800 pottery vessels and the bones of more than 200 people. Although a settlement from that period has been discovered in the near vicinity, it would appear that this burial ground not only served the needs of that community but also may have been a traditional burial center for a much larger population. It is possible, therefore, that the existence of central grounds in sacred cultic areas explains the relatively small number of burial caves near the towns themselves. However, in the Lisan vicinity and further south, other settlements and an additional cemetery have been found. So one must accept this conclusion with a certain reservation (Photo 11).

The principal economic activity of the new settlers was cultivation at the beginning, in contrast to the pastoral nature of the Chalcolithic communities. The production of flint implements becomes less important, the percentage of tools is much smaller, they are made with less care, and arrowheads are rare. The "Canaanite sickle blade" appears, an implement made of rectangular pieces of flint with one sharp edge, shiny from high usage, and the other shaped in order to be fixed in a bone or wooden handle. This is a distinctly agricultural tool that remained in use down to the Israelite period. The cultivational nature of the new settlers is also clarified by the distribution of their settlements, as Gophna has discovered. We find the settlements of the Early Canaanite period in the Jordan Valley, the Jezreel Valley, the Coastal Plain, and the Shephelah, and also in the central hill country. However, on the southern coastal plain, they generally do not go beyond the line of Nahal Shikma, and throughout this period they are almost never found in the southern Shephelah or in the Negeb. Arad, in the eastern Negeb, is an exception to this rule. Actually, one must view it as the southern outpost of the communities in the Mt. Hebron foothills; it did not begin in the earliest phase of Early Canaanite I. This geographical settlement pattern makes good sense in the light of the different characteristics of the two occupation waves: the bearers of the Chalcolithic culture were seminomads who took advantage of the pasturage in the semiarid regions during the winter and spring. The area of Nahal Shikma was a border between the Mediterranean and the more arid Irano-Turonian climate, i.e., it served as a natural border for the settlements whose principal economy was based on permanent cultivation. This explanation cannot, of course, be squared with the assumption of contemporaneity of the two cultures. The families of shepherds in the southern regions would need the sustenance of summer pasturage in the more northerly districts, but these were now taken up by the new settlers in Early Canaanite I. Study of the skulls from the tombs points to a fundamental difference between the people of the two cultures. Of course, there are some variants among the skull types, but the people of the Early Canaanite belong to the Mediterranean type with an elongated cranium as against the Armenoid, broad cranium type of the Chalcolithic culture. Evidently, the people of Early Canaanite I came in several waves and settled in the various parts of the country. They can be divided according to certain ceramic types as distinguished originally by Wright, three in particular, which characterize the different stages of Early Canaanite I: (1) a distinctly red burnished ware typified by jugs and juglets with large handles extending up from the rim of the vessel (Plate 9:11); (2) pottery with a definite gray burnish, including mainly large bowls, carinated on the upper part and having a flat base. Under the rim one sometimes finds a decoration of buttons, and others are on a high, windowed base (Plate 9:13); (3) pottery with a decoration of red bands covering nearly the entire vessel in various directions and groupings, sometimes in waves and sometimes intersecting, particularly deep bowls and round juglets having lug handles on the shoulder (Plate 9:21).

Opinions are still divided concerning the connections and the periods in which these groups appeared and disappeared, especially since most of the vessels are known not from stratified occupation but from tombs, the span of usage of which may have been considerable. However, it is clear from the regions where these vessels are distributed that at least some of them are contemporary. The first two groups having the bright burnishing are in the north, while the painted third group is southern. The gray burnished ware was first discovered in the Jezreel Valley, thus Wright called it the "Esdraelan culture." At various sites in the northern part of the country the two burnished groups appear, sometimes separately and sometimes together. At Jericho, red burnished vessels were found in tombs and on the tell itself. Gray burnished vessels were found in nearby Tulul Abu el-'Alayiq. Red burnished ware has shown up with the painted pottery in some centrally located sites such as Gezer, Ai, Mizpah (Tell en-Nasbeh), and Jerusalem, and all three groups have been found together in some tombs such as Tell el-Far'ah (North). In tomb A13 at Jericho the painted ware came from the upper phase and the red burnished from the lower. Therefore, it would appear that the painted pottery is the latest of the three. Contemporary with it in the northern part of the country is a reddish-brown and pink-painted wash called "grain wash." The red burnished ware is evidently the earliest of the three groups, and the differences between them are regional. It is possible that their penetration began mainly from east to west toward the coastal plain, as assumed by Gophna; also, the waves of settlers seem to have arrived in the country at certain intervals beginning with the north and later reaching the south.

As in most periods, not much is known about origins. The burnishing technique is reminiscent of an Anatolian tradition, and it is possible to find some resemblance between it and the Neolithic of Crete, Rhodes, and even Malta. The forms of some vessels point to a connection with Mesopotamia in the Uruk period. The painted wares have some analogies in northern Syria. On the other hand, there is no Egyptian influence, but rather the opposite. Some forms of the Canaanite wares had already penetrated into Egypt during this period, viz., the Egyptian predynastic (Nagada II). It is clear, therefore, that one must seek the origin of these settlers in the north. Inasmuch as there are no written documents, one is unable to say with certainty what their language may have been. It is only possible to conjecture, on the basis of place-names, that in the Early Canaanite period a Semitic language, similar to the later Canaanite and Hebrew, already dominated. Most of the new towns, the names of which are known to us in later periods, were founded, as mentioned previously, in this period; the morphology of their names is almost exclusively Semitic, e.g., Beth-yerah, Jericho, Beth-shean, Megiddo, Gezer. Place-names generally do not change, even during times of population and language changes. If, when the towns were founded, a different language had been spoken, one would expect the appearance of other linguistic elements in their names.

The founding process of the fortified cities and the circumstances that led to it are also not as clear as they should be. It is almost certain that the impetus was not local but that Eretz-Israel shared in a widespread development all over the Near East with its inspiration coming from the major centers of civilization in Mesopotamia and Egypt. This is the Uruk-Jemdet Nasr period of Mesopotamia, when monumental buildings were erected and cities were first fortified which developed into the Proto-Literate period preceding the early Sumerian dynasties. In Egypt, this is the Gerzean period and the Proto-Dynastic. From various Egyptian imports, it is now clear that the later phase of Early Canaanite I in this country overlaps the beginning of the First Dynasty of Egypt.

Establishment of the organized cities and the large monarchies took place in the entire Near East during the end of the fourth and the beginning of the third millennium B.C.E., and it is clear that the impetus to this process did not come from Eretz-Israel. It is also evident from the various elements in the pottery and material culture that there is a connection between Mesopotamia and Eretz-Israel. In particular, one must note the cylinder-seal impressions in the Jemdet Nasr style discovered in several places.

Although the earlier phases of Early Canaanite I are still not thoroughly elucidated, everyone agrees that the establishment of the towns is not the first step in the new settlement. The first communities were unfortified villages and the construction was generally simple and poor. The two groups of burnished pottery disappear before the first fortifications; only the third group, the painted ware, announces the main phases, viz., those of urbanization, of the Early Canaanite period.

As mentioned above, one does not know the reason for establishing the fortified towns that henceforth make their imprint on the country's occupation. Evidence is steadily increasing for a certain Egyptian penetration at the beginning of the First Dynasty, particularly in the south of Eretz-Israel in the later stage of Early Canaanite I. This is a period in which the first fortified towns were evidently built, e.g., Beth-yerah, Tell el-Far'ah, and Ai. There is probably a connection between these two phenomena, but it is difficult to assume that the massive fortifications in all parts of the country, even in the inner regions and in the north, were founded in response to Egyptian pressure. Likewise, one may not assume that in this period a central, organized government was established, dependent upon these cities and in rivalry with Egypt, as proposed by Lapp. The picture of the fortified towns reminds us in every respect of the royal Canaanite city-states of a later time as we know them, especially in the el-'Amarna Age and from the Bible. The existence of independent, rival city-states, each dominating a very limited area, is characteristic of the regime in the country during the entire Canaanite period except, perhaps, for a brief interim during the so-called Hyksos Age. There is no evidence to the effect that things were different in the Early Canaanite period, particularly since there is no city known to us large enough or sufficiently well fortified to rank as the "capital" of such a hypothetical kingdom.

Perhaps it was the rivalry between a city and its neighbor that required the strong fortifications? Or maybe they were directed against the traditional waves of settlers that penetrated the country during certain periods, as shown by the appearance of new ceramic types. It could be that all of these factors combined and perhaps were augmented by historical circumstances that are still a mystery to us.

The cities of this period are a revolutionary innovation in the history of Eretz-Israel, and most of them are larger and stronger in their fortifications than the towns of later periods. Towns like Beth-yerah and Tel 'Erani spread out over an area of more than 200 dunams (about 50 acres). In many places, the Early Canaanite city was much more extensive than the fortified towns built on it in later periods. Most impressive are the fortifications of Beth-yerah, Megiddo, and Ai among the towns of this period that have been extensively investigated. Beth-yerah is a large city on an area of about 250 dunams situated beside the southwestern shore of Lake Chinnereth near the outlet of the Jordan, the ancient course of which passed around the tell on the north and west. This city was founded in the earliest phase of the Early Canaanite period and existed during the entire third millennium B.C.E. At the end of the Early Canaanite, the site was abandoned and, except for sporadic settlement here and there, the tell was not inhabited until the Hellenistic Age, after nearly two thousand years. This is also an instructive example of the preservation of a place-name in spite of such great gaps in its occupational history. The name Beth-yerah is known only from sources late in the Second Temple period but, in fact, it is certain that a name associated with the lunar deity was not coined at that time. Rather, we must recognize here the name of an early Canaanite city preserved even by the later Jewish residents in the area for a very long time.

Beth-yerah was surrounded by a brick wall eight meters thick, made of three units dependent one upon another. This massive wall existed without essential changes down to the end of Early Canaanite, in spite of the waves of destruction that passed over the city and an appreciable rise in the levels of occupational debris.

The wall of Megiddo from Stratum XVIII was built of bricks on a stone foundation, preserved to a height of more than four meters. This wall was also made, unit after unit to the length and breadth, to a thickness of eight meters. The excavators were of the opinion that the brick was only four to five meters. This conclusion was based on a series of rooms built against the wall on the outside that they associated with the early phase of the stratum. On the basis of these rooms, the various excavators conjectured that this was not the city wall but only a support wall or an internal fortification. But for that purpose a wall so substantial was not necessary. It is more probable that these rooms preceded the main fortification (Stratum XIX) and, as at Beth-yerah, the city fortification was originally established by a series of blocks or units.

The fortifications of Ai (et-Tell) are most impressive; they are made of large stones. The wall reached a breadth of six meters and is preserved to this day to a maximum height of seven meters. In no later period were such massive fortifications constructed. The wall at Ai surrounded a town of about 110 dunams as against 30 to 40 dunams of Jebusite Jerusalem, for example, or 40–50 dunams of Canaanite Shechem.

These cities in particular have been described, not because they are unique of their kind, but because they have been better investigated than most of the other sites. Today more than thirty towns are known in various parts of the country. In the north central Shephelah, for example, there existed four large cities at intervals of approximately 30 km. one from the other: Tel 'Erani with an area of about 250 dunams, surrounded by a brick wall at least eight meters thick; Tel Yarmuth with an area of about 300 dunams, protected by a massive stone wall; Gezer, including more than 100 dunams, evidently fortified by a wall of dirt or bricks covered with stone; and Tel Aphek, whose area is about 120 dunams, surrounded by a brick wall on a stone foundation between three and four meters thick in the Early Canaanite period. This is a concentration of large towns surrounded by large fortification walls without parallel in any other period.

A more complete concept of a town from Early Canaanite has been emerging in recent years, thanks to the excavations at the southern-most city known thus far, Arad in the eastern Negeb. Therefore, Arad will serve as a representative example of one of the urban centers of this era, an approach justified in addition because the present author was a partner in its discovery (Fig. 8).

The fortified city was founded at the beginning of Early Canaanite II, i.e., about the twenty-ninth century B.C.E. It was preceded by a Chalcolithic settlement and a unwalled community from Early Ca-naanite I, Stratum IV. Concerning the date of Stratum IV, we have the testimony of a sherd with the name of Narmer, the first Pharaoh of the First Dynasty of Egypt, about 2900 B.C.E., incised on it. The new occupation from the end of Early Canaanite I did not directly replace the Chalcolithic village but is separated from it by a certain time gap, estimated at two hundred years or more.

The very choice of this place is an indication of the new nature of the community: no water source beside one of the wadis, but rather a relatively higher place dominating the surrounding area, convenient for the fortification of a large town. It may be that this spot had already attracted Chalcolithic settlers, and the new occupants had chosen the depression surrounded on three sides by the continuation of this ridge

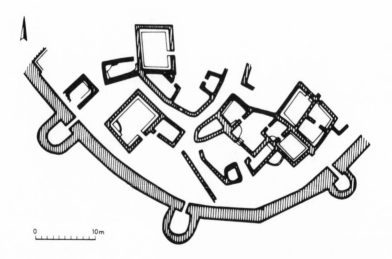

0 _____ 10m

FIG. 8. Arad. A portion of the general plan of the town

in the form of a horseshoe. In this manner, a closed area was obtained for settlement covering nearly 100 dunams, protected from the desert winds. This is a large area which can compete in size with that of other towns such as Megiddo, Jericho, and Lachish and was probably intended from the very beginning for a large, organized population on an urban scale.

It would appear that this topographical formation also helped to solve the problem of water supply. At the lowest place in the horseshoe, there is an artificial depression, the remnant of a big water cistern in which water could be collected from the entire town area. A large public pool was discovered recently in the excavations at Ai. Additional cisterns for catching rainwater were surely hewn out of the limestone rock within the town and outside of it. The Arad ridge is formed of Eocene limestone which holds water well even without coating or plastering. Evidently, the climate has not changed in any appreciable manner from that period to present times. Furthermore, it is obvious from the geological structure of the area that near Arad there is no well or other water source. The water supply came, therefore, solely from the collection of rain. This is limited to a few winter days, and does not exceed an annual average of between 150 and 200 millimeters. The residents of the ancient city had already contrived to overcome that limitation and succeeded in collecting rainwater in pools and cisterns, keeping it for their use throughout the entire year for the needs of a large city, the population of which may be estimated in the thousands. This was an impressive achievement for people of such an ancient period! Not much time had passed before the city was surrounded by a wall, the second phase of ancient Arad (Stratum III). At Arad, it was possible to establish the course of the entire wall to its length of about 1,170 m., 900 m. of which were exposed and/or excavated. It is the first time in Eretz-Israel that a good picture was obtained of a city layout from that period with the course of its wall. This is not because Arad was more important than other towns or that excavations on a larger scale were conducted there. The reason is the special factors of the Negeb. In every other place, life was taken up again on the ruins of the more ancient settlements, and these covered the earliest strata with later deposits causing great damage to the older structures; thus, for example, at tells like Megiddo and Jericho, traces of the same period were uncovered at great depth beneath many later strata, so they could only be excavated in limited areas at the bottom of deep trenches. Even at Ai, the largest part of which was not reoccupied in later periods, the excavated areas are more limited. This is because of massive Byzantine terraces, clearings, plantations, and cultivation which covered the ancient city, causing appreciable damage to its buildings. None of these disturbances is present at Arad. The greater part of the ancient city was not resettled in any later age. Neither is most of its surface area suitable for cultivation, and only in the center of the town was the ground broken by the superficial Bedouin plow. The ancient remains were covered by a horizontal layer of loess forming a protective covering easy to remove. In most places, it is not necessary to dig more than a few centimeters before revealing the tops of walls from the ancient buildings. The course of the city wall can be established around most of its perimeter by surface observation, and in many segments its foundation could be uncovered merely by sweeping. Therefore, this is the first time that complete quarters of a city from that ancient period have been revealed, something that could only be achieved by the expenditure of considerable means and at great effort in other places.

Since the town was not built on top of a hill, as is the case with other tells, but rather in a depression surrounded on three sides by a ridge, the situation of the wall is also unique. On a normal tell, the wall is built at a convenient location on the slope and the top of the tell is usually the most strongly fortified internal area. At Arad, the wall was built on top of the ridge at the watershed; it forms a sort of semicircle with some protrusions in conformity with the curvings of the ridge. A person approaching the city from that side could see only the wall and its towers, while the houses were hidden from view, being located on the incline sloping inward. Only to the southeast, at the end of the ridge, did the wall turn down to close off the city on its lower side. At this point, therefore, it was obliged to make a 90-degree turn on both sides to traverse the valley in a more or less straight line, i.e., across the ends of the "horseshoe." Someone looking at the city from that direction could see over the wall and observe the buildings as they ascend the slope of the shallow crater.

The wall was built of fieldstone and its width was two to two and a half meters. It would seem that its superstructure was also of stone since an abundance of rocks was found all around it and the manufacturer of bricks would have required a good deal of water. Along the whole length of the wall there were semicircular tower/buttresses protruding about three meters from its outer line. A passage about 70 cm. wide led through the city wall into each of these towers. The distances between the buttresses were not standard; they were adjusted according to the local topography. In a segment of about 190 meters excavated more extensively on the southern side, there were seven buttresses, indicating that the town must have been surrounded by about forty such towers at an average distance of 20 to 25 meters from one to the next. This is an impressive picture testifying to the knowledge and the effort invested in fortifying the city (Photo 12).

Within the city itself, one of the quarters at the southern corner was excavated and also a certain portion nearer the center. From them, one may discern the principles that guided the construction of the town. The houses were usually built at a certain distance from the wall so that along the inside there remained a sort of street that occasionally widened out. However, this principle was not preserved consistently, and the street was blocked here and there by houses or rooms built against the wall. Beside the entry to one of the towers, for example, there was a room against the wall, and one may assume that it had some function in the town defense, either as quarters for the troops or for storing weapons.

The houses were arranged in *insulae* of various sizes including several dwelling units around a central courtyard. Between the house groups there were alleys, and, as usual, there was evidently one entry from the alley to the entire complex of dwellings. It is possible, therefore, to conjecture that every group of houses belonged to one clan (Fig. 9).

The architecture of the dwellings reflects great uniformity and a crystallized tradition. The basic unit is a "broad house," i.e., a rectangular room with the entry on one of the longer sides. The house was sunk about 50 cm. below the surface, and thus one descended into it by two or three steps. In a few of the houses a stone was preserved with a hole through the center for the door socket to the left of the entryway. Thus, the houses must have had wooden doors that swung on an axis, and their position was consistent and uniform: The doors were on the inside and opened inward, toward the left. The "furnishings" found in the houses consisted of stone benches extending around the length of the walls, sometimes encompassing the entire room, and usually with a flat stone slab serving as a sort of table in the center. On the floors were found stone-lined depressions in which large jars could

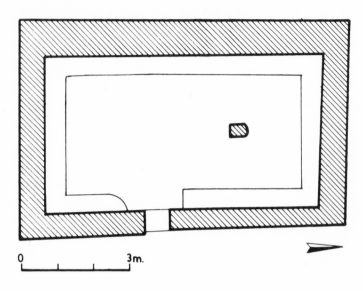

FIG. 9. Arad. Plan of a typical house

be stood. Sometimes a small additional room was attached to the house, apparently a storehouse or kitchen. The entrance to this room was usually from outside. The larger houses usually had in their center, at a fixed distance apart, stone slabs that surely were the bases for wooden pillars supporting the roof.

As is usual in archaeological excavations, the uppermost houses are found in a more disturbed condition. One finds only the wall foundations preserved to a certain height above floor level. This is the reason that, in most cases, one can only distinguish the foundation plan of the structures, whereas there is very little data concerning the upper portion. Therefore, special interest is attached to a terra-cotta house model discovered at Arad in one of the ancient houses. The purpose of the model is not clear, but it would seem that the craftsman intended to represent a typical "Arad house." It is a rectangular house having a flat roof and one opening on the long side. The doorway reaches almost to the roof, so it seems likely that the height of the houses was not much more than that of a man. In the opening itself, a double lintel was molded, apparently an outer and an inner, which corresponds to the door that opened inward. There are no windows in the model, so the door was evidently the only light source. The house walls are decorated with horizontal and vertical red stripes on a white background. We do not know if this decoration was applied only to the model or whether the real houses may have been plastered and ornamented on the outside (Photo 14A). The size of the dwellings varies, and their length runs anywhere from three to eleven meters or more. Apparently, this is due to the respective size of the families, perhaps also to the rank of the occupants. At the same time, it is probable that the public buildings were built according to the same standard, a practice demonstrable elsewhere. In the central part of town, not far from the main water installation, there was a complex of buildings exceptional in size. The excavator, R. Amiran, believes that these are temples, but the theory has not been proven since cult objects and ritual installations have not been found in them.

It is known from other excavations that temples were in fact built during this period according to the same "broad house" plan, as demonstrated at Megiddo and Jericho and also at the temple in Engedi from the end of the Chalcolithic period. However, we must admit that without specific finds the question must remain open. The architecture of these structures is common to both private and public buildings, to temples, and evidently to palaces. If, with regard to the large structures near the center of Arad, one must still wait for additional finds to illuminate their function, the location of at least one public building in the eastern corner of the city is known for certain. It was built on the end of the northeastern ridge of the "horseshoe": a high and impressive point dominating the surrounding area. The Chalcolithic settlement had been concentrated around this hill, and on top of it were built the settlements and later fortresses from the Israelite period on. Because of the later buildings that cover the ancient town on this hill to a considerable height, excavations only penetrated in a few places to the earliest strata, where two details were clarified: (1) the wall does not continue here across the top of the ridge as elsewhere but circles around this hill and continues on the northern and eastern slopes; (2) on the inward slope of this hill, the extremity of a massive building from the Early Canaanite period was discovered. Its curved end was cut at the edge of the slope, and to the east it disappears under the heavy wall of the Israelite fortress. Although a segment of only a few meters was revealed, the quality of its construction and its thickness prove that it was a public building. From this, it may be deduced that the eastern hill was encircled by the wall and included within the city because of the large public building standing there. Was it here that the temple of the city was built, on the most prominent point dominating the town and the entire region?

Much to one's regret, one has no clear answer, but this point has been stressed because of one surprising fact: on the same hill there was erected, some fifteen hundred years later, the Israelite temple of Arad. Was that a coincidence? Did this prominent hill impress and attract settlers again and again? Perhaps the Bedouin in the region preserved the ancient tradition of this sacred hill even during the long gap in permanent occupation?

The ancient town continues to present many questions for which there are no unequivocal answers. What was the economic basis for such a large town? Beside many of the dwellings there were found

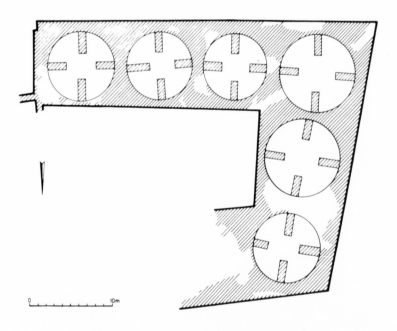

0   10m

FIG. 10. Beth-yerah. Round granaries

rectangular or rounded stone platforms, evidently the bases for grain silos. In one section near the western wall, four round circles were found filled with stone, somewhat reminiscent of the structure with ten circles discovered at Beth-yerah, which seems to have served as a public granary.

In the various rooms, appreciable quantities of carbonized grain and legumes were found. It is probable that the city residents had not abandoned cultivation, and the abundance of granaries may have been intended to assure a supply of grain during the frequent drought years. Among the animal bones found was a plethora of bones of sheep and goats, so one may assume that raising small animals was an important branch of the economy. One of the most interesting finds was a stone stele with an incised drawing found in one of the houses. Two schematic figures are depicted in the drawing, one standing and the other lying down. Was this meant to be an ancient mythological representation of the god of grain and fertility who had died and risen in the annual cycle, perhaps under the influence of Dumuzi-Tammuz from Sumer, as suggested by Amiran? It would appear that the town had strong commercial ties with Egypt. The Egyptian vessel with the incised name of Narmer, evidently from the earliest level (Stratum IV), has been mentioned already. In the two levels of the fortified city (Strata III–II), more Egyptian vessels were found. On the other hand, in Egyptian tombs from the First Dynasty, pottery has been discovered which originated in Eretz-Israel or Syria. It was found in tombs from the mid-First Dynasty: a jar with a distinct red burnishing, ledge handles, and a "pillar handle" spout with a cup replacing a small dipper juglet. This jar is quite typical of Stratum III at Arad, and in the various rooms, large attractive jars of this type were found (Photos 13, 14). On the other hand, in tombs from the later phase of the First Dynasty, there were vessels decorated with geometric patterns characterized by an ornamentation of triangles filled with dots, commonly designated "Abydos ware," since it was first discovered in tombs there. In contrast to the occasional vessels known up to now from different places in Eretz-Israel and Syria, Stratum II at Arad is full of these vessels, a fact which indicates that Arad was one of their places of origin (Plate 10).

These vessels give an important chronological correlation between ancient Arad and the kings of the First Dynasty of Egypt. Amiran's later research has led to the conclusion that the city at Arad existed beyond that date and on toward the end of the Second Egyptian Dynasty. The

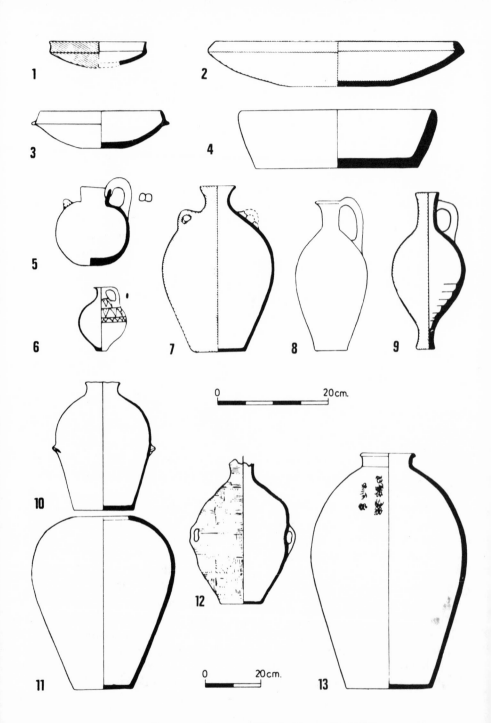

PLATE 10. Pottery of Early Canaanite II–III

imported vessels also testify to the lively trade connection with Egypt in which Arad must have played a dominant role. We do not know what commodities were brought to Arad or exported from it, or whether it may have been mainly a way station. One of the items was possibly asphalt, found in some of the rooms. Asphalt was a much sought after material among the Egyptians, particularly for embalming and the caulking of boats. It was certainly brought to Arad from the Dead Sea, and it may have been shipped on to Egypt. Just recently, there have been discovered in the Negeb highlands and in southern Sinai some seminomadic settlements of this period with pottery from both Egypt and Eretz-Israel, evidence which testifies to the diverse cultural connections (e.g., Nebi Salah; Photo 16).

It is interesting that there is a correlation in time between the total abandonment of Arad before the end of Early Canaanite II and the weakening of connections between Eretz-Israel and Egypt during the course of the Second Dynasty. This fact tends to support the assumption that the existence of a city so large and well developed in the Negeb, unparalleled in any other period, was related to the intensification of Egyptian influence and a strong commercial tie with Egypt (Photo 15). In contrast to Arad, the existence of which may be estimated at about two hundred years at the most, the Early Canaanite period is very long, lasting close to a millennium. During the course of this extensive period, one may discern innovations and changes in the material culture, but in the final analysis it was an era of general uniformity and continuity. Its division into four phases (Early Canaanite I–IV) is founded mainly on the appearance of new pottery types. Early Canaanite I is characterized, as previously mentioned, by the red and the gray burnishing followed by the grain wash in the north and the painted pottery in the south. Everyday ware, such as holemouth jars, jars with ledge handles, and open bowls with folded rims carinated toward the outside, begins in the last phase of Early Canaanite I and continues with minor changes to the end of the Early Canaanite period. Early Canaanite II is typified principally by the appearance of two new wares: (1) "metallic" pottery, jars made of a thin, uniform material, fired at a high temperature and having a metallic ring—and usually smoothed by a toothed instrument leaving traces of combing in various directions, sometimes cross-hatched; (2) Abydos ware, so called because of its original discovery in Egyptian tombs from the First Dynasty, jugs and jars with geometric decoration in red paint,

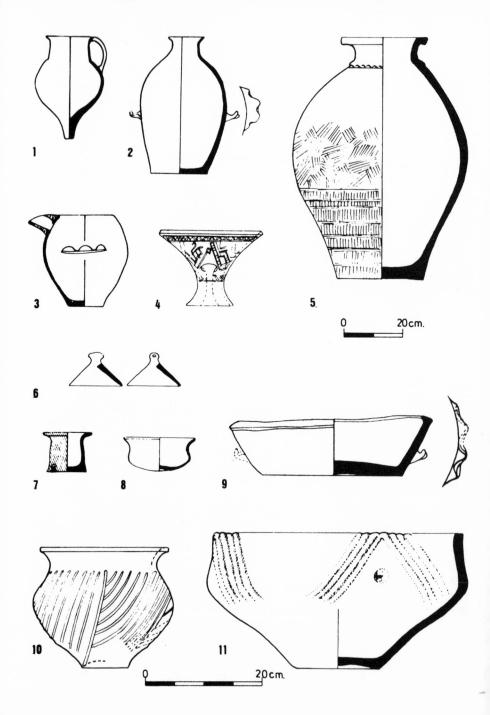

PLATE 11. Pottery of Early Canaanite II–III

including zigzag lines and triangles filled with dots.

The main distinguishing feature of Early Canaanite III is the Beth-yerah (Khirbet Kerak) ware, so designated from the large quantities present in the initial discovery at that site. This is a unique type of pottery that originated in the Anatolian area. It includes a limited repertoire of vessels, mainly wide carinated bowls (some with ear handles), jugs, stands, craters, and covers. All of the vessels are made by hand without any use of the wheel, and the shapes are quite different from those usually found in the country at this time. The quality of the material is far from excellent; it is brittle and fragile, and the firing is not uniform. However, the wares are distinguished by a special technique of slip and a special burnishing which give them a particular beauty. Sometimes the vessel is entirely red, but often it is red on the inside and black on the outside, at least in part. The ornamentation is molded in the form of prominent lines and buttons, and the covers are sometimes decorated by an animal head (Plate 11:10, 11). This special ware appears suddenly during the course of about the twenty-seventh/twenty-sixth centuries B.C.E., and at least at Beth-yerah it was quite ubiquitous. For this reason, it seems to have been brought by a new wave of settlers that arrived in the Jordan Valley from the north. Notably, there is a decided resemblance between this pottery and the gray burnished ware at the beginning of the Early Canaanite period, both in form and technique, which fact may indicate a similar place of origin for the two cultures. However, the penetration of this new wave seems limited; it hardly went beyond the northern district of the Jordan Valley. The ware is found in appreciable quantities in Beth-shean (Strata XII–XI) and in tombs at 'Afula, but it is much rarer at other sites in the valley such as Megiddo. Although isolated examples also appear in the south, e.g., at Jericho, Ai, Aphek, Gezer, and even Lachish, it is clear that the new settlers did not penetrate into those areas, and those few vessels must have arrived there through trade.

Early Canaanite IV is the last phase after the period of Beth-yerah ware. Its delineation is still quite indistinct, since this is principally a time of decline of that culture without substantial innovations. It should be noted that some of the tells had already been destroyed by then, e.g., Ai, but on the other hand, this is the first stage of settlement at other mounds in the south, such as Tell Beit Mirsim and Beth-shemesh.

We must admit that the internal division of the Early Canaanite

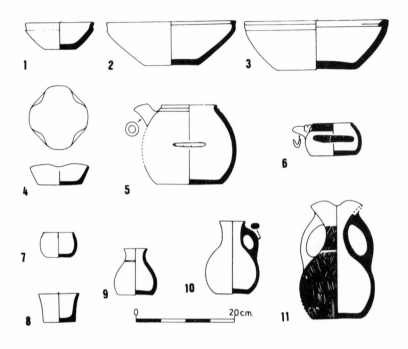

PLATE 12. Pottery of Early Canaanite IV

period is still insufficiently clear and precise, and this fact accentuates once again the basic uniformity of the culture during this long era in the history of the country.

Our knowledge about the various cities is still quite scanty due to the limited areas excavated. As previously mentioned, the massive walls characterizing most of the cities are quite impressive, but still there existed unwalled settlements alongside them. Clearly defined gates have been discovered at three places: Beth-yerah, Tell el-Far'ah (North), and Arad. At all three sites, this was a direct passage with a maximum width of about two meters. At Tell el-Far'ah, the entryway was protected by two rectangular towers that projected outward on each side of the gate.

Except for the granary at Beth-yerah, only a few public buildings are

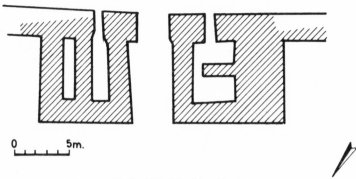

0 _____ 5m.

FIG. 11. Tell el-Far'ah (North). Gate

known, among them temples, which certainly played an important role in the life of the city, as seems likely from the names of the towns. In the ancient Semitic languages, including Hebrew, temples were called "House of (the god)," as in the Bible one finds "House of Yahweh," "House of Baal," etc. The various towns whose names contain the element Beth- ("House of"; also spelled Beit [Arabic], Bet [Modern Hebrew]) are certainly named after a central shrine there, e.g., Beth-yerah, Beth-shean, Beth-shemesh, Beth-anath. The same was evidently true of towns that simply bore the name of a deity, e.g., Jericho, Ashtaroth. Of course, it is frequently difficult to establish if one has found a temple building, since cultic implements could also be found in private buildings and the architecture is not always unambiguous. Some of the larger broad houses at Arad are considered by the excavator, R. Amiran, to be temples, but their size is not decisive, and distinctly cultic objects have not been found in them. Likewise, two structures have been uncovered at Ai, the function of which is debated. On the top of the acropolis near the western corner of the town a large, distinguished building was found with four marvelous ashlar pillar bases in Egyptian style. The plan is that of a broad house like the Arad structures, and it was surrounded by corridors and revetment walls. The excavator called this building a "palace," while others are of the opinion that it served as a temple, though without proof, since it did not have a platform or any distinct cultic vessels. Near this building, against the city wall, there was found another structure which the

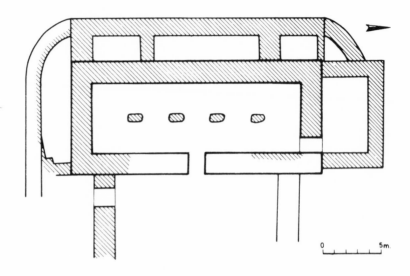

FIG. 12. Ai. "Palace"—Temple

excavator called a "temple" since some distinctively cultic vessels of pottery and alabaster were found there. This building was comprised of small nonuniform rooms, and many have expressed doubt if it really was a temple. Perhaps one may conjecture that the "palace," on the top of the tell, was the central temple of the city while the "temple" nearby was nothing but one of its storehouses where some of the ritual objects were stored. But all this interpretation remains conjectural. On the evidence of the Beth-yerah ware found there, the two buildings were erected in Early Canaanite II and existed during Early Canaanite III. The alabaster vessels found there were Egyptian imports from the First Dynasty and had been kept for several hundred years in the temple treasure.

The situation at Megiddo is much clearer; here one may speak about a "sacred quarter" beginning in Early Canaanite I and continuing, in spite of all the changes and gaps that followed, to the end of the Late Canaanite. The first temple erected there, in Stratum XIX, is a broad room of the Arad type and, like the "palace" at Ai, with pillars supporting the roof. There is a raised, plastered platform opposite the entry-

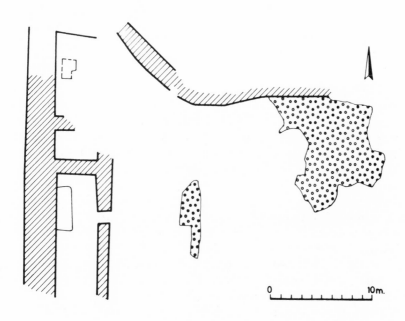

FIG. 13. Megiddo. Temple (Stratum XIX)

way. This platform and the location of the building in the later sacred
area leave no room for doubt that it is a temple. Beside it was a similar
room suggesting the possibility of a pair of shrines. In front of them
was an extensive sloped courtyard paved with stone slabs, some of
them double, testifying to repairs made during the long period of
usage. On the slabs of the two strata, there were found incised figures
of human beings and animals and various designs, most of them apparently hunting scenes. In this stratum (XIX), Megiddo was still an unwalled settlement, and it would appear that the rooms surrounding the
temple extended to the edge of the tell. In the following stratum,
during Early Canaanite II (Stratum XVIII), a massive city wall was built
and the temple area served then as a sort of acropolis encompassed by
an additional wall. The nature of the buildings in this period is not
clear, but it is evident that in its second phase the great altar platform
was built adjacent to the temple site; this latter is one of the most

impressive cult installations ever discovered in the country. It is a round platform, about eight meters in diameter, built of small field-stones to a height of 1.40 m. above the foundation with a flight of seven (!) steps leading up to it from the east. It is surrounded by a tremendous wall, and in the intervening area there were found many fragments of pottery and animal bones, surely the remains of gifts and offerings. In Early Canaanite III, there were built beside the platform three new temples unique to themselves. These shrines were assigned by the original excavators to the Middle Canaanite period, but in the light of a reexamination by Dunayevsky and Kempinski, it is clear now that this assumption was erroneous. Kenyon had already noted the fact that a paved area found above the platform included vessels from Middle Canaanite I (locus 4009), and that a repaired wall of the temple beside the platform (4040) contained an "eye-ax" from the same period. This means that the platform had gone out of use before Middle Canaanite I and the adjacent temple was repaired in that period. Kenyon's suggestion to assign the temples to an earlier phase of the same nomadic interim cannot stand up to criticism, and it is certain now that these temples belong to the later phases of the Early Canaanite at Megiddo. Confirmation of this dating may also be seen in the pillar

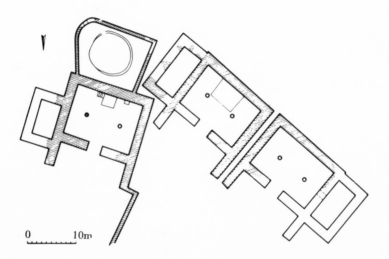

FIG. 14. Megiddo. Temples of the megaron type

base found in one of the rooms of the building next to the temples in Stratum XVI (Early Canaanite III) identical in its stonecutting to the unique pillar bases of the temples.

These three temples are identical in plan, and even their measurements are quite similar. Each one is comprised of a broad room with a vestibule entrance at the front created by lengthening the two outer walls about five meters beyond the closing wall of the court. This plan is reminiscent of the Aegean megaron type, known principally from the Early Bronze Age in Asia Minor and northern Syria (Tell Khuweirah), and even the compact construction of the temples resembles the arrangement of the megaron buildings in Stratum II at Troy. At the same time, one must stress that the typical megaron is a long room, as against the broad room of the Megiddo temples. Was it that elements of the Aegean megaron were adapted to the broad-room construction so commonplace in Eretz-Israel since the end of the Chalcolithic period?

Even in their internal arrangements, the three temples resemble one another. In the center of the southwestern wall, opposite the entryway, there was a rectangular platform in the tradition of Canaanite temples of all periods. In the center of each were found two pillar bases worked in an irregular form, obviously carrying pillars for supporting the roof. Two more such pillar bases were found at the edge of the vestibule, thus forming a broad portico divided symmetrically by the two pillars.

The three temples were built near the round altar platform, one to the north of it and two in a line to the west of it. Opinions are divided as to whether their construction began at the same time or whether they were built in various stages. First was built the western pair, according to Kenyon; or first the single temple (4040) to the east, according to Dunayevsky and Kempinski. Between them and the city wall, a large public building (3177) stood at first, perhaps the ruler's palace. In the later stage (Stratum XV), a new building was erected in its place (3160), in the center of which were two rows of broad stairs ascending toward the temples, which evidently served one after another. It would seem that this was a special eastern gate to the city and the acropolis, and the elaborate approach ramp was built there for festive processions leading to the temples and the altar platform. This climax in the development of the Megiddo "sacred area," which took place in Early Canaanite IV, preceded only by a short time the total decline of the city at the end of the Early Canaanite period (Fig. 15).

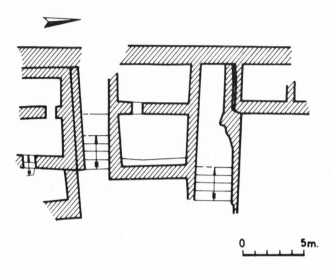

FIG. 15. Megiddo. The eastern gate

It is surprising how this splendid culture of well-developed city-states is still mute and protohistoric in spite of the influences from the great cultures of the ancient East so much in evidence. It is also clear that the connections with Egypt were intensive, particularly during the early stages. Byblos, a city on the Phoenician coast, was under strong Egyptian influence throughout the Old Kingdom, but most of the contacts with it were at least partially by sea. Concerning relations between Eretz-Israel and Egypt beginning with Early Canaanite I, one sees evidence from the appearance of Canaanite pottery types in the Gerzean culture, including the ledge handles so foreign to Egypt. The Egyptian ware from the First Dynasty has been uncovered at various sites in the south, e.g., those in Nahal Besor (Photo 15), Arad, Tel Halif, Tel 'Erani, Ashkelon, Maghar, and Azor. At Arad and Tel 'Erani, sherds were found with the incised *serakh* sign of Narmer, first of the First Dynasty Pharaohs. On a royal palette of Narmer discovered in Egypt, Pharaoh's victory over a fortified city is depicted, and the wall of the town has towers reminiscent of a Canaanite city during the same period. Concerning the lively intercourse and perhaps even a certain

Egyptian foothold in the southern part of the country, there is evidence from the way station discovered by Gophna beside En ha-Besor on the trunk route to Egypt. Its beginning was in the last stage of Early Canaanite I, and Egyptian vessels from the early First Dynasty were found there (Stratum IV). In the ensuing stratum (III), a building was uncovered, constructed of bricks of Egyptian type, containing pottery with Egyptian seal impressions from the middle of the First Dynasty. Stratum II is evidently Canaanite. Therefore, it is not impossible that during certain stages of the First Dynasty, the Egyptians may have ruled over parts of Eretz-Israel; in any case, it is obvious that they conducted military campaigns and that commercial ties between the two countries were intense. We have already mentioned the extensive imports from Canaan of Abydos ware, found in tombs of the First Dynasty.

Although the connections with Egypt died out during the Second Dynasty, and Egyptian pottery is no longer known in Eretz-Israel during the later stages of the Early Canaanite, there are testimonies to Egyptian military campaigns even in these later periods. In a tomb from a place called Dashasheh dating to a reign of the Fifth Dynasty, there is a depiction of the conquest of a Canaanite town. A more detailed document comes from the reign of Pepi I, first and greatest Pharaoh of the Sixth Dynasty (about 2325–2275 B.C.E.). From the document, we learn that the Egyptian army under the command of Weni conducted several campaigns against the "Sand Dwellers," presumably in Canaan. Most illuminating is the description of the campaign in which a force that arrived by sea preceded the land force and disembarked beyond a prominent topographical feature called "the Gazelle's Nose," apparently the Carmel headland. The description indicates a conquest of fortified towns and other settlements, and the cutting down of fig trees and vines, typical fruit trees of the Canaanite landscape (Photo 17).

Weni's campaign marks the complete downfall of the Early Canaanite culture. One may not assume that the Egyptian campaigns brought this about but rather the opposite, that these were conducted at a time when the cities in Canaan were growing steadily weaker. Perhaps the Egyptians took advantage of the opportunity or possibly they came in order to make preparations against an invasion threatening both Canaan and Egypt from the north. What is clear is that the destruction of the cities of Canaan was general and absolute; not one town that has been investigated thus far escaped this fate. The precise date for the destruction of some of these cities is still cast in doubt. Arad was destroyed already in Early Canaanite II, and it would appear that Tell el-Far'ah (North) also saw its end near the close of that period. However, most of the other towns continued to exist down to almost the end of the Early Canaanite, and were evidently destroyed during the twenty-third century B.C.E., e.g., Beth-yerah, Beth-shean, Megiddo, Aphek, Ai, and Jericho. Of course, during this same time a few settlements were established in the southern part of the country such as Beth-shemesh and Tell Beit Mirsim, and an appreciable settlement also developed in Transjordan. Yet these were evidently declining remnants of the collapsing civilization. Around 2200 B.C.E., the country returned to a seminomadic stage, and the Early Canaanite culture was destroyed, never to rise again.

This was a time of upheavals and revolutions in the entire ancient East. In the reign of Pepi II, Byblos was destroyed by fire and the sea links with Egypt came to an end. With the end of the Sixth Dynasty, there is the First Intermediate period in Egypt, a time of social turmoil and the absence of a strong central government, with increasing pressure from Asia. In the same period, the kingdom of Akkad fell, leaving Mesopotamia fragmented for some time into small rival kingdoms that collapsed under the pressure of the Gutians from the north and the Amorites from the west. The last two centuries of the third millennium were an intermediate period in the Near East when the old kingdoms had fallen, and nomads and seminomads engulfed broad areas. Even though solid historical data concerning Eretz-Israel is lacking, it is obvious that the total destruction of the Early Canaanite culture must be viewed in the general framework of events throughout the region.

MIDDLE CANAANITE I

This period, which extends across the last two hundred years of the third millennium B.C.E., actually concludes the protohistoric era in the history of Eretz-Israel.

The commonly accepted terminology, Middle Canaanite I, established by Albright (his Middle Bronze I), is maintained here despite the fact that this terminology is infelicitous. Much more precise is the proposal by Kenyon and others to call it "Intermediate EB–MB" or "Intermediate Canaanite," because this is actually a distinct interim period not essentially connected with the preceding or the succeeding cultures. But then one would have to call the Middle Canaanite IIA by the term Middle Canaanite I, as Kenyon has done. Such a change of accepted terminology causes endless confusion. It is better, therefore, to continue to maintain the term Middle Canaanite I as an agreed definition for this same intermediate period separating the Early Canaanite from the Middle Canaanite II of Eretz-Israel.

The culture of Middle Canaanite I is entirely different in all its elements from what preceded. It is difficult to exaggerate in stressing this change, which finds expression in the sharpest manner in all the concrete phenomena of its material culture: pottery, weapons, burial practices, the nature of the communities, and their diffusion.

The pottery is new in form, technique, and decoration. The shape of the vessel is generally round with an open calciform rim. The body of the vessel is made by hand, in contrast to the rim, which is thrown on a fast wheel. The join, usually quite obvious on the inside, is frequently decorated by a plastic ornamentation of incisions, protrusions, or combing. The painted and red burnished decorations of Early Canaanite disappear completely, and the clay is entirely different, testifying to a new technology of preparing and firing: instead of the thick, brownish-red biscuit, it is thin and gray, and the firing is more uniform. The oil lamp has four pinched spouts (Plate 13:12). Among the few legacies from the previous period, there is the hole-mouth jar. It continues to serve as a storage and cooking vessel, although the new technique is obvious in both the clay and the form of the rim. This vessel is almost entirely absent from the tombs, and thus is missing from most published repertoires from that period. The preservation of this isolated vessel in daily use is natural since one may not assume that the new settlers came to an entirely vacant land, and the exception only emphasizes the overall essential difference. Along with the vessel, there also appears the ancient ledge handle attached to the standard jars of the period, but even it receives a special form—the "folded ledge handle" (Plate 13:14).

The weapons are of copper, having new forms and a more perfected technology: daggers are particularly widespread. Bars of copper found in several places testify to the diffusion of the local metal industry, certainly brought by these settlers from their place of origin (Photos 17 and 18).

The burial customs are completely different from all of those in the

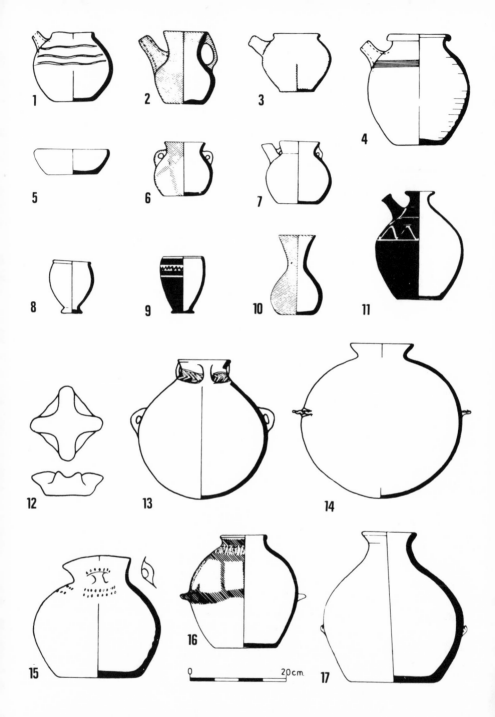

PLATE 13. Pottery of Middle Canaanite I

past or those which followed. Instead of the "family tombs" with many graves in extended use, individual interment was the norm, and only rarely have two skeletons or additional isolated skeletons been found in the same tomb. On the other hand, great effort was expended in hewing out the tomb itself, which was a cave approached through a vertical shaft. The skeletons were usually placed in secondary interment, disarticulated and incomplete. In the Golan there are many dolmen fields. Here "tables" were made of giant stones, sometimes covered with a mound of rocks (tumulus). According to the recent investigations by C. Epstein, they served, at least partially, in Middle Canaanite I (Photo 19). More widespread are the tumuli groups in the Negeb situated prominently on the tops of ridges. In only some of them have human bones been found, and in a few only scattered bones. It may be that the deceased was buried first in one of the tumuli while the tribe was spending time in the Negeb, and in due course the bones may have been transferred to one of the shaft graves in the northern part of the country. Stone "walls" sometimes surround the fields of tumuli in the Negeb, and in some cases they extend for a distance of several kilometers in a straight line, completely ignoring the more serious topographical interruptions. Obviously, here is a world of burial customs and ritual for the dead unprecedented in the cultural history of Eretz-Israel.

The settlements were poor and temporary, and their houses are more reminiscent of sheds and booths than real buildings. There are no fortifications, and in no place have public buildings been found thus far. The impression is that after the complete destruction of the Early Canaanite towns, a seminomadic population roamed freely about the country for nearly two hundred years. Kenyon points out that part of the area on the tell at Jericho remained uninhabited while traces of a settlement were preserved on the nearby slopes. There was a deep stratum with pottery from this period but practically without structures, and in her opinion it was created by extended usage on the part of a population camping in tents and booths. This picture of open, temporary settlements, not even situated on the ancient tells so convenient for fortification, is typical of Middle Canaanite I throughout the land. The distribution of settlements is also unique and connected with their special nature. On the one hand, their remains are found in every part of the country—the valleys, the hill country, Transjordan, and even in Galilee and the Negeb. They penetrate into the interior and

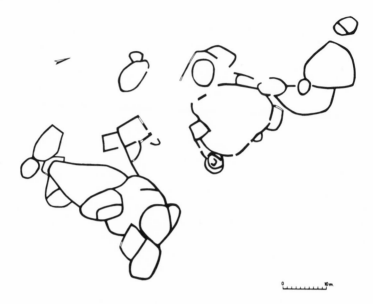

FIG. 16. Nahal Boqer. A typical settlement

the peripheral zones, into forested areas or into the arid steppe that had heretofore remained uninhabited. Under an Israelite settlement from the period of the conquest, beside Peqi'in, in Upper Galilee, was found a dwelling cave from Middle Canaanite I. This is an isolated and forested mountain region that was not really occupied until the Israelite period, and these were none other than nomadic pastoralists who had migrated hither with their flocks. More impressive is their penetration into the southern regions of Transjordan or the southern Negeb, two peripheral areas for which this was the first occupation to any appreciable degree throughout their history. In Transjordan, this was more extensive and had its beginning already toward the end of Early Canaanite IV, surely because of the more convenient living conditions in that area in contrast to the arid southern deserts. In Transjordan, a certain continuity is also descernible in the ceramic types between Early Canaanite IV and Middle Canaanite I. It would appear that the new settlers came into contact here with the remnants of the older population that had sought refuge in Transjordan, but from thence the

Middle Canaanite I clans spread out into Cisjordan.

However, these are not population surpluses in a time of increase in search of additional living space. That conclusion is clear in the light of the geographical gaps in more convenient northern areas. For example, in the northern Negeb between Beer-sheba and Arad, the district of the biblical Negeb, there has not been found even one settlement from that period, in spite of their diffusion in more southerly and westerly regions, and in spite of the fact that the annual rainfall is greater there, making pasturage more lush. The concentration of Bedouin in this region exceeds even today that in the southern highlands. How, therefore, can one explain the fact that the settlements of Middle Canaanite I "skipped" over the Negeb? It is probable that this was a seminomadic population wandering with its flocks when necessary, perhaps during a time of trouble when the people were gradually being driven from the more fertile areas. This may be the reason that the northern Negeb remained as a sort of barrier between the settled area and the retreating seminomads (Fig. 16).

This is also the picture reflected by the settlements in the Negeb. So

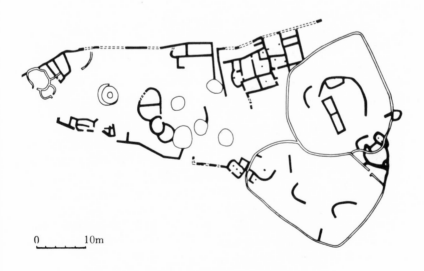

0 _____ 10m

FIG. 17. Har Yeroham. The central settlement
(Stratum I, outline; Stratum II, solid lines)

far, that is the only area where one may examine a complex of such communities, which are almost never preserved in more northerly regions. Tens of settlements like these have been discovered throughout the Negeb highlands, from the vicinity of Aroer to the north down to Kadesh-barnea, and even beyond it, to the south. Most of them are small sites, comprised of large and small stone circles, surely the remains of cattle pens, and booth and tent dwellings. A few of the communities were somewhat larger, and in the vicinity of Be'er Hafir there was found a kind of "town" made up of circle after circle. A unique site was excavated near Be'er Yeroham by Kochavi. It was built on the top of a ridge very difficult of access and surrounded by a stone fence. The houses were rectangular and characterized by rows of pillars made up of stone disks for supporting the roof. Special finds there were a potter's oven and a group of copper bars indicating that craftsmen lived there and were responsible for manufacturing the implements typical of that culture. On an adjacent ridge, there was a ritual high place, a raised stone platform with 12 cup holes surrounded by a fence. It would appear that the larger communities such as those at Be'er Hafir and Be'er Yeroham were central settlements around which the nomads were concentrated (Fig. 17).

At sites of this period in the various parts of the country, one may discern several "families" according to differences in the pottery and burial practices, some of which may be regional-tribal, though at least part were chronological distinctions. The earlier phases include many more elements of the Early Canaanite period, and it would be natural that with their arrival, the new settlers adopted elements from the local culture. However, these features disappeared rather quickly, and evidently additional waves of settlers were no longer finding anyone from whom to inherit such things. The Negeb settlers belong to the later "family," a fact which supports the assumption that they had been driven there toward the end of the period.

In Phoenicia and central Syria, these settlements developed to the proportions of flourishing towns, perhaps through collaboration with the former populace as elucidated particularly at Byblos and Hamath on the Orontes. At the latter place, several phases of an established, well-built community were discovered, though it is doubtful whether the place was fortified. Carbon-14 tests have established dates between 2200 and 2000 B.C.E., and there is no basis for the assumption that these occupants penetrated into Eretz-Israel itself during a later pe-

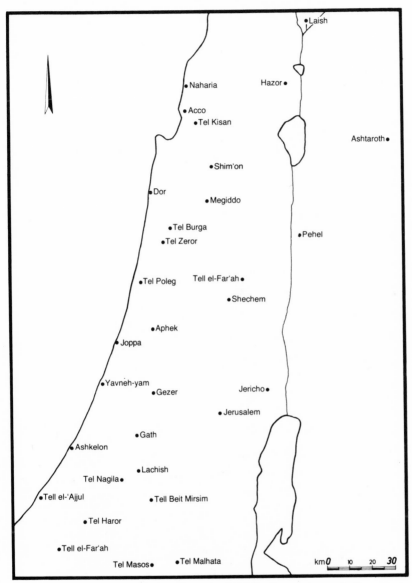

FIG. 18. Map of sites from the Middle Canaanite period

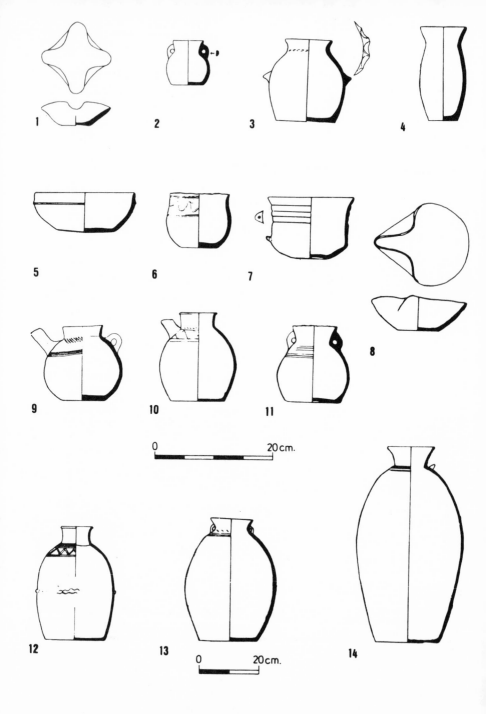

PLATE 14. Pottery of Middle Canaanite I

riod. On the other hand, in Eretz-Israel all of the settlements discovered thus far were poor and temporary, and there is no structural connection with the earlier or later strata. This is a unique, foreign intermediate wave, and the towns of Middle Canaanite II belong to another culture having practically nothing in common with the people of Middle Canaanite I. The general picture does not support the theory that their temporary settlements eventually developed into new towns. They disappeared and were blotted out just as they had appeared. First, they were evidently driven to the periphery of the land and into its hilly regions, and after a short time, they simply vanished.

For that reason, one must absolutely reject the widely accepted theory that associated the people of Middle Canaanite I with the appearance of the "Amorites." The latter are a West Semitic people found in the land during Middle Canaanite II, as will be shown farther on. There is still no historical information about Middle Canaanite I. Its material culture seems to point to a northern origin with even some connections with the Kurgan culture of the European steppes, a culture of pastoral nomads with developed metallurgy, shaft graves and tumulus burials, and beakers ornamented with incisions. The influence of this culture is felt in Europe and Asia at about the same time. These people do not found settlements that become the towns of Middle Canaanite II, but rather they and their temporary communities vanish the way they came, apparently under pressure from newer waves of settlement such as that of the "Amorites."

For this restoration, there are also chronological consequences. With the rise of the Twelfth Dynasty in Egypt, the Egyptian interest in Eretz-Israel and Syria increases once more, and now for the first time there is historical information about the land, its towns and their rulers. This material shows a country bearing a West Semitic population in the midst of an energetic process of settling down, a picture that corresponds to the early stages of Middle Canaanite II. Thus, it is obvious that around 2000 B.C.E. the intermediate wave of Middle Canaanite I comes to an end, being a sort of unusual epilogue to the Early Canaanite period. As already stated, this was a time of population movement and the decline of cultures and kingdoms in the entire Near East, and the penetration of the Middle Canaanite I people was an exceptional aftermath that temporarily filled a hiatus thus created. Its disappearance, like its arrival, is shrouded in mystery, but it opened the way for the Amorite wave that followed it.

MIDDLE CANAANITE II

The Middle Canaanite II and Late Canaanite periods, taken to-gether, lasted about eight hundred years, from 2000 to 1200 B.C.E. From the standpoint of culture and history, they represent a continuity worthy of the name "the Canaanite period," in the fullest sense of the term. This is Canaan in its rise, its flourishing, and its decline as reflected in ancient Israelite tradition. It is the first really historical period in Eretz-Israel from which written documents have been pre-served—historical, administrative, and literary—that give flesh and blood to the sinews of the bare archaeological finds. This is also the period in which the Hebrew tribes penetrated into various districts of the country and finally crystallized into the people of Israel, the first and only people to make the country its natural homeland.

During the course of the period under discussion, Eretz-Israel was in a close relationship to Egypt that varied from intensive diplomatic and commercial ties to a firm, institutionalized Egyptian rule. Most of the historical information available derives from Egyptian sources in which one encounters, for the first time, nearly all the Canaanite towns known from the Bible. The secondary division of this period into Middle and Late Canaanite, more than being dependent upon ar-chaeological data from the country itself, is closely tied to the division of Egyptian history into the Middle Kingdom with the Second Interme-diate (the so-called Hyksos Age) on the one hand, and the New King-dom (the Age of the Empire) on the other. Decisive historical dates do not always correspond to sharp, meaningful transitions in the material culture, and one must again remember that there is no division suit-able to all the data. With regard to the terminology of these periods, a conservative approach is taken here: every new term would only add to the confusion and obscurity. As a definition of the chronological phases, the accepted division into Middle Canaanite IIA and IIB, Late Canaanite I and II is good enough, even though from a substantive standpoint they are essentially four phases of one period.

The complete isolation of Eretz-Israel during the First Intermediate, and the nature of the nomadic population, are faithfully depicted in the words of one of the last Pharaohs in the Tenth Dynasty (perhaps one Akhthoes), about 2040 B.C.E., to his son Meri-ka-re: "Lo, the miserable Asiatic, he is wretched because of the place he is in: short of water, bare of wood, its paths are many and painful because of mountains; he does not dwell in one place, food propels his legs; he fights since the time of Horus, not conquering nor being conquered; he does not announce the day of combat, like a thief who darts about a group. . . . Do not concern yourself with him; the Asiatic is a crocodile on its shore: it snatches from a lonely road, it cannot seize from a populous town." This is a striking description of the population of Eretz-Israel during Middle Canaanite I and of its lack of association with Egypt. The situation changed entirely during the period of the Middle Kingdom (1991–1786 B.C.E.). The first of its kings, Amen-em-het I, built the "Wall of Egypt," a line of forts in the eastern part of Wadi Tumilat (the land of Goshen), intended to keep check on movement between Asia and Egypt. For the continuation, there are available both historical documents and archaeological finds that testify to the connections with Egypt and illustrate the composition and character of the populace in this country. In all of the texts, the local rulers have typical West Semitic names ("Amorite"), showing that they are the predominant element in the population at this time. They are already in the land during the twentieth century B.C.E., as seems probable from the story of Sinuhe, which opens with the death of Amen-em-het I; its events take place in the reign of his son, Senuseret I (1971–1928 B.C.E.). That Egyptian runaway first got as far as Byblos, but apparently the Phoenician coastal town was again in close relations with Egypt. Therefore, he continued on his way, first to the "land of Kedem," a desert region east of Eretz-Israel and Syria, and henceforth to the country ruled by one of the princes of "Upper Retenu," his name being Ammu-inshi, a typical Amorite name with the element *ammu* and perhaps *ns* (meaning "man"). Retenu is the new name of Eretz-Israel and southern Syria, the derivation of which has yet to be established clearly. Its rulers are called *hq3 hst,* meaning "ruler of a foreign land," a title applied henceforth to the local rulers, and afterward also borne by the members of the foreign regime, the so-called "Hyksos," in Egypt. The title is appropriate for a population undergoing rapid transition to sedentarization, while its organization is still mainly tribal, supporting itself on fruit trees, field crops, and cattle. In the story, reference is also made to envoys on their way to Egypt, evidence for the strengthening of ties already in the mid-twentieth century. The most important information about Eretz-Israel during the Twelfth Dynasty is derived from the execration texts. These make up a register of magic curses pronounced against rulers and dignitaries among the opponents of Pharaoh; among them were the rulers of districts and towns in Eretz-Israel. The older group of the two main collections of execration texts from the end of the twentieth to the beginning of the nineteenth century B.C.E. is written on bowls, broken and buried in a sacred place. They contain about 20 names of towns or districts in Eretz-Israel and Syria, the majority of which are unknown in later sources. Evidently, there were tribes and names of districts that have vanished during the course of time, but alongside them mention is made for the first time of historical towns in Eretz-Israel, such as Jerusalem and Ashkelon, and the residents in the vicinity of the Phoenician harbor towns of Byblos and Ulassa. The second group, about a century later, is written on clay figurines shaped like shackled prisoners including 64 names, most of which represent known cities such as Jerusalem, Ashkelon, Aphek, Acco, Achshaph, Shim'on, Pehel, Hazor, Laish, Ashtaroth, and Tyre. All of these and others are royal Canaanite cities, well known to us from the Bible some five to six hundred years later. The differences between the two groups is evidence concerning the rapid transition to an urban regime that began as early as the twentieth century, and was completed during the nineteenth. Concerning this phenomenon, we also have the evidence of the number of rulers in each town, sometimes three or even four in the earlier group of execration texts with only one or perhaps two in the later group. All of the rulers' names whose form and composition can be analyzed are West Semitic ("Amorite"), and thus the uniform ethnic character is clear: its language was a relative of biblical Hebrew. At the head of the famous caravan depicted in the tomb mural from Beni Hasan during the Twelfth Dynasty bringing stibium to Egypt is found the ruler of a foreign land, Abi-shar ('bs'), with a distinctly Amorite name. There is not sufficient information to decide whether the strong ties and the Egyptian interests developed as far as real political control. The turquoise and copper mines in southern Sinai are one of the evidences for the nature of the contacts. Not only were the activities of the Egyptian expeditions renewed and augmented during the Twelfth Dynasty, but also the inscriptions of that time contain evidence of the participation by contingents of workers from Canaan (Retenu), and the reliefs depict good relations rather than the extermination of enemies. Another witness is in the Egyptian sphinxes sent as gifts to the local courts. Sphinxes of the Thirteenth Dynasty were found at Ugarit, Qatna, Byblos, and addi-

CHRONOLOGY OF MIDDLE CANAANITE IIA–B

PERIOD	TELL BEIT MIRSIM	MEGIDDO	ALBRIGHT'S DATES	ALBRIGHT'S PARALLELS	CORRECTED DATES	CORRECTED PARALLELS
Middle Canaanite IIA	G	XIV	19th–18th cents.	End of XII Dyn.	20th cent.	XII Dyn.
Middle Canaanite IIA	F	XIIIB XIIIA	18th cent.	XII Dyn. XIII Dyn.	19th cent.	XII Dyn.
Middle Canaanite IIB	E₁	XII	18th–17th cents.	Early Hyksos	18th cent.	XII Dyn.
Middle Canaanite IIB	E₂	XI	17th cent.	Middle Hyksos	18th–17th cents.	Early Hyksos
Middle Canaanite IIB	D	X	17th–16th cents.	Late Hyksos	17th–16th cents.	Late Hyksos

tional places in Syria, and stelae of Egyptian noblemen have turned up in various places as far as Anatolia, including tells in Eretz-Israel such as Megiddo, Gezer, and Tell el-'Ajjul (Beth-'eglaim, the predecessor of Gaza). Smaller objects, such as scarabs, are known from many places throughout the land. Great importance is attached to the stele of a high Egyptian official named Thut-hotep found at Megiddo; from his tomb in Egypt, it is established that he lived during the reigns of Amen-em-het II and Senuseret II and III (1929–1843 B.C.E.). As there are practically no royal annalistic texts from the Thirteenth Dynasty, it is impossible to know whether these gifts symbolize good commercial relations or Egyptian domination. Quite exceptional is the inscription of Khu-sebek, who took part in a campaign to Shechem under Senuseret III. This text tells about Egyptian campaigns to this country in the nineteenth century that penetrated even into the internal hill regions.

Although these Egyptian sources from the Twelfth Dynasty are partial and fortuitous, they furnish significant information about Eretz-Israel in this period and permit one for the first time to connect archaeological finds with historical sources. One must pay careful attention to the fact that the relations with Egypt are steadily intensified during the twentieth and nineteenth centuries, and they develop from contact through emissaries and commerce in the twentieth (e.g., in Sinuhe) to an obvious Egyptian superiority and military campaigns in the nineteenth century. Throughout that entire period the names of the rulers of the land are West Semitic (Amorite) and, according to the later execration texts, the composition of towns in the country is reminiscent of the Canaanite cities known from later sources.

The situation thus depicted by no means corresponds to the culture of Middle Canaanite I in Eretz-Israel, which has been seen to be nomadic, having a distinctiveness from Middle Canaanite II, and lacking all connections with Egypt. The cultural and ethnic continuity reflected in the sources strengthens the theory that this was a new wave of occupation in Middle Canaanite II, which opened an energetic period of new settlement in the history of the land when most of the ancient urban communities were rapidly reconstituted. Although there is no room for doubt that these were waves of new settlers from the north, having many contacts in particular with the Syro-Phoenician coast, from the standpoint of settlement pattern and society, they carried on, in large measure, the regime of the Early Canaanite period. Thus, one must assume that the transition from Middle Canaanite I to

Middle Canaanite IIA in Eretz-Israel approximately overlaps the beginning of the Twelfth Dynasty in Egypt, i.e., it started not later than the beginning of the twentieth century B.C.E. There are still no datable Egyptian finds within Eretz-Israel itself. On the other hand, pottery having the general characteristic of Middle Canaanite IIA has been found in the royal tombs of Byblos with inscriptions from the reigns of Amen-em-het III and IV, so it follows that those wares at Byblos belong to approximately the nineteenth century. Evidently, that date is also valid for Eretz-Israel, and the transition from Middle Canaanite IIA to IIB began about 1800 B.C.E. In the light of these considerations, the Middle Canaanite II period may be divided into two more-or-less equal phases: Middle Canaanite IIA starts in the twentieth century and goes through the nineteenth, while Middle Canaanite IIB begins in the eighteenth and continues into the sixteenth century. This chronology seems to correspond quite well to the finds in the various tells around the country (Plate 15).

Occupation levels from the period under discussion have been discovered at numerous sites, but two key places where stratigraphic continuity has been established from Middle Canaanite IIA and IIB are Megiddo and Tell Beit Mirsim. Comparison between the strata of these two tells as worked out by Albright still holds, with only the reservation that he compressed the span of the earlier phases a bit too much. The chronological table on page 93 is basically derived from Albright's book: I have only added a column with dates corrected in the light of the following considerations.

There is no reason to assume that Strata G through F in Tell Beit Mirsim and Strata XIV through XIII at Megiddo can be limited to a period of a century or less.

It seems much more probable that they correspond fundamentally to the Twelfth Dynasty of Egypt and cover as much as two centuries. This assumption now derives support from Kochavi's excavations at Aphek, where four substantial building phases have been discovered from Middle Canaanite IIA which in thickness and quality are not inferior to those of Middle Canaanite IIB.

As mentioned above, there is a uniform continuity in the ceramic types of Middle and Late Canaanite, and the various phases are direct developments from what preceded. Pottery is made on a fast wheel and well fired, except for the simple cooking pot in the form of an open bowl with a flat base and a strip-of-rope design below the rim. This pot

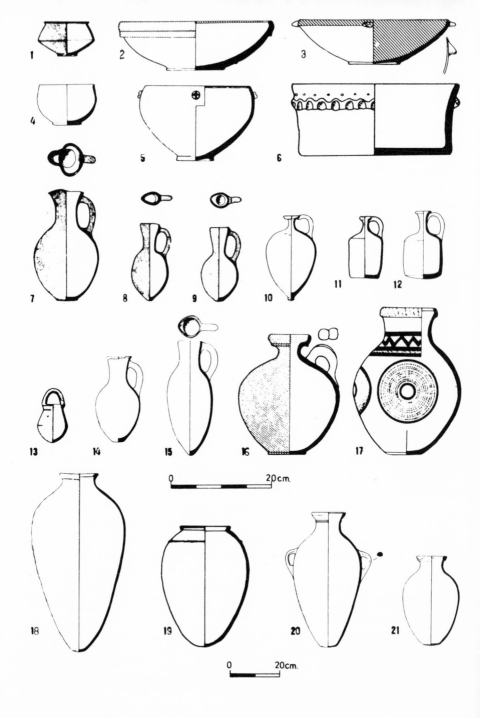

PLATE 15. Pottery of Middle Canaanite IIA

continues to exist through Middle Canaanite II, and its beginning may go as far back as the end of Middle Canaanite I (Plate 15:1). Ledge handles disappear; hole-mouth jars and jars with flat bases become the exception. The storage jars now have flat bases which gradually become more pointed toward the end of the period. Juglets appear with a handle springing from a trefoil rim. The rounded bowls are reminiscent at first of bowls from Early Canaanite, but carinated bowls become dominant; these have a high and delicate carination that later becomes lower and more pronounced. The bowls and the juglets mostly have a thick red slip and an excellent, continuous burnishing. Apparently the potters' intention was to imitate metal vessels. A silver bowl from Byblos is a marvelous reflection of the bowls from Middle Canaanite IIA (Plate 16:2). In the metal industry, bronze now replaces copper, and new types of weapons appear: short, broad daggers, narrow axes with matching extremities, and lanceheads with a socket. The burial customs are also entirely different from those of Middle Canaanite I. Instead of the ubiquitous single burials, the burial cave is again revived and serves families for many generations, as was customary in the Early Canaanite period. An innovation is the individual burials on the tell itself under the floors of dwellings, which are very widespread throughout Middle Canaanite II. Many of the representative complete finds come from such burials, and their association with the various strata is frequently inadequate. Here the skeletons are complete, but in the caves they were regularly pushed aside to clear space for additional interments, and the custom of disarticulated secondary burials is discontinued. The tombs are also a testimony to a sedentary people as contrasted to the nomadic population of the previous period.

Intensive permanent settlement was renewed in the earliest phase of Middle Canaanite IIA, in part on tells that had been occupied in the Early Canaanite, e.g., Laish (Dan), Hazor, Megiddo, Tell el-Far'ah (North), Jericho, Aphek, and Gezer, but to some extent also at places being occupied now for the first time, e.g., Shechem and, as recently shown, at Tel Zeror and Tel Poleg on the Sharon (Photo 21).

It is possible that some of these communities were founded as open villages but quickly developed into thoroughly urbanized centers with fortifications characteristic of the ancient city. There is no certainty as to whether Stratum XIV at Megiddo was already fortified, but in Stratum XIII the two main excavation areas revealed a wall built of bricks on a stone foundation to a thickness of 1.8 m. and the addition of

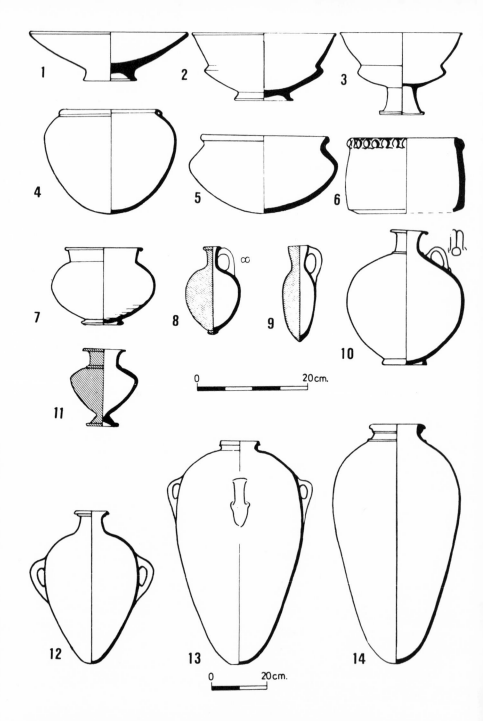

PLATE 16. Pottery of Middle Canaanite IIB–C

salients at fixed distances. A more impressive wall, 3.25 m. thick, was found at Tell Beit Mirsim, although it is not clear whether its construction should be associated with Stratum G or F. At Aphek, a wall 2.5 m. thick was found, also having salients or thickened segments at fixed distances, and it is connected with occupation levels from Middle Canaanite IIA. Fortifications in Middle Canaanite IIA are particularly obvious at Tel Zeror and Tel Poleg, inasmuch as at both places the communities were founded in that period and do not continue into Middle Canaanite IIB. At Tel Zeror, a brick wall was found, 4 m. thick, situated atop a rampart surrounded by a moat. At Tel Poleg, a brick wall 2.7 m. thick was found, and the material discovered on the adjacent floors is entirely parallel to Strata G and F at Tell Beit Mirsim and Strata XIV–XIII at Megiddo. The older wall at Shechem is also of stone construction, to a thickness of 2.5 m., and although the date of its erection is still debated, one cannot assume that the city was unfortified during the Egyptian campaign in the first half of the nineteenth century B.C.E. Also at Jericho, there was evidently a brick wall in one of the early phases of Middle Canaanite IIA, while at Tell el-Far'ah (North), the excavator assumed that the earliest settlers in Middle Canaanite II used the remains of the wall from the Early Canaanite period, which was repaired and strengthened. Fortifications of the early phases of Middle Canaanite II are still problematic in many places because of the massive fortifications erected directly on top of them during the later course of the period. These fortifications are associated with earthen ramparts and sloping glacis impressive in themselves. They symbolize a new era and are usually denoted by the general term "Hyksos fortifications."

This name continues to be used for lack of a better definition. But one must admit its limitations and refrain from deriving generalized historical conclusions. Hyksos is an Egyptian term designating the Second Intermediate period in the history of Egypt, when foreigners gained control over parts of that country and erected their new capital at Zoan (Tanis) in the Delta. This domination took place with the decline in power of the Thirteenth Dynasty in about 1720 B.C.E., and the main Hyksos dynasty is the Sixteenth, whose kings ruled between 1674 and 1567 B.C.E. The word Hyksos means nothing more than "rulers of foreign countries" (hq3 hst), and it is the designation for the rulers of Eretz-Israel and Syria in sources from the Twelfth Dynasty.

Concerning the form of Hyksos domination and the nature of their kingdom, opinions are still divided.

The transition in this country from Middle Canaanite IIA to IIB took place before the establishment of Hyksos rule in Egypt, around 1800 B.C.E. Fortification of the towns was achieved with the aid of *terre pisée* ramparts (using the accepted French term), supported by sloping glacis. These became the exclusive type and are found at every settlement in the period, both those previously existing that were now refortified and also the new ones. At Megiddo, there was found in Stratum XI a thin wall, the main defense of which was a glacis. Tell Beit Mirsim was surrounded in Stratum E by a *terre pisée* rampart, and during the course of time there was erected on it a wall sloping outward. At Shechem, the area of the city was slightly widened by a "cyclopean" wall battered on the outside and made of giant irregular stones with smaller stones in between. The fortification of Jericho in this period was a rampart and a plastered glacis which inclined partially to the outside of the ancient line of the walls at this tell. At Tell el-Farʻah (North), a stone wall was supported by an earthen rampart with a retaining wall. At Gezer there was discovered a rampart to the height of five meters laid against a wall of four meters, altogether ten meters thick. A "cyclopean" wall was also found at Gezer during the latter phase of Middle Canaanite II, evidently the last stage of the Hyksos fortifications.

Even more impressive and instructive are the fortified "enclosures" erected during this period beside ancient cities and in some new places. Their fortification consisted of an earthen rampart with a sloping glacis, usually with a moat at the foot on the outside, from which was dug the great quantity of soil used to raise the rampart. The rampart was usually strengthened by a stone nucleus of bricks and retaining walls, but there was no wall on top of it (Fig. 19).

The largest enclosure in the country is that at Hazor, which was built to the north of the older tell and enclosed more than 700 dunams. Within the area thus incorporated, various structures were found from the seventeenth and sixteenth centuries (Stratum III). It would appear that during this period the enclosure had developed so that it surrounded a real city; the population may be estimated in the tens of thousands. Its beginning was earlier (Stratum IV), but the only building found thus far that relates to this phase is a small segment of the early gate. Therefore, controlled data are still lacking for fixing a more

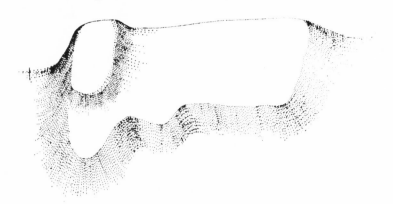

Fig. 19. Hazor. The enclosure

precise date for the erection of the enclosure. However, in the case of Hazor, there is a historical datum of great importance. At Mari, Hazor is the only southern city mentioned except for neighboring Laish (mentioned in one epistle). Emissaries from Babylon returned by way of Mari after a long stay at Hazor. To Hazor were sent appreciable quantities of tin for the manufacture of bronze. Hazor's king appears at the same rank with the large centers in northern Syria: Carchemish, Halab, and Qatna. These were the great political capitals of the age, and at Carchemish and Qatna enclosures were discovered similar to those at Hazor. Therefore, one may infer with certainty that Hazor of the Mari Age was a mighty city having an enclosure. The Mari archive preceded the 32d year of Ammurapi, king of Babylon, i.e., 1760 B.C.E. according to the Middle Chronology, which must be followed today because of archaeological and historical data. The great Hazor was founded, therefore, at the latest by the beginning of the eighteenth century, i.e., in the transition from Middle Canaanite IIA to IIB. A similar dating was established for the rampart of nearby Laish, which also appears in the aforementioned Mari archive. The rampart was built at this latter place on the slopes of the ancient tell on top of occupation strata and tombs from Middle Canaanite IIA. A foundation offering deposited in the nucleus of the rampart, evidently during the course of construction, belongs in the excavator's opinion to the transition from Middle Canaanite IIA to IIB. The discovery of smaller enclosures in various parts of the country, even outside of the older fortifications on the tells, shows how widespread was this type of defense construction. Here one should mention in particular the enclosure at Tel Burga northeast of Caesarea, which has an earthen rampart surrounding an area of 250 dunams within which was a settlement of about 50 dunams having pottery from Middle Canaanite IIA. Along the coast there were discovered rampart enclosures at Joppa, Yavneh-yam, and Ashkelon. At Yavneh-yam the rampart is partially submerged in the sea, but one may estimate the enclosure at 500 dunams. The pottery is from Middle Canaanite IIA, and since there does not appear to have been an earlier settlement on this site, it is likely that such was the date for the rampart's construction.

City centers in the Shephelah at Lachish and Tel Nagila are refortified by ramparts and glacis after a long period of cessation in occupation since the Early Canaanite period. The southern strong points of the Hyksos were built in the western Negeb along the course of Nahal Besor. The largest and most westerly of them was Tell el-'Ajjul (Beth-'eglaim). The rectangular area surrounded by a rampart and moat is about 150 dunams, and this is the first occupation on the site except for a large cemetery from Middle Canaanite I. Its closest competitor to the east was Tel Haror (Tell Abu Hureireh), apparently ancient Gerar, the city of Abimelech, where an enclosure was also established encompassing an area of at least 150 dunams with a high tell beside it, itself surrounded by a rampart (Photo 20). Farther south along Nahal Besor, a mighty Hyksos fort was established at Tell el-Far'ah (South) also defended by a rampart and a moat. Its area was only about 30 dunams, but its identification with Sharuhen in the light of both Egyptian and biblical sources shows that this was one of the principal Hyksos strong points in the south, which the Egyptian army was obliged to besiege for three years during the reign of Ahmose, founder of the Eighteenth Dynasty.

In the eastern Negeb, two neighboring Hyksos enclosures were built along the course of Nahal Beer-sheba. The enclosure at Tel Masos was evidently erected first, having in its center one of the local wells; it encompassed an area of about 20 dunams. Six kilometers to the east of it is situated Tel Malhata, where a rampart and glacis were erected to include an area of 10 to 15 dunams. At Tel Masos, pottery was found from the transition between Middle Canaanite IIA and IIB. Here also one may take advantage of a historical consideration to fix a more

precise date for the founding of the site. Recent archaeological researches actually leave little room for doubt that Tel Masos should be
identified with biblical Hormah as one of the only two pre-Israelite
sites in the eastern Negeb, the largest and best-established community
B.C.E. (Josh. 12:14; Judg. 1:17; I Sam. 30:30). A place, the name of
which is written *h3m*, is mentioned at the head of the later execration
texts, and among the inscriptions from the Sinai mines during the
reign of Amen-em-het III (1842–1797 B.C.E.) there is an allusion to
twenty Asiatics *('3m)* from *h3m.* The identification of this place with
biblical Hormah and with the most southerly Hyksos enclosure in
Canaan is highly probable, and thus strengthens the assumption that
the enclosure at Tel Masos was erected there at the beginning of the
eighteenth century B.C.E. This is one of the enclosures that existed for
only a short time. Tel Malhata nearby inherited its place and existed
down to the end of the Middle Canaanite II.

There is still no consensus concerning the origin of the Hyksos
fortifications and their military significance. Although earthworks for
fortification are no innovation in themselves, the great enclosures,
some of which are found void of structures, at least in the first stage
of their existence, point to large concentrations of civilian and military
personnel. It is also possible that they were intended for chariotry and

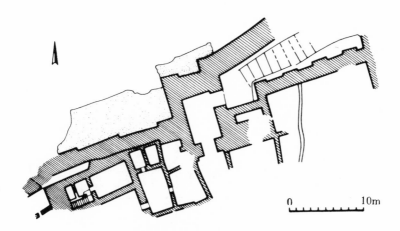

0 _____ 10m

FIG. 20. Megiddo. The Gate from the Middle
Canaanite period

horses, and represent the revolutionary military innovation of the period. Concerning this possibility, there is evidence first and foremost from the new plan for gates instituted in that era. The gate area, which had to have a convenient approach, was the most vulnerable point in the city fortifications, and thus it always received special attention. Only a few gates from Middle Canaanite IIA are known, and all of them have an angular entryway with a 90-degree turn inside the gate tower: the gate of Stratum XIII at Megiddo and apparently the gates of Stratum E at Tell Beit Mirsim and Tel Poleg.

In Middle Canaanite IIB, a new gate becomes ubiquitous with a direct entryway, the plan of which is used exclusively with Hyksos fortifications. The gate passage is divided by three piers on each side, and its width, which runs between two and four meters, would suffice for admitting one or two chariots. These piers were short from the beginning and served to protect the door sockets just inside the outer set of piers. In the course of time, a tendency took root to lengthen the piers sufficiently to form two pairs of guardrooms on each side of the central passage. This kind of gate, which had its beginning, as mentioned above, in the Middle Canaanite IIB, enjoyed a long life, and was the most widely used throughout all of the Canaanite and the Israelite periods. These were the "cities fortified with high walls, gates, and bars" (Deut. 3:5, etc.) in the biblical allusion. Good examples from Middle Canaanite IIB are known from Hazor, Megiddo, Shechem, Gezer, Beth-shemesh, Yavneh-yam, and Tel Sharuhen (Fig. 21).

The Middle Canaanite IIB is a flourishing period in occupation and economy throughout the land, virtually unprecedented. As mentioned

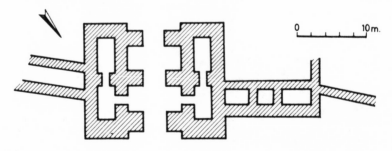

FIG. 21. Hazor. Gate from the Middle Canaanite period

previously, this prosperity had already begun before the Hyksos' entry into Egypt, but it intensified under the Sixteenth Dynasty. In the absence of historical sources, one is unable to establish to what degree there may have been a stable central government based, perhaps, originally on Hazor and afterward on the Hyksos capital in the Delta, Zoan-Tanis-Avaris. The many Hyksos fortifications are evidence of the fact that it was, at best, a feudal regime dependent upon many local

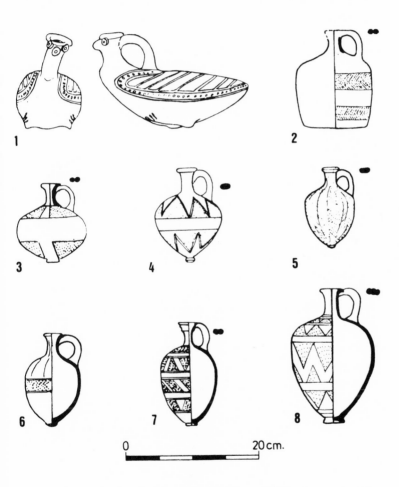

PLATE 17. Tell el-Yehudieh ware from Middle Canaanite IIB

rulers competing with one another, a conclusion which may be deduced from the frequent destruction levels found at every site. This may be viewed as the beginning of the alignment of Canaanite kings that crystallized during the Late Canaanite period into larger political units.

The economic wealth was certainly derived mainly from the extensive commerce that followed through Eretz-Israel between Egypt and all of the expanse of the Fertile Crescent and beyond, as evidenced by the Hyksos scarabs found in abundance in every region, distributed as far as Anatolia and Crete. There is great uniformity in the pottery, the quality of which is excellent, although certain differences may be noted between the northern and southern parts of the country (Plate 17). The main vessel for export, which saw a wide distribution, was the juglet named after Tell el-Yehudieh in Egypt where it was first discovered: a pear or cylinder-shaped juglet with grayish-black color and

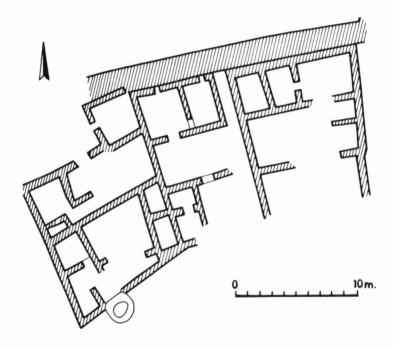

Fig. 22. Megiddo. The city wall and attached structures

geometric dotted designs filled with white coloring. It is widespread in Middle Canaanite IIB but, as is now certain, had its beginning already in Middle Canaanite IIA. It would appear that this juglet was related to the export of the perfume so renowned from Canaan to Egypt and to Cyprus. Many of the splendid vessels and precious objects come from tombs, and it must be noted, in particular, that the ornamented bronze toggle pins and the decorated bone and ivory inlays are marked by a strong influence from Egyptian art. In the Jericho tombs, where the climate is dry, remains have been preserved of organic materials, household implements, furniture and clothing. At Tell el-'Ajjul, warrior graves were discovered with the skeleton of a horse in the center, buried along with the deceased. The richness of the accompanying objects in the latter site, among them many gold ornaments, testifies to the affluence of the local nobility (Photo 21).

At some sites, there have been discovered large buildings that must have served the rulers of the native aristocracy. The palace erected at Megiddo beside the temple was redesigned and expanded in Stratum XII: it has a large central court surrounded by rooms on all sides. In the gate area there were uncovered in Stratum XII three affluent houses, one beside the other, two of them with a central court and rooms on two sides, and a third with a court fronting on the street

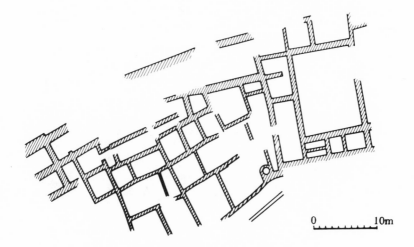

FIG. 23. Megiddo. A palace (Stratum X) and the buildings beside it

surrounded by rooms on three sides. These houses continued to exist in Stratum XI, but in Stratum X, a new palace was built with thick walls instead of the two eastern houses, and it had an expansive central courtyard with channeling and bathing installations, surrounded by rooms on all sides. This is the beginning of the palace near the gate which continued to expand throughout the existence of the Canaanite city at Megiddo until it took over the entire area. A similar development is noted in other cities in Syria and Eretz-Israel. In Alalakh (Stratum VII, seventeenth century B.C.E.), the palace is still situated beside the temple, but in the ensuing strata it was transferred to the gate. At Hazor, the corner of just such an expansive palace was discovered near the Solomonic gate, and in the same area there was certainly an acropolis gate at Hazor in Middle Canaanite II also. One of the great palaces found in Eretz-Israel is Palace I at Tell el-'Ajjul, which covered an area of more than two dunams, also having a broad central court surrounded by rooms on three and perhaps four sides. The thick walls indicate that this building, like the other palaces, was more than a single story.

Also, in a relatively small area of Tell Beit Mirsim, Stratum D, there was discovered a "noble's house," with an inner courtyard and two rows of rooms behind it, the thick walls of which indicate the existence of a second story. Near it were discovered additional houses with thinner walls, but they are also expansive and have very regular ground plans with an inner court and rows of rooms on two sides. The impres-

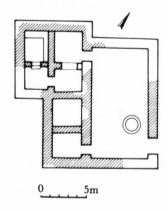

FIG. 24. Tell Beit Mirsim.
    "Nobleman's house"

0   5m

sion is that this was a noblemen's quarter, one of whom was *primus inter pares*.

In the absence of historical documents, one cannot know the ethnic composition of the Canaanite population and its rulers in this period. Under the Twelfth Dynasty and the Mari period, all of the names of rulers known from the sources are West Semitic (Amorite), but with the raising of the curtain anew at the beginning of the New Empire, many of the rulers have names with Hurrian elements, and the country

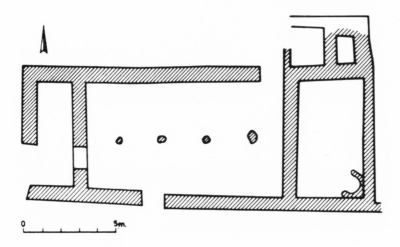

FIG. 25. Naharia. The temple

itself is now called Khurru, "Land of the Hurrians." There is no doubt, therefore, that many Hurrian elements, and with them an Indo-European ruling class, arrived in the country during the Hyksos era, and, in fact, in Alalakh (Stratum VII, seventeenth century) there are numerous Hurrians, although the ruling dynasty is still West Semitic. However, the complete continuity of material culture, and the continuation of the exclusive domination of the West Semitic Canaanite language in the country show that the makeup of the population did not change appreciably. It would seem that it was mainly the noble families which came into power by the aid of associated warrior groups. Some of the city destructions must have been the result of such events. One significant innovation that can be attributed to the new rulers is a novel type of temple, the temple tower. Most impressive is the cultic high place at Gezer from Middle Canaanite IIB, where ten stelae of different sizes were erected in a row with a large rectangular stone basin in the center serving for libations. Beside Naharia, another cult place was discovered with numerous offerings accompanied by a small rectangular building (Photo 22A). A larger structure was built there in a later phase, perhaps belonging to the temple type with an angled entryway, known from Assyria. The development of the "sacred area" at Megiddo is most illuminating. After the destruction of the Early Canaanite temples and the intermediate phase of Middle Canaanite I, the old cult area remained open and was surrounded by a temenos wall separating it from the adjacent residential area. In Stratum XII, one finds a small ritual chamber beside which was a group of stelae in an open area, and this cult place contined to exist in Stratum XI. Only in Stratum X was a new temple built on this site, a temple tower that remained in use until the end of the Canaanite city (Stratum VIIA; Fig. 26). A similar building was discovered at Shechem. This latter was also constructed in the second phase of Middle Canaanite IIB, and it continued to exist until the end of the Canaanite town there. The plan of these temples consists of one long room with a cultic niche on the innermost side and two tower chambers, one on each side of the broad entryway. The walls have a thickness of three to four

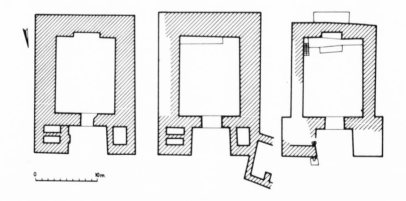

FIG. 26. Megiddo. Temple towers

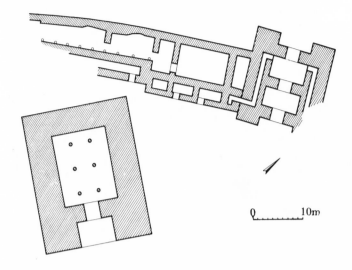

FIG. 27. Shechem. Temple tower and gate

meters, and they prove that the building had more than one story; the
upper stories were reached by a staircase in one of these chambers.
The form of the temple is that of a fortified tower; thus, the temple at
Shechem in the days of Abimelech where the elders of Shechem had
assembled is called "the Tower of Shechem" (Judg. 9:47, 49). This
type of fortified temple comes to the country from the north; it is well
known in northern Syria at Tell Mardikh (between Aleppo and
Hamath) and at Alalakh (Stratum VII), where there is a broad-room
building. Similar to it is the earliest of the orthostat temples at Hazor
(Stratum III) having one broad room with two tower chambers in
front of it; it even dates from approximately the seventeenth century
B.C.E.

Concerning the extensive commerce through the length of the Levant during the Hyksos period, there is testimony from Cypriot ware,
the importation of which began late in Middle Canaanite IIA (Megiddo
XII; Plate 18) and became ever more widespread during Middle Canaanite IIB (Megiddo XI–X) and Late Canaanite. Toward the end
of the Middle Canaanite period, there is a bichrome ware that be-

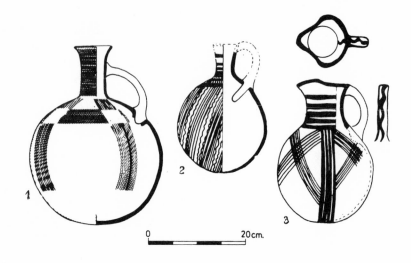

PLATE 18. Cypriot ware from Middle Canaanite IIC

gins in Megiddo X and Stratum II at Tell el-ʿAjjul, where it is found with scarabs of Apophis. The bichrome ware, which is especially plentiful at the beginning of the Late Canaanite period—so much so that it serves as a trademark for that era (Megiddo IX)—includes a special type of jug and bowl with geometric decorations in red and black, interspersed with figures of living things, especially birds and fish. The uniqueness of this ware strengthens the supposition that a "school" from one pottery center produced these vessels over the course of about one century. Their main distribution is along the Levantine coast from Alalakh in the north to Tell el-ʿAjjul in the south and in eastern Cyprus. This distribution of the ware reveals its origin in that area. Recent researches based on the composition of the material have fostered the opinion that the bichrome ware is also a Cypriot product (Plate 19).

LATE CANAANITE

More than any other era, this is a period measured by Egyptian history, viz., from the New Kingdom. It takes in the reigns of the

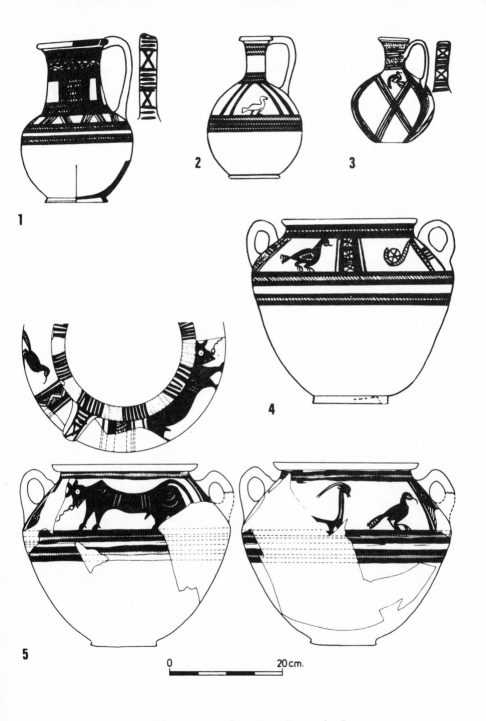

PLATE 19. Bichrome ware from Late Canaanite I

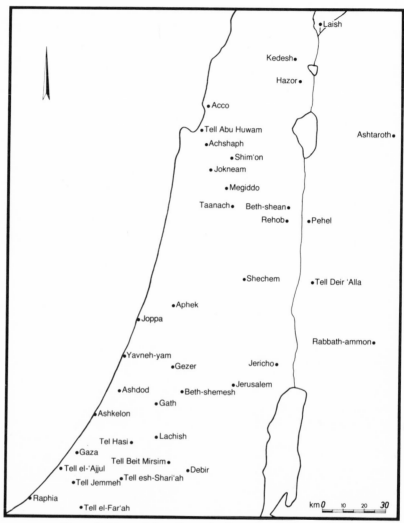

FIG. 28. Map of sites from the Late Canaanite period

Eighteenth and Nineteenth Dynasties, the days of the Egyptian Empire when Egypt dominated Eretz-Israel and parts of Syria. This is the time of the Egyptian province of Canaan, concerning which there is an abundance of historical documents giving life to the inert archaeological finds. This is fundamentally a historical division; there is no break in material culture between Middle Canaanite II and Late Canaanite I. Of course, at the various tells excavated, a destruction in about the mid-sixteenth century is discernible, so it is obvious that the expulsion of the Hyksos from Egypt left its mark on the country from the standpoint of occupation. One does not know if this is due to direct activity on the part of the Egyptian army under Ahmose, since there is only one source that deals only with the siege of Sharuhen (Tell el-Far'ah [South]) for three years. One must remember that this is an eyewitness account from the tomb of a military officer and may be only an example of the reduction of the Hyksos strong points in the country, one by one. In any case, this same officer testifies that the grandson of Ahmose, Thutmose I (1525–1512 B.C.E.) went as far as the border of Naharina, the Hurrian kingdom of Mitanni in the Upper Euphrates region, so it is obvious that the Egyptian army passed through all of Eretz-Israel and parts of Syria during its campaigns.

Destruction of the various cities was followed by an appreciable economic and occupational decline. Some of the Hyksos enclosures and strong points were abandoned, never to be resettled—e.g., Tel Malhata in the eastern Negeb; and poor settlements were found at Tel Nagila in the southern Shephelah and Yavneh-yam on the coast. At other towns, the excavators have established an occupational gap in the first stage of Late Canaanite I, e.g., at Jericho, Tell Beit Mirsim, and Shechem. One must entertain certain reservations about this assumption because it is founded mainly on the absence of bichrome ware, the commonly accepted trademark of the period. As mentioned, its beginning is toward the end of Middle Canaanite, and it is distributed principally among the coastal sites, apparently being imported from Cyprus. Its absence from tells farther inland may be accidental, therefore. To this day, scholars have not succeeded in establishing other clear criteria for distinguishing the pottery of Late Canaanite II. Even the division into Late Canaanite I (1550-1400) and Late Canaanite II (1400–1200) is consequently historical in principle, with the latter stage including the el-'Amarna Age and following. The pottery of Late Canaanite I represents a transition in which the characteristic shapes

PLATE 20. Pottery of Late Canaanite I

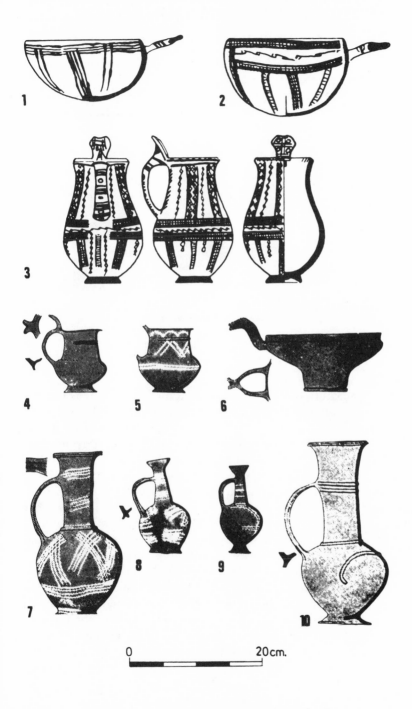

PLATE 21. Cypriot ware from Late Canaanite I

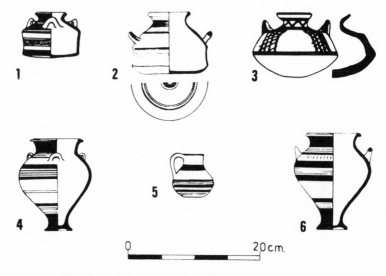

PLATE 22. Mycenaean ware from Late Canaanite I

of Late Canaanite II were crystallized without a sharp break being felt during the course of the entire period. Imported vessels from Cyprus (Plate 21) and Mycenae (Plate 22; Photo 22), which gradually achieved a great diffusion, beginning in the el-'Amarna period, provide a useful chronological tool. One must also remember that the pottery from every stratum is principally associated with its culmination, and one cannot expect whole vessels, except those from tombs, to derive from phases during which there was no heavy destruction of the city. Therefore, it is probable that in most of the towns, occupation continued, but in the first phase there is no evidence of significant public building projects, and the mighty Hyksos fortifications continued to serve for local defense. This is a period of economic decline and a recession in the international trade that had enriched the Canaanite cities (Plate 20). It would seem that the decline and abandonment of various towns brought about an essential change in the alignment of the Canaanite city-states. Of course, one may not assume that a fundamental alteration occurred in the status of the Canaanite kings, who shifted from being vassals of the Hyksos rulers to being vassals of the Pharaohs of the New Kingdom. However, it would seem that now the power of certain central towns was in the ascendancy as their kings imposed their control over broader areas; in addition to the urban capital they also dominated various local towns in the immediate vicinity (Photo 22).

This alignment is clearly delineated in the el-'Amarna archive. That corpus was found in the capital built by Amenhotep IV (Akhnaton) and includes letters from his reign and that of his father, Amenhotep III (1400–1360 B.C.E.). The archive is a unique treasure that sheds tremendous light on the general diplomacy of this era and on the Egyptian province of Canaan, in particular. The letters were written on clay tablets in Akkadian cuneiform, which had become widely disseminated since the Old Babylonian period as the international lingua franca for diplomacy and commerce in the entire Middle East. These tablets were dried and usually baked, so they are able to withstand the ravages of nature buried under layers of destruction. A number of such tablets have been discovered at tells in this country: a dozen from Taanach, a handful from Megiddo, Shechem, Jericho, Tell el-Hesi, Aphek, and Kumidi in the Lebanese Beqa'. It would seem that only the hand of fortune has prevented the discovery of a real archive thus far in one of the tells of this country.

Among the 300 or so el-'Amarna letters, about half are letters from the kings of Canaan in which the writer usually mentions the name of his town by means of his title "the man from the city of . . ." The general picture that emerges is one of disputes and mutual accusations between the various cities amid groveling and the affirmation of loyalty to the Egyptian authorities. In some letters, the writer claims ownership over his cities in the plural, and some kings are accused of stealing towns one from the other. In Eretz-Israel itself, one hears about only fourteen royal cities in different parts of the land, viz., Ashtaroth in Bashan, Hazor and Pehel in the Jordan Valley, Megiddo and Shim'on in the Valley of Jezreel, Acco and Achshaph in the Plain of Acco, Gezer, Gath, and Lachish in the Shephelah, Ashkelon and Yurza in the south, and finally Shechem and Jerusalem in the hill country. This list is not complete; there are some epistles where the name of the city is not indicated, but it would seem that not many are missing. All of these now became royal centers dominating extensive areas in the hill country and more limited areas in the valleys. This is principally the picture of the kings of Canaan as depicted also in the Bible.

The capital of the Egyptian province was at Gaza, called pa-Canaan, "the (city of) Canaan." The Canaanite kings rendered obedience to the Egyptian high commissioner located there, and their main obligations were paying taxes, furnishing manpower for corvée, recruitment of support troops, especially chariotry, during the time of an Egyptian campaign, maintenance of logistic supply for the Egyptian forces passing through, and in particular securing the highways in each city's domain. Egyptian garrison troops were stationed in some key cities such as Jerusalem, Megiddo, and Byblos on the Phoenician coast. In addition, there were special Egyptian bases under direct Egyptian administration, where storehouses and government workshops were located. Along the coast, one is familiar from Egyptian sources with Gaza and Joppa in the south, and with Ulassa and Sumur on the Phoenician coast. At Joppa the existence of the Egyptian base is confirmed by an archaeological discovery, the doorpost of the city gate bearing the incised name of Ramses II. This royal Egyptian inscription symbolizes the direct Egyptian ownership of the town. With the intensification of ties between Egypt and Phoenicia, and the strengthening of sea-lanes and coastal shipping, the various coastal towns began to flourish, some of them having been founded in this period. Cities such as Gaza and Raphia appear for the first time in sources of this era. In the excavation of the tell at Sheikh Zuweid, south of Raphia, apparently ancient Laban (Petrie published it under the name Anthedon), the first occupation level was Late Canaanite. The same is true for the important harbor city of Dor on the Carmel coast, which began in this period, as did the small harbor town at Tell Abu Huwam, located beside the mouth of the Kishon north of Haifa. Even Ashdod, which had its beginning toward the end of Middle Canaanite, achieved prosperity in Late Canaanite, and inscriptions from Ugarit on the northern Syrian coast refer to it as an exporter of fish and fabrics.

The main Egyptian base at the internal crossroads of the land was Beth-shean, as revealed mainly by the excavations conducted there. The principal effort was concentrated in the "sacred area" on top of the mound where a series of temples was found containing cult objects, architectural fragments, and numerous stelae with Egyptian inscriptions. One of the texts from the reign of Ramses III even gives the name of the builder, Ramses-user-khepesh, who was most probably the commander of the Egyptian garrison force stationed there. Even though all indications are that the temples were built by the Egyptians as an integral part of their military base, their ritual was not devoted to Egyptian deities but rather to the local Canaanite gods. Near the early temple (Stratum IX) was found a stele erected by an Egyptian in honor of "Mekal, the god of Beth-shean." In one of the later temples (Stratum V), a stele of the goddess Anat was found; this may have been the "house of Ashtaroth," where the Philistines placed Saul's weapons after his death on Mt. Gilboa (I Sam. 31:10), and the main temple may have been the "house of Dagon" where they displayed his skull (I Chron. 10:10).

The Beth-shean temples existed there through five continuous strata (IX–V), for the dates of which there is still no general agreement. The excavators depend mainly upon foundation offerings of Egyptian scarabs found in the various temples in the high place area and under the walls: from Thutmose III in Stratum IX, Amenhotep III and IV in Stratum VII, and Ramses I in Stratum VI. On the other hand, a lintel bearing the name of Ramses III found in Stratum V in secondary use, evidently came from the commander's house of Stratum VI. At first glance, these would appear to be conflicting testimonies, since scarabs can generally furnish nothing more than a *terminus a quo,* and the date of every stratum may be later; however, the continuity and the consistency of foundation offerings in every one of the temples is impressive, so it may be that the excavators are correct. In Stratum VI, two building phases were found, and it is possible that the lintel from Ramses III belongs to the second stage. Furthermore, there are two additional reasons for dating the temple of Stratum VII to the el-'Amarna Age: (1) the resemblance to two small temples at el-'Amarna, the Egyptian capital in that period; (2) the find of a capital in the shape of a papyrus flower in that stratum. A similar capital was found in the palace of Stratum VIII at neighboring Megiddo which is also dated to the el-'Amarna Age. From a historical standpoint, it seems likely that the Egyptian base at Beth-shean was established under Thutmose III like those at Gaza and Joppa, though the earliest testimony to its existence is from the el-'Amarna letters.

The plans of these temples differ from stratum to stratum. In IX, there were evidently two neighboring shrines surrounded by a series of service rooms, corridors, and courtyards, but their ground plans are not uniform, and it is difficult to grasp the significance of the rooms and the various installations. In Stratum VIII, only the bases of basalt columns were preserved, and one may only conjecture that this monumental structure was also a temple. The first clear temple belongs to Stratum VII. It is comprised of a central hall (holy place), the roof of which was supported by two pillars, with benches around the walls. To the north of it there was a small, broad room serving as a holy of holies. One ascended into it by a set of steps leading to a platform built against the back wall, evidently where the statue of the deity had stood. That statue must surely have been visible from its elevated place, even out in the holy place, perhaps in partial darkness; and in front of the steps there was an incense altar, the smoke of which must have filled the entryway and intensified the aura of mystery. These were the main cultic accouterments which are henceforth characteristic of all Canaanite temples. They were transferred by inheritance even to the Israelite period except that the stele replaces the divine statue, as has been learned from the temple at Arad (Fig. 29). The ground plan was not essentially changed in Stratum VI. Only the holy of holies and its platform were now moved to the center of the room, with small storerooms on either side, and there was a wider staircase at the entryway from the holy place to the holy of holies (Fig. 30).

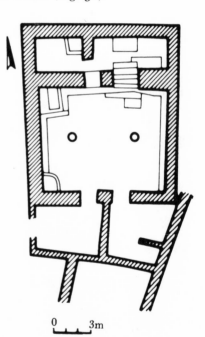

FIG. 29. Beth-shean. Temple
(Stratum VII)

0 ____ 3m

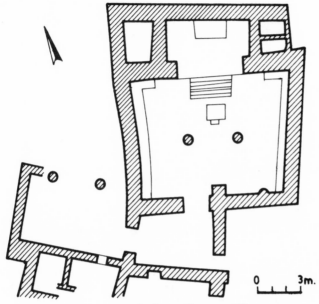

FIG. 30. Beth-shean (Stratum VI)

In Stratum V, which belongs entirely to the Israelite period (second half of the twelfth to the eleventh century B.C.E.), two new adjacent temples were built. Not only is their ground plan completely different, but the direction is also changed: in contrast to the north-south alignment of the earlier temples, the new shrines have an east-west orientation, typical of Israelite temples. The southernmost shrine is larger, apparently the house of Dagon (I Chron. 10:10), and it had two rows of pillars giving it the form of a basilica. The smaller northern temple was evidently the house of Ashtaroth (I Sam. 31:10); there were four pillars, but its internal division and its installations were not preserved. From the varying sizes of the pillar bases, one may deduce that most of them were taken from older buildings, and the construction of Stratum V cannot be compared with the monumental construction of Strata VII–VI. At the same time, it is instructive that the tradition of the sacred area and its temples continued at Beth-shean even after the weakening of Egyptian domination down to the time of Philistine control there in the reign of Saul. And, of course, Beth-shean is referred to in the Bible as one of the Canaanite cities which held out against the pressure of the Israelite tribes during the period of the Judges (Judg. 1:27; Fig. 31).

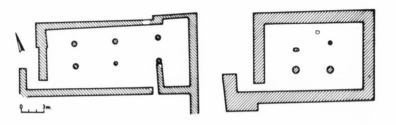

FIG. 31. Beth-shean. Adjacent temples (Stratum V)

The Pharaohs of the Nineteenth Dynasty also immortalized their deeds in the area by means of three victory stelae found in the excavations at Beth-shean. The one from the reign of Ramses II only indicates that he conducted a military campaign to the region during his ninth year (about 1282 B.C.E.). Two stelae from the reign of his father, Seti I, contain a more detailed historical description. The first, from his first year (1309 B.C.E.), depicts the rescue of Beth-shean by Pharaoh's army after the two neighboring kings of Pehel and Hamath had attacked it. To this period one may perhaps assign the destruction of Stratum VII. A second stele, from later in his reign, describes the suppression of rebellious 'apiru (Hebrew?) clans in "Mt. Yarumta." This is none other than Remeth-Jarmuth of the Israelite tribe of Issachar (Josh. 19:21; 21:29), north of Beth-shean. Thus, one may conjecture that clans of that tribe had already penetrated into the area toward the end of the fourteenth century.

It is probable that the Egyptians were only continuing to maintain the tradition of Canaanite temples at Beth-shean—and, in fact, series of Canaanite temples have been discovered in archaeological excavations at other major towns such as Hazor and Lachish. Already mentioned are the "temple towers" at Megiddo and Shechem, which were in existence throughout the entire Late Canaanite period, being destroyed only during the course of the twelfth century B.C.E.

Hazor remained the largest city in Canaan throughout the entire Late Canaanite. The vast enclosure was surrounded by a rampart; it was fortified and had almost entirely been built up inside during Middle Canaanite and maintained its existence alongside the high tell. In Late Canaanite (fifteenth-thirteenth centuries), there are three strata in the city's occupation, Strata XV–XIII in the general numbering of the main tell; Strata II–IA in the local numbering of the enclosure. To one of these stages, if not to the city from Middle Canaanite, the biblical statement must refer: "Hazor formerly was the head of all of those kingdoms" (Josh. 11:10). In all of the main excavation areas, both in the enclosure and in the upper city, temples were found, three in the former and one in the latter. This picture of a multiplicity of temples is surely typical of a great Canaanite city, but it should not be assumed that Hazor consisted entirely of temples. In two of the temples in the enclosure, remains were visible on the surface before excavation; that is why they were chosen for digging. The temple in the upper city was found near the conjectured city gate beside the palace.

The most elaborate of the Hazor temples was discovered at the northern extremity of the enclosure, viz., the "orthostat temple." Orthostats, smooth slabs of basalt, lined the walls of the last temple (Stratum IA), but there is no doubt that they originated in one of the earlier temples that had stood on that spot (Stratum II or III).

Reference has already been made to the earliest of these shrines from the Middle Canaanite (Stratum III), reminiscent in its general plan of the temple towers at Megiddo and Shechem, although its walls are not so thick. This temple continued to exist as such also into Late Canaanite I (Stratum II), except that the courtyard in front of it was now equipped with a monumental entryway. In the center of the court, there was found a rectangular platform, apparently the base for an altar, and near it there was a drainage channel made from discarded incense stands. A sacrificial altar in the temple courtyard is in itself a piece of equipment that passed on as a heritage to Israelite ritual. Among the fragments of cult objects discovered in the courtyard were several examples of clay liver models bearing Akkadian inscriptions with magic formulae. The practice of hepatoscopy for signs of the future is mentioned also in the Bible (Ezek. 21:21 [Heb., v. 26]) and was very widespread in Mesopotamia, from whence it was diffused to the entire ancient East.

This temple went out of use at the end of Stratum II (about 1400

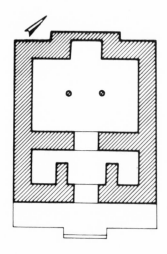

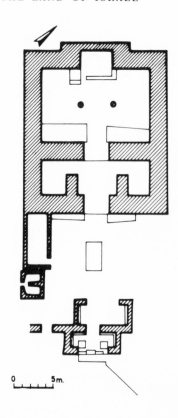

FIG. 32. Hazor. Temples from
the enclosure
(Strata III and II)

B.C.E.), but the new temple built there in Stratum IB was also erected
on the same foundations and preserved its same general plan. Like its
predecessors, it was made up of a main cultic room in the form of a
broad room with its roof supported by two pillars. On the northwestern side (every temple in this series was oriented in that direction),
there was a raised niche where the statue of the deity must have stood.
In front of the main room, there was a narrow vestibule with two
towers, one on each side, one of which contained two narrow chambers, evidently for a staircase. Thus far, the temple is identical to the
former "temple towers," the only essential modification being the
added vestibule, narrower than the temple itself. It is doubtful if this
room was roofed over, inasmuch as two pillar bases were found, one
on each side of the entry to the central room. These free-standing

pillars, having no structural function, are reminiscent of the two ornamented pillars standing at the entry to the Solomonic Temple—Jachin
and Boaz (Fig. 33).

Both sides of the main entry to the temple were ornamented by
orthostats carved with lions in relief standing as symbolic guardians of
the shrine. One of them was actually found in a pit excavated nearby,
where the lion was surely buried by devotees who feared the wrath of
the deity after the destruction of the temple.

Concerning the god venerated at this temple, one learns something
from the cult objects found in the last phase, most of which certainly
originated in the earlier temples. Among the offering tables and ritual
implements found scattered on the floor of the holy place, there was
a flat incense altar made of basalt bearing the symbol of the sun god,
viz., the sun disk with four rays. The same symbol was carved on the
chest from a fragmented basalt statue mounted on the back of a bull.
The tradition of a deity standing astride a bull symbolizing his power
also finds expression in the Israelite period in the making of the

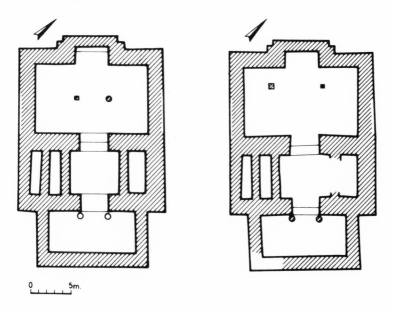

FIG. 33. Hazor. Temples from the enclosure (Strata IB–IA)

"golden calf" by Aaron in the desert and by Jeroboam son of Nebat at Dan and at Bethel. In Israelite ritual, emphasis is upon the calf alone, who carries and symbolizes the unseen divinity.

The closest parallel to the "orthostat temple" of Hazor is found at Alalakh in northern Syria. Not only were orthostats found there in various strata, and even a pair of lions decorating the entry, but there is also a great similarity in ground plan: the temple from Middle Canaanite (Stratum VII) is a characteristic "temple tower," having a broad room for a holy place and a narrow entry vestibule with towers on both sides. The temple from the fifteenth century (Stratum IV) is also similar; the last two temples, from approximately the thirteenth century (Strata IB and IA in Alalakh), are identical in their plans to the temples of IB and IA at Hazor. This is an illuminating example of Canaanite cultural uniformity, and of the reciprocal influence among the great urban centers throughout the Levant.

Some would see in this ground plan a close prototype of the Solomonic Temple. Only at first glance can one say that both have a tripartite division consisting of a vestibule, a holy place, and a holy of holies. In the Solomonic Temple, the Holy Place is the main cult room with its offering table and the incense altars, and it is distinctly a long room. This function is fulfilled in the Hazor temples by the inner room, which is definitely a broad room. The holy of holies with the principal cultic artifacts is a central niche in the holy place at Hazor. To the entry vestibule of the Solomonic Temple, one can match the central space at Hazor, but the former does not have towers or similar staircase chambers. In the outer unit of Hazor, there is no parallel with the Solomonic Temple, although the two pillars at the entry to the vestibule are the same. Various details in distinctly Canaanite ritual which find expression in the Hazor temples were also adopted into the Israelite cultic repertoire, but the basic architectural concept of the building is completely different.

A second temple, smaller and simpler, was found in the southwestern corner of the enclosure built against the rampart, viz., the stelae temple dedicated to the moon god. Its ground plan is simply that of a small broad room with a raised cultic niche on the southwestern side. It existed throughout the later stages of the city in the fourteenth and thirteenth centuries (Strata IB–IA), and here also one may say that the ritual objects in the later phase must have originated largely in an earlier stage. On the niche, there was set up a row of smooth basalt stelae with one stele in the center bearing the relief of two raised hands holding a circle and a crescent, a symbol of the moon god. On the left side stood a statue, a figure seated on a throne with an inverted crescent hanging around its neck. To the right of the stelae was a small lion orthostat which certainly must have originated at the entryway of one of the earlier temples. In the area outside the shrine, a workshop was found containing a ceramic mask and a ritual standard made of bronze covered with gold, which bears the relief of a goddess holding two snakes in her hand with the crescent above. Snakes are an ancient symbol of fertility, and are even found in Israelite ritual from the age of Moses to the reign of Hezekiah. It is also possible that this standard and perhaps also the two raised hands are meant to represent the consort of the moon god. The stele symbolizing the presence of the

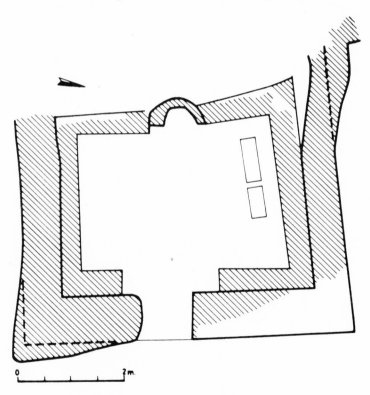

FIG. 34. Hazor. Temple (Stratum I)

deity and possibly related to a memorial of patriarchs and historical events became a central artifact in the Israelite cult. The simple ground plan of the shrine with one broad room and the central cultic niche is reminiscent of the ancient Israelite temple discovered at Arad and depicted in the biblical description of the Tabernacle (Fig. 34). The temple in the upper city of Hazor was also comprised of only one room, but it was a distinctly long room in contrast to the broad rooms of the shrines in the lower city. It began in Middle Canaanite (Stratum XVI), and during its last phase an orthostat threshold similar to that in the lower city was added on to it. The head of a similar orthostat lion was also found near the entryway. Except for votive ceramic vessels, no cult objects were found that could testify to the nature of this temple. According to the latest investigation it would appear that it had gone completely out of use already at the end of Stratum XV, but a number of stelae and a libation bowl standing in front of them demonstrate that the ritual on this site continued to the end of the Canaanite period (Stratum XIII).

Also at Lachish, the principal royal city in the southern Shephelah, there was discovered a series of temples but, surprisingly, they were outside the city in the Hyksos moat which has earned them the title, "the fosse temples." Three shrines were found there built one after

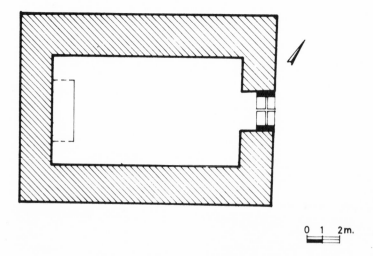

0 1   2m.

FIG. 35. Hazor. Temple (Stratum XIII)

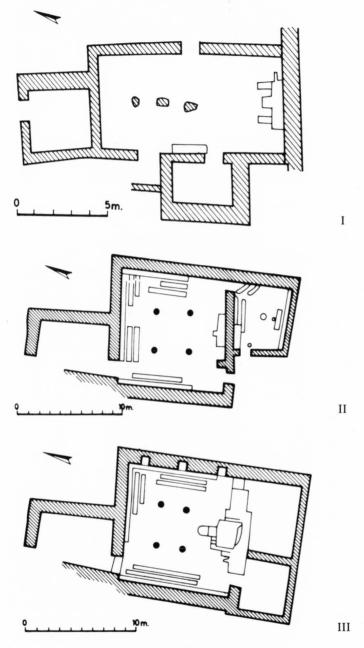

I

II

III

Fig. 36. Lachish. The fosse temples

another in Late Canaanite. It is possible that the stable Egyptian authority in the southern part of the country permitted their existence
outside the city area, and, in fact, Lachish is not mentioned in even one
of the topographical lists from the Egyptian campaigns.

The fosse temples were small, simple structures, actually comprised
of only one cult room with a raised platform built against the southern
wall. The earliest temple was a small room 5 by 10 m. in size with a
roof supported by two pillars, having a tiny storage room on one side.
The two entries to the temple were not on one axis opposite the holy
of holies, as in all the Hazor shrines, but on the two long sides to the
right and to the left. This building belongs to Late Canaanite I (six-
teenth-fifteenth centuries). In the *favissae* round about, discarded cult
offerings were buried, including samples of bichrome ware, a Mycenaean krater of the Mycenaean II type unique in this country and a
scarab of Thutmose III. Of special significance for dating is a plaque
with the name of Amenhotep III (1417–1379 B.C.E.) found under one
of the walls of Temple II. Thus, it is clear that Temple II was not built
before the el-'Amarna period, and Temple III existed during the thirteenth century as evidenced by a faience ring bearing the name of
Ramses II. Several scarabs from the reign of Amenhotep III, and
especially one of the large "lion hunt" scarabs of faience from his tenth
year, confirm the strong ties with Egypt during his reign. The building
was broadened in the time of Temples II and III, so that the cult room
was now 10 by 10 m., with four pillars for carrying the roof. The
entryway was transferred to the northwestern corner, to the northern
wall opposite the platform, and in front of it there was a small vestibule. Rooms were also added behind the platform, one in Temple II
and another in Temple III, and a few rows of benches were built
around the walls that must have been intended for cultic objects.

Expensive votive objects were found mainly in the *favissae,* not only
pottery vessels, among them an abundance of Mycenaean imports, but
also objects of ivory, bone, glass faience, metal, stone, various beads,
Egyptian scarabs, and cylinder seals. On a decorated pottery jug from
one of the pits of Temple III found with a scarab of Ramses II, there
was an inscription in old Canaanite writing (Proto-Canaanite) containing the words, *mtn . . . (l)'lt,* "a gift . . . (to) the goddess." This permits
the assumption that the fosse temple was dedicated to the goddess
Ba'alath, the chief Canaanite deity, whose name was memorialized in
the Proto-Sinaitic inscriptions of Serabit el-Khadem as well (Photo 23).

At Tell Deir 'Alla in the eastern Jordan Valley near the Jabbok, perhaps the biblical Succoth, a late Canaanite cult place was discovered which seems to have occupied most of the area on the unfortified hill. Incense stands, clay models of temples, and many votive objects including Mycenaean imports leave no doubt that this was a temple, but thus far it is most difficult to evaluate its ground plan or its character. The temple at Tell Deir 'Alla existed throughout the Late Canaanite, and in view of an Egyptian faience vessel with the name of Queen Ta-useret, last of the Nineteenth Dynasty rulers (1202–1194 B.C.E.), found in the destruction debris of the last temple, it is clear that it was destroyed at the beginning of the twelfth century. This area was in fact outside the sphere of Egyptian authority (cf. the borders of Canaan, Num. 34:12), and the temple was apparently venerated by the entire population, so that it could exist undisturbed even without fortification. It is possible that this is the "house" at Succoth, mentioned in the narrative of Jacob, from whence he continued his journey to "Shechem, which is in the land of Canaan" (Gen. 33:17–18).

Two isolated but very substantial buildings outside the city area were also discovered at Rabbath-ammon and Shechem respectively. Both of them consist of rectangular structures with a central court surrounded by rooms on all sides—the smaller structure at Rabbath-ammon and the larger at Shechem. In the middle of the courtyard, there was found the base for a pillar in both buildings. There is no foundation for the widely accepted theory that these buildings were temples, and that the pillar bases served as altars or stelae. It is probable that the internal space was roofed over and that the central pillar supported the roof.

Apart from fragments of an incense stand found in the courtyard of the Shechem building, there were no cultic objects discovered there, and the small amount of pottery, as yet unpublished, was dated by the excavators to the end of Middle Canaanite. On the other hand the date of the building near Rabbath-ammon is much clearer because of the many Cypriot and Mycenaean imported wares found in it: they belong to the fourteenth and thirteenth centuries B.C.E. The small objects found in this latter building were particularly rich and include decorated vessels of bone and ivory, Egyptian stone vessels, gold ornaments, beads, and an appreciable number of arrow and javelin heads, daggers, bowls, and a bronze Egyptian sickle sword. No clear ritual vessels were found among these objects; they are simply evidence of

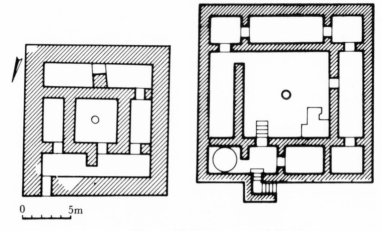

FIG. 37. Villas: Rabbath-ammon and Shechem

the wealth enjoyed by the local residents (Fig. 37).

Nor does the ground plan correspond to any temple design. On the other hand, a close architectural comparison can be made with Egyptian buildings from el-'Amarna in which a row of rooms surrounds a rectangular internal courtyard having one, two, or four pillars. It would appear that the roof of this internal chamber supported by those pillars was higher than that of the other rooms to permit the entry of light.

A house with similar ground plan was discovered at Beth-shean (house 1500, Stratum VI). It is also a rectangular building with an internal chamber having two pillars and rooms on all sides. At Beth-shean it is obvious from the finds that this was the dwelling of the Egyptian commander. Another example of this architectural type is the "governor's house" at Tell el-Far'ah (South). This is again a rectangular structure with a central court having rooms on all sides with only the pillar missing—perhaps it was made of wood. Since the entire structure was built of bricks, it is important to note the Egyptian finds, such as a fragment of a pitcher with the cartouches of Seti II (1214–1208 B.C.E.), and remains of an ivory inlaid box with a picture of the governor seated on his royal throne and a hunting scene. It is generally assumed that the governor of the Egyptian garrison at that place, mentioned in Egyptian inscriptions, lived in this fort. Therefore, one may conjecture that the buildings at Shechem and Rabbath-ammon were also fortified villas and that the latter, with its thick walls and narrow entry, served as the fortified tower of the Egyptian commander who controlled the area (Figs. 38, 39).

One of the most interesting discoveries in recent years is the Egyptian temple uncovered at Timna by Rothenberg. That temple was built in front of an impressive cliff (the so-called "pillars of Solomon"), near the work camps of the copper mines in Nahal Timna in the southern Arabah, about 25 km. north of Elath.

Rothenberg's researches have shown that apart from early exploitation in the Chalcolithic and later use in the Roman period, the copper mines were only worked in one era, viz., the Nineteenth and Twentieth Dynasties during the thirteenth and the first half of the twelfth century B.C.E. There is no basis for associating them with the reign of Solomon and the Israelite monarchy according to the formerly accepted view. The Egyptian temple contained pottery similar to that discovered in the mines and the various camps in association with votive objects bearing Egyptian inscriptions, including the names of Pharaohs from Seti I to Ramses V. It is clear, therefore, that the Egyptians are the ones who developed the copper mines of Timna in that period, a development that adds plausibility to their sudden interest in Edom and Moab, as revealed in the inscriptions of Ramses II.

The mining temple is an Egyptian shrine dedicated to Hathor, the Egyptian goddess of mining. It consisted of one small room built against the cliff with a rounded niche in its center and a large court-

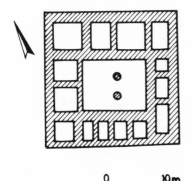

Fig.38. Beth-shean. "House 1500" (Stratum VI)

0   10m.

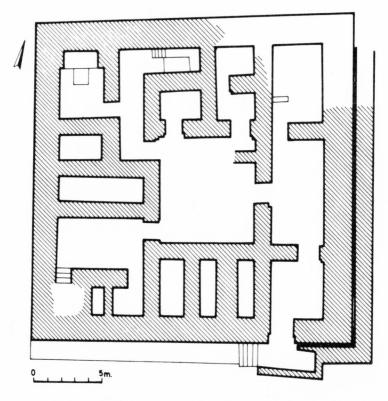

FIG. 39. Tell el-Far'ah (South). The "governor's house"

yard, 9 by 7 m., in front. Among the cult objects most outstanding are the Hathor figures carved in stone, some on typical "Hathor pillars," others with the cow ears characteristic of that goddess (Fig. 40). In the last phase of the temple, a row of pillars was set up along the left-hand wall of the courtyard, among them one with the face of Hathor obliterated and also a large stone bowl. These stones must have served as stelae, so prevalent in Semitic ritual, while the bowl was for libations. Thus it would appear that in this last phase the temple was reconstituted by different elements, perhaps the local workers who had gained control of the area when the Egyptians went away. On the last floor, there was an appreciable number of cloth pieces; therefore, the

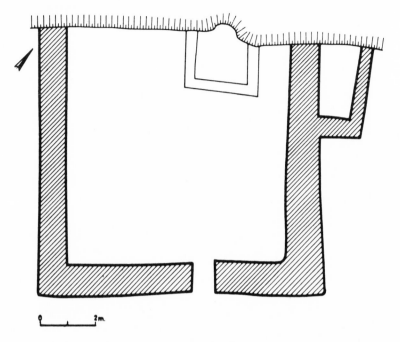

FIG. 40. Timna. The Egyptian temple

excavator conjectures that the entire shrine was covered by a tent, in accordance with nomadic custom and the description of the tabernacle in the wilderness.

Apart from the many votive objects found in the temple (Photo 25), there was a most interesting type of ware that also turned up in the mining camps. It has three types, sharply distinguishable one from another: (1) regular pottery from the end of Late Canaanite and the beginning of Israelite I; (2) "Negeb ware" made by hand in a more primitive method by nomadic potters wandering around the area, which ware will be discussed in our survey of the Negeb in Israelite I (Plate 23:11–14); (3) a decorated ware, unique in itself, which may be rightly called "Midianite" (Plate 23:1–10). This latter ware also has simple forms, mostly bowls with a flat base, but also a few juglets and jars. However, the vessels are made of creamy, yellowish clay, well fired

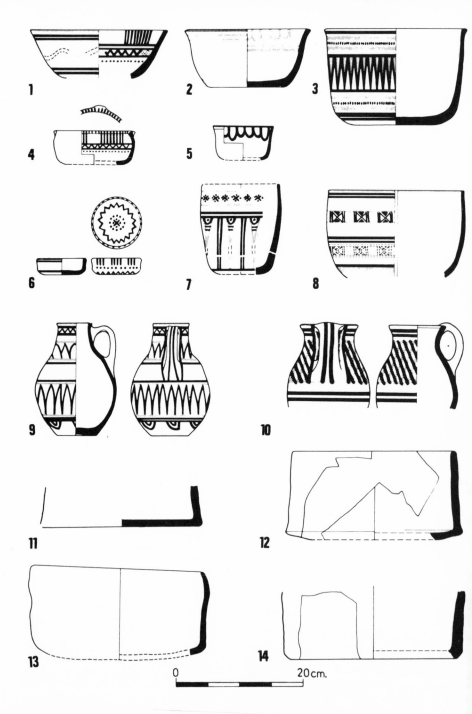

PLATE 23. Midianite pottery from the end of the Late Canaanite period

and so perfectly smoothed that the signs of burnishing can be seen; their ornamentation is distinctive, usually bichrome in reddish-brown to black colors. The decoration is made up of a wide variety of geometric patterns, with stripes, intersecting lines and coils, triangles, dots, circles and semicircles, etc.; there are also schematic figures of men and birds. The same ware has been discovered in various sites by surveys conducted in northern Hejaz, east of the Gulf of Elath. This is the region where we find the Midianites, according to the Bible and later sources, and the great diffusion of this special pottery in the land of Midian during the thirteenth-twelfth centuries, and apparently earlier, justifies its definition as "Midianite ware."

It is still quite difficult to establish the sources for this ware, but some of the geometric patterns and, in particular, the bird decorations are reminiscent of the decorated ware from Nuzi, one of the Hurrian cultural centers east of Assyria. It is interesting that in the Bible a tradition has been preserved to the effect that the Hurrians (Horites) preceded the Edomites in the land of Edom. So there is probably preserved here an echo of that highly developed culture which flourished in Midian and southern Edom during the Late Canaanite period.

There is one more instructive detail which has associations with the biblical tradition from the wilderness wanderings: the astounding Midianite culture provides a realistic basis for the traditions about the strong ties between Moses and Midian. It also explains the striking contrast in the relationships with Midian in the various narratives. In the story about the march through Transjordan to Canaan, and the long stay on the Plains of Moab, a fathomless enmity is depicted between Israel and Midian. This reality corresponds to the early wave of conquest in the fourteenth century which we will deal with further on, when Midian had possession of Seir and the King's Highway, and the tribes had to make their way through this area. In the thirteenth century, on the other hand, during the second occupation wave, the Edomites had already pushed out the Midianites from that area, so there was no longer a conflict of interest between the Israelite tribes and the Midianites, who had been pressed southward.

The classic example of a flourishing Canaanite urban center in the Late Canaanite period is Megiddo. In the various quarters of the town, substantial houses, spacious and well built, have been uncovered; among them the Egyptian house of rectangular type with a central courtyard is again most prominent. A large and especially attractive building of this kind was found to the east of the gate (area DD), and in the middle of its courtyard there was a carefully carved pillar base (Fig. 41).

The royal house was to the west of the gate, dominating the adjacent gate plaza. The beginning of a prominent house with its dimensions goes back at this site to the end of Middle Canaanite (Stratum X), but in the Late Canaanite strata (IX–VIIA), it was greatly expanded at the expense of the neighboring houses. Its massive outer walls give it the character of a fort: in Stratum IX it had two wings: the western was totally destroyed because of later constructions and the eastern contained a large court surrounded by rooms (Fig. 42).

Stratum X, distinguished by its bichrome ware, was destroyed during the famous campaign by Thutmose III in 1468 B.C.E., an action in which the Canaanite city-state alliance, headed by the kings of Kedesh (on the Orontes) and Megiddo, with the backing of Mitanni, was crushed. Although Megiddo itself only capitulated after a seven months' siege, and the town was doubtless plundered and burned after its conquest, obviously it was immediately restored by its occupants, since there is complete continuity in its structures. The palace of Stratum VIII, which certainly must have been built in the second half of the fifteenth century and seems to have stood until the el-'Amarna Age, is the most impressive and best preserved of all, and its finds testify to the prosperity of the occupants. This phenomenon typifies the Egyptian administrative practices in the country. Their rule was based on the vassal city-states, so they did not interfere in their restoration. A stable government and the prosperous trade routes dominated by Megiddo brought the city to one of its most flourishing zeniths in spite of the heavy tax burden imposed by the Egyptian authorities.

Palace VIII is a rectangular structure with a length of 50 m., and the width of its walls, often as much as two meters or more, permits the deduction that it had more than one story. In the eastern wing there is a large courtyard with rooms on two sides and a wide entryway leading directly from the gate plaza. Beside it was a large room paved with seashells that had a rectangular basin in its center and that evidently served as a washroom. In the western wing, there was an additional courtyard from which a monumental entryway with two pillars led to two large paved rooms, one of which was possibly a throne room. A pillar with an Egyptian papyrus blossom design found in the eastern courtyard seems to have originally belonged with those pillars.

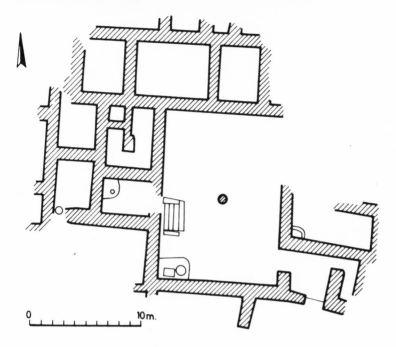

FIG. 41. Megiddo. Nobleman's house

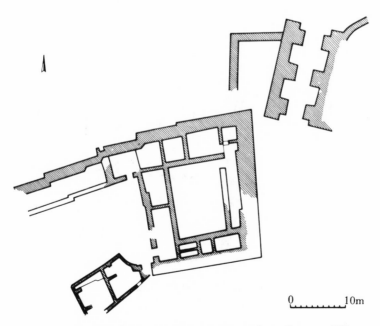

FIG. 42. Megiddo. The gate and the palace (Stratum IX)

As previously mentioned, similar capitals were found in Stratum VII at Beth-shean (Fig. 43).

Concerning the wealth of Megiddo's king during that period, there is the evidence of a treasure of golden implements, ivory plaques, jewelry, and objects of art of various expensive materials found under the floor of one of the small northern rooms. The occupants of this palace must have hidden it there in the hope of preserving it in the face of some impending disaster, but it remained buried under the debris of the building until it was uncovered by the excavators nearly 3,300 years later. This is the richest collection of valuables and luxury items from the Late Canaanite period ever discovered in this country. To Stratum VIII one may also assign the fragment of a cuneiform tablet found below the excavation dump in the gate area. The text is a passage from the Gilgamesh Epic, the first of its kind discovered here.

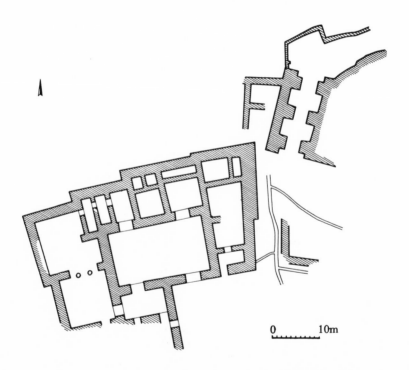

0 _____ 10m

FIG. 43. Megiddo. The gate and the palace (Stratum VIII)

It surely derives from the archive of the palace scribe, and bears witness to the broad spectrum of cultural influences at Megiddo during the el-'Amarna Age (Fig. 44; Photo 24).

The palace also continued to dominate this area during the two ensuing strata (VIIB–VIIA). It is true that the outer walls became somewhat thinner, but the eastern wing with the great courtyard remained without essential change. Only the rooms of the western wing were modified, and at the expense of the courtyard and the monumental entryway a continuous row of chambers was built. In the last stratum of the palace (VIIA), a special addition of three contiguous rooms was added to the west of these other rooms, the latest ones being sunk into the ground to a depth of more than a meter. Since there was found in them a rich treasure of ivories as well as jewelry and

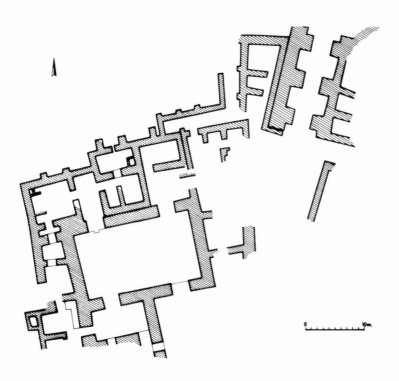

FIG. 44. Megiddo. The gate and the palace (Stratum VIIB)

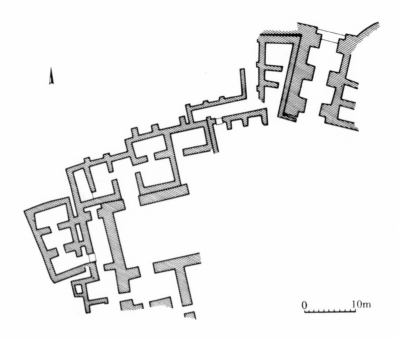

FIG. 45. Megiddo. The gate and the palace (Stratum VIIA)

valuables of gold, alabaster, and other precious materials, it would appear that this basement was constructed as a "treasury" for the palace. The collection of ivories is the richest from the Late Canaanite ever found here. It is a most impressive representative of that glyptic art in which the craftsmen of Canaan had become expert, attaining unrivaled achievements in this field. The cartouche of Pharaoh Ramses III on an ivory box indicates that at least some of the ivories originated in that period, and the last king at Megiddo was no less opulent than his ancestors. It must be assumed that some of the ivories originated in the thirteenth century because of the richness and the varied styles, in particular those ivories in the style of the Hittite kingdom. This treasure probably included the inheritance of the ancestors of the last king at Megiddo, collected during the course of Strata VIIB and VIIA.

One of the most impressive phenomena, typifying the broad spectrum of Canaanite culture and the strong ties with the entire Fertile Crescent, is the multiplicity of writing styles found in the country and the languages written. True, most of the inscriptions are short and broken, but it is probable that only a very small amount of the whole has survived, and the variety itself testifies to the many influences at work in the country. Already mentioned are the hieroglyphic Egyptian inscriptions such as victory stelae and inscriptions on statues from Beth-shean, Chinnereth, and Megiddo, the monumental inscriptions on the doorposts of the gate at Joppa—all of them products of the Egyptian authorities. To them must be added, apart from the many scarabs, inscriptions on ivories from Megiddo and hieratic texts on ceramic bowls discovered at Lachish and Tel Sera' in the Negeb, this latter probably being ancient Ziklag. The most widespread was Akkadian cuneiform written on clay tablets; this was the diplomatic lingua franca of that era. Remnants of an archive of letters similar to the epistles from el-'Amarna were found at Taanach, as mentioned above. But isolated texts have also turned up in various places; they include letters and administrative and literary documents (Photo 24). There is no doubt that in every one of the main Canaanite city-states there was a scribe learned in Akkadian cuneiform who conducted the local correspondence. Unique clay tablets have been found at Tell Deir 'Alla in a stratum from the beginning of the twelfth century. Although the tablets have yet to be deciphered, they remind one of the Minoan linear scripts; this is evidently due to influence from the Aegean region. Traces of an inscription carved on a stele from Balu'ah in Moab seem to be in a similar script.

All of these are types of script widespread in neighboring countries, but even more important are the forms of writing created in Eretz-Israel and Syria during the second millennium B.C.E. The latter are the ancient alphabetic scripts from which all forms of alphabetic writing have developed during the course of time—including those in use in our day. The invention of alphabetic writing, which limits the number of signs to thirty or less instead of the hundreds of signs in hieroglyphic or cuneiform writing, thus making it accessible to the masses, is one of the great revolutions in the development of human civilization. This invention came into being and thrived in Eretz-Israel and Syria during the second millennium and is Canaan's greatest contribution to human culture. It is an ingenious innovation, perhaps by one man, but it was made possible by the location of Canaan at a crossroads and a meeting place of cultures in the ancient East (Photo 23; Fig. 46).

There are two types of alphabetic writing: the Ugaritic cuneiform and the Phoenician linear. Rich archives in Ugaritic script have been discovered in the northern Syrian coastal city of Ugarit since 1929; they contain a wide range of material from the city administration and a treasure of West Semitic mythology now made known for the first time, containing many parallels to the Bible in language, expressions, and content.

Isolated examples of this script have also been discovered in Eretz-Israel at Beth-shemesh, at Taanach, and on a copper knife blade found near Mt. Tabor; they testify to the diffusion of this script throughout the Levant. This form of writing, which includes only thirty signs (those found here have even fewer, due to the slightly more limited consonantal repertoire), is an alphabetic script adapted to the material and writing system of cuneiform. It was widespread in the fourteenth century B.C.E., and its beginning was probably not much earlier than that. The names of the letters in the alphabet and their order correspond to the Canaanite alphabet, and it would also seem that the choice of some of the wedge combinations for the individual letters was influenced by the Proto-Canaanite form of writing. It is evident, therefore, that the Ugaritic script was a transitory experiment in adapting the new linear script to the ubiquitous clay writing material of cuneiform (Fig. 46A).

The linear alphabetic script is the greatest Canaanite achievement. It is first found in the Egyptian turquoise mines at Serabit el-Khadem in southern Sinai alongside Egyptian votive inscriptions; since then, the term "Proto-Sinaitic" has become commonly accepted. The small number of texts and their brevity prevented a thorough decipherment of all of the signs, but most of them have been clarified, and the language with its main fundamentals is fairly certain, thanks especially to the researches of Albright and Cross. It is "Canaanite" (West Semitic), and these inscriptions were written by workers from Canaan engaged in their trade here, either in the service of the Egyptian expeditions or alongside them. A recurrent combination in these texts is the five letters *lb'lt*, "to (the) Lady," a title of the principal Canaanite goddess identified with the Egyptian Hathor, mistress of the mines.

This is an acrophonic writing system. The signs represent a more simplified form of hieroglyphic (Fig. 46B). But now each symbol no longer expresses the entire concept of the picture but rather the first

Latin Script	Greek Script	Arad, Stratum VI	Arad, Stratum X	Gezer Calendar	'Izbet Sarta	Proto-Sinaitic	Late Hebrew/Aramaic
A	A						א
B	B						ב
G	Γ						ג
D	Δ						ד
E	E						ה
V	Y						ו
Z	Z	(xı)					ז
H	H						ח
	Θ						ט
I	I						י
K	K						כ
L	Λ						ל
M	M						מ
N	N						נ
	≡						ס
O	O						ע
P	Π						פ
							צ
Q							ק
R	P						ר
S	Σ						ש
T	T						ת

FIG. 46. Development of the Hebrew alphabet

letter of the word in the Canaanite language, for example: *'aleph* is the picture of an ox head *('alpu)*, *beth* is the picture of a house, *daleth* of a fish *(dag)*, *kaph* of the palm of the hand, *mem* of water, *nun* of a snake, *'ayin* of an eye, *resh* of a human head, etc. In other words, the name of each letter is also the name of the subject it depicts. It is worthy of

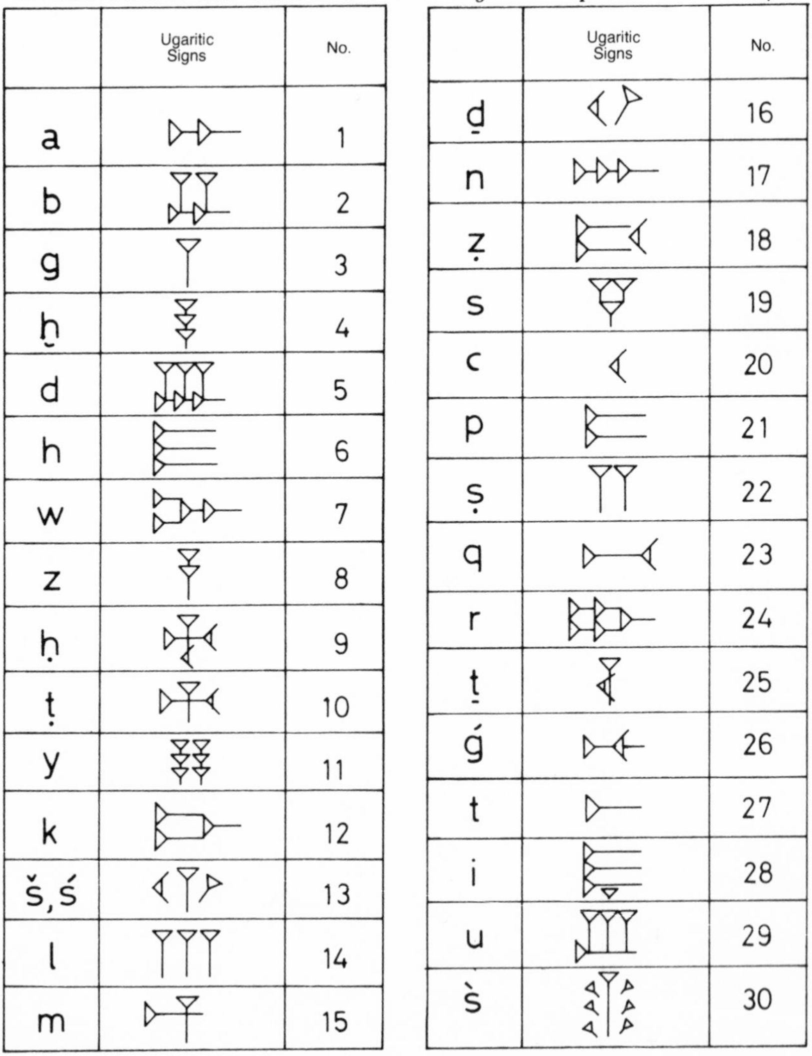

	Ugaritic Signs	No.		Ugaritic Signs	No.
a		1	ḏ		16
b		2	n		17
g		3	ẓ		18
ḫ		4	s		19
d		5	ʿ		20
h		6	p		21
w		7	ṣ		22
z		8	q		23
ḥ		9	r		24
ṭ		10	ṯ		25
y		11	ǵ		26
k		12	t		27
š, ś		13	i		28
l		14	u		29
m		15	ṡ		30

FIG. 46A. The Ugaritic alphabet

note that the acrophonic meaning of
each letter is still quite obvious, and
these letter names must have been assigned to them at the very beginning.

The date of the Proto-Sinaitic inscriptions is still a subject of debate:
between the Middle Kingdom and the
beginning of the New Kingdom (seven-
teenth-fifteenth centuries B.C.E.), but
a few brief inscriptions in a similar
script that have been discovered at
several tells in the country in strata
from the Middle Canaanite (Shechem,
Gezer, Lachish, Tel Nagila) testify
to its beginning in that period and
its diffusion in Canaan. The Proto-
Sinaitic script is the archetype of the
Canaanite-Phoenician script, from
which it was borrowed in the tenth or
ninth century in Greece and subsequently transmitted during the course
of time to the other countries of the
west. A richer collection of Phoenician inscriptions is available only
from the beginning of the tenth century at Byblos and also beginning in
the tenth century in Eretz-Israel, but

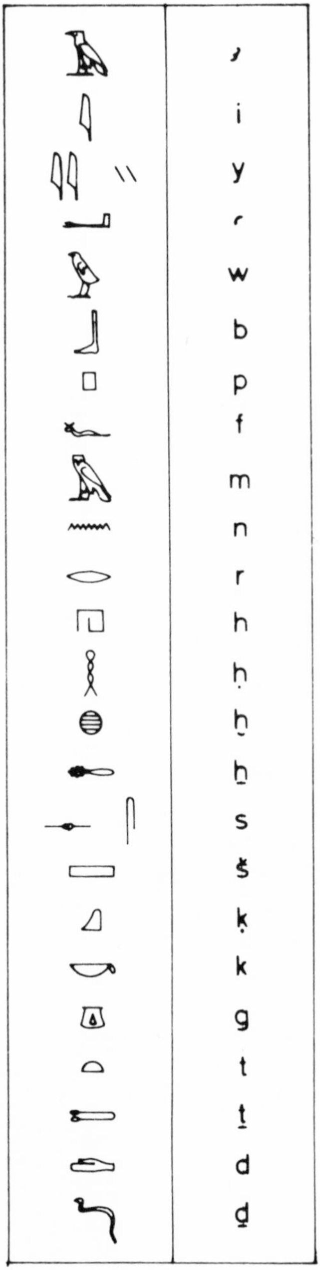

FIG. 46B. Egyptian hieroglyphic signs
(after Gardiner,
Egyptian Grammar)

short texts in the "Proto-Canaanite" from Lachish and Beth-shemesh indicate that, by the thirteenth century, the script had already taken on its general linear form with only a few minor changes. Just recently, there was discovered at Khirbet Raddana, north of Jerusalem, a text of two and a half letters incised on a jar handle representing a distinct transition between the Proto-Sinaitic and the Proto-Canaanite of the thirteenth century. They are written vertically like most of the Proto-Sinaitic texts, and the first letter, aleph, is still reminiscent of the ox head in spite of the schematic shape of an angle bisected by a line like that found at Lachish. That inscription should evidently be dated to the fourteenth century, and it serves as the first example of the transition from Proto-Sinaitic pictographs to the schematic letters of the Canaanite-Phoenician script during the Late Canaanite period. The short inscription from Khirbet Raddana also has special importance for the beginning date of Israelite settlement, a question that will be treated in the coming chapter. Khirbet Raddana is a small hill-country settlement, typical of the Israelite occupation in its location, its houses, and the shape of its vessels, so this is the first epigraphic evidence for the date of its founding no later than the fourteenth century B.C.E. The establishment of such new settlements overlaps in time the decline of Canaan. It begins in a period of ethnic changes, and the decline of regimes and cultures in the entire Near East, and is comparable only to the decline of the Early Canaanite culture. This was a period when new ethnic elements were penetrating into the Fertile Crescent, especially the "sea peoples" from the west and the waves of Aramaean and Hebrew tribes from the east. These developments brought successive population displacements, ethnic movements, and destruction of cities and kingdoms, including the great powers that had dominated the entire region during the Late Canaanite. The kingdom of the Hittites fell at the end of the thirteenth century along with the important city-states in northern Syria such as Ugarit and Alalakh. Assyria and Babylon and Egypt broke up into smaller units without a strong central government, thus ceasing to be major influences in Canaan after the mid-twelfth century. Canaan receded more and more to the Phoenician coast, to the rugged coastal area from the Plain of Acco in the south to Byblos and Arvad in the north. Here it continued to hold out with its main attention turned toward the sea, and it enjoyed a revival as a maritime commercial power throughout the Mediterranean beginning with the tenth century. In Eretz-Israel itself, the Canaanite city-states were condemned to a decline and eventual dissolution after a final period of flourishing in the el-'Amarna Age. This decline took place during a period of two hundred years or more. No city escaped this fate, and after the end of the twelfth century, none of them still survived. Jericho had not been a real town during the Late Canaanite, but only a fort on top of the mound; its "Middle building" was evidently destroyed in the second half of the fourteenth century, as apparently was Bethel at a date not too far from that. Some of the cities in the Shephelah that have been excavated were destroyed near the end of the thirteenth century, viz., Lachish, Tell Beit Mirsim, Tell el-Hesi, Beth-shemesh. At Lachish there was found in the destruction level a bowl with an Egyptian hieratic inscription indicating a quantity of produce, apparently the registration of taxes being paid, and the date "Year Four." Various scholars have assumed that the fourth year of Merneptah is meant, and that Lachish was destroyed somewhere around 1220 B.C.E.; however, a date somewhat later is also possible— for example, in the reign of Ramses III, at the beginning of the twelfth century. In the recent excavations an additional fragment of a similar inscription has turned up with the date, "Year Ten (or more)." Perhaps even more decisive is a scarab with the name of Ramses III found at Lachish (and the metal fragment from the city gate bearing his cartouche). Since there is evidently an occupational gap between the destruction of the Canaanite city at Lachish until the end of the eleventh century, these inscriptions may be taken as evidence that the Canaanites held out until the beginning of the twelfth century. The destruction of Hazor also seems to have taken place near the end of the thirteenth century. Prior to its total destruction there was an earlier phase of drastic decline (Stratum XIII) on the high tell. Stratum IA of the lower city was much poorer than its predecessors, and it is doubtful whether the lower enclosure was still fortified. The two latest Canaanite strata include Mycenaean IIIB pottery dated to the thirteenth century, to the second half of which the last stratum must be dated.

Other Canaanite cities, principally in the valleys and along the coast, held out for an additional fifty to a hundred years. These were the Canaanite cities not conquered by the various tribes. Canaanite Taanach and Megiddo were destroyed only around 1125 B.C.E. That date is fixed with great precision at Megiddo by two Egyptian inscriptions: on an ivory box with the cartouche of Ramses III found in the ivory treasure of VIIB, and on a statue base of Ramses VI which originated most likely in the same stratum. Canaanite Shechem, the capital of Mt. Ephraim, continued to exist for some time into the twelfth century until it was destroyed as a result of the conflict with Abimelech, son of Gideon. Isolated cities even held out until the beginning of the Israelite monarchy, e.g., Jebusite Jerusalem or Canaanite Gezer, which was only destroyed in the reign of Solomon.

IV

THE ISRAELITE PERIOD

THE SETTLEMENT AND THE JUDGES—ISRAELITE I

THE Israelite period begins in the chronology of Eretz-Israel about 1200 B.C.E.; this is the Iron Age, which lasted for about 600 years until the destruction of the First Temple (587 B.C.E.). These designations are quite general and schematic, and one must keep that fact in mind. The penetration and the settlement by the Israelites in the various regions of the country begin prior to this time, in the thirteenth century—by general consensus—and, as will be seen, quite probably in the fourteenth. Certain Israelite settlements and the characteristic pottery types from the period of the conquest therefore relate, from a chronological standpoint, to the Late Canaanite period. On the other hand, iron came into use only at a later time. It first appears during the fourteenth-thirteenth centuries in the Hittite kingdom, where it was protected as a monopoly. It really began to be disseminated with the fall of the Hittite empire at the end of the thirteenth century, but it penetrated Eretz-Israel only at a later stage. During all of the Israelite I period (twelfth-eleventh centuries), bronze was still the common metal, and the use of iron was quite rare. At Megiddo all of the metal implements in Strata VIIA and VI are made of bronze, except for one iron knife from the latter. This is also the case with Megiddo tombs: iron objects are extremely rare, and in addition to two rings only two knife blades were found associated with pottery from the twelfth-eleventh centuries, in contrast to the abundance of bronze implements. At the Israelite settlement of Tel Masos, which existed from the end of the thirteenth century to approximately the end of the tenth, all of the metal implements are made of bronze except for a sickle and a knife blade. At Beer-sheba, there were two iron sickles in Stratum VI from

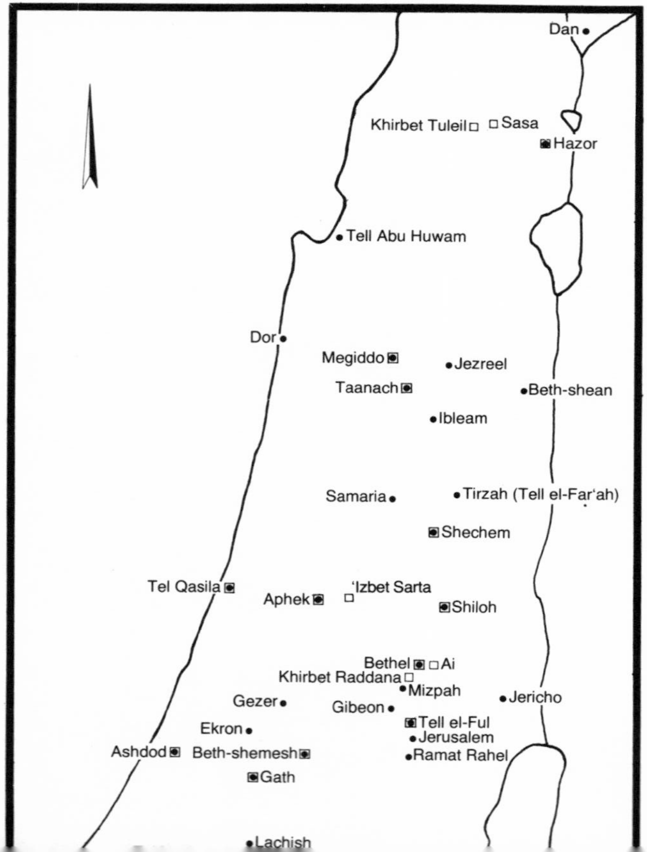

FIG. 47. Map of sites from the
Israelite period

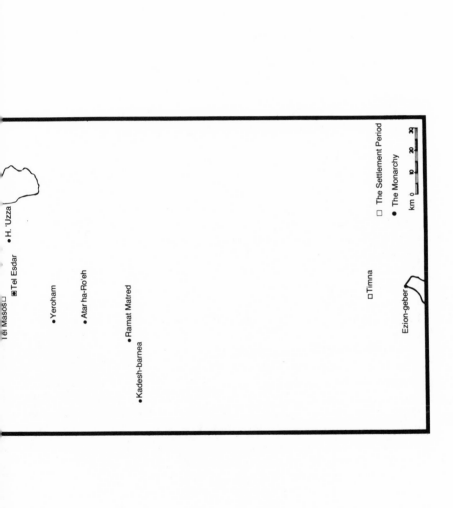

Tel Masos□ ■Tel Esdar ● H. 'Uzza

● Yeroham

● Atar ha-Ro'eh

● Ramat Matred

● Kadesh-barnea

□ Timna

Ezion-geber

□ The Settlement Period

● The Monarchy

km 0   10   20   30

the early tenth century B.C.E., and an iron plow blade was found at Gibeah of Saul (Tell el-Ful) in the fortress from the reign of Saul, near the end of the eleventh century. Thus, it is clear that the appearance of iron in Israelite I is rare and sporadic, and that iron has no significance in the technology of that time. It begins to be widespread only at the beginning of the monarchy, whence it achieved a dominant use in tools and weapons.

The assumption is generally accepted that the Philistines brought the knowledge of ironworking to the country and kept it as a monopoly until their power was broken by David. That assumption is based in fact on one verse describing the situation in the reign of Saul: "There was no smith to be found throughout all the land of Israel; for the Philistines said, 'Lest the Hebrews make themselves swords or spears'; but every one of the Israelites went down to the Philistines to sharpen his plowshare, his mattock, his axe, or his (goad, LXX)" (I Sam. 13: 19–20). Actually, the verse does not deal specifically with ironworking, and since the tools found in the Israelite sites of this period are made of bronze, it may be assumed that metalworking in general was intended. At Beth-shemesh, which was near to Philistia, there were found in Stratum III ovens and furnaces of the bronze industry (which had their beginning in the previous stratum from the end of the Canaanite period), along with an abundance of Philistine pottery.

Of course, the distribution of iron with the breaking of the Philistine hegemony corresponds, at first glance, to the above-mentioned assumption, but thus far there is no substantial archaeological evidence for the widespread diffusion of iron in Philistia in the period under discussion. In the only Philistine capital that has been extensively excavated—Ashdod—iron implements were not found from the early Philistine strata. At Tel Qasila, a city evidently founded by the Philistines on the bank of the Yarkon, there is in fact no iron from the two earlier strata (XII–XI), and its first appearance is at the end of the eleventh century (Stratum X). Of course, in the temple discovered there, there was in the early stratum (XII) an iron blade with an ivory handle, but it is precisely such an exceptional find that testifies how greatly iron was regarded as a precious and rare metal. Likewise, even in the temple of Stratum X there was an iron bracelet, a phenomenon noted in Israelite I, when the new metal was rare and costly, serving mainly for jewelry.

An isolated piece of evidence may be cited from Tel Sharuhen (Tell el-Far'ah [South]). In the tombs which, according to their contents, belong to the Philistines there was found, alongside many bronze implements, also an iron knife and an iron dagger with a bronze grip. Thus it would seem that even though iron appears here and there, it is still rare and costly, even in Philistia. Therefore, it is doubtful whether the Philistines had a monopoly on its production. Its distribution at the end of the eleventh century may be related to the intensification of commercial ties with the north at that time, especially by sea routes, as attested by the appearance of a new imported product, the Cypro-Phoenician ware.

The year 1200 B.C.E. does not, therefore, correspond with the introduction of iron, which comes later, nor with the destruction of the Canaanite cities, which was partly earlier and partly later, nor with the beginning of Israelite settlement, which was also earlier. Neither does this mark a break in pottery types: the ware of the Israelite communities begins earlier, and Philistine pottery only in the mid-twelfth century, while local types have a thorough continuity. Nevertheless, the year 1200 remains the most appropriate date for designating the beginning of a new period, one of the decisive turning points in the history of the country.

In the fourteenth and thirteenth centuries, Cypriot and Mycenaean ware is widely diffused, evidence of the strong commercial ties all across the Fertile Crescent and among the islands of the Aegean and Greece. These imports come to a complete end around 1200 with the fall of the Mycenaean sea power, this also being the approximate date for the destruction of Troy. It is the date of the collapse of the Hittite empire and the destruction of the great city-states in northern Syria such as Alalakh and Ugarit. Although the first blossoms of this new period begin to appear before that, and traces of the older period are felt afterward, this is a cutting-off point. Henceforth Eretz-Israel remains in isolation for more than two hundred years, except for a brief Egyptian resurgence at the beginning of the Twentieth Dynasty. This is the climax of the great ethnic movement for which there are few precedents in human history. The penetration of the Israelite tribes and related Hebrew groups into Eretz-Israel is a marginal feature of this movement, which changed the entire ethnic and political order of the eastern Mediterranean and the lands of the Fertile Crescent. It included the entrance of the Dorian wave into Greece, the movement of the sea peoples across the expanses of the eastern Mediterranean basin, the Phrygian thrust into central Anatolia, and the Aramaean migration into Mesopotamia and Syria. These waves brought an end to the city-states that had characterized Eretz-Israel and Syria during a long period, except for the cities of Phoenicia that preserved the spark of Canaanite culture. The new tribal league that appears on the stage of history maintained in its communities a broader national tie, and with it begins the era of the national states that henceforth stamp their imprint on Eretz-Israel and its surrounding territories.

The Israelite settlement and that of the related Hebrew tribes in Transjordan is essentially different from every previous occupation wave in the country's history. Throughout the entire Canaanite period there were striking differences in the density of settlement in the various districts. The valleys were intensely settled, with strong and important kingdoms on the coastal plain and the Shephelah, in the Jezreel and Jordan valleys. On the plains there were flat and fertile lands convenient for cultivation, and at the foot of the hills most of the copious springs flowed forth, and the main roads skirted around the valleys. Among the hill regions only the most northern enjoyed a dense settlement—northern Transjordan from the Yarmuk basin northward, and the northern part of Upper Galilee to the north of the highest Galilean peaks. Most of the hill regions were only thinly settled, and appreciable areas were forested with thick scrub that was a formidable obstacle to settlement and agriculture. The southern and highest part of Upper Galilee and nearly all of Lower Galilee, except for the lateral valleys and the southern highlands, were not occupied. In the central hills the Canaanite occupation was concentrated along the backbone, down the watershed road that ran from Debir, Hebron, and Jerusalem in the south to Bethel, Tappuah, Shechem, Tirzah, and Dothan in the north. The western and eastern slopes of the hill country were practically not occupied. The same picture prevails in Gilead and in parts of southern Transjordan, where the few communities were concentrated along the length of the King's Highway on the mountain plateau.

It is clear that there were periods when settlement flourished and expanded in contrast to times of decline and contraction, but the picture of settlement does not fundamentally change. Only here and there did isolated communities also penetrate into the more internal regions, and during the zenith of the Hyksos period two of their fortifications are found in the northern Negeb. Of course, toward the end of the Early Canaanite period and especially in Middle Canaanite I, settlements appeared in new areas, particularly in Transjordan and the southern Negeb, but this was a temporary wave of seminomadic occupation which disappeared after a short time without leaving a trace.

These unoccupied areas or those very sparsely settled are the very regions of the principal and most intensive settlement by the tribes of Israel and their relatives. The reason is clear from the sources and from archaeological research: since at the beginning they lacked the strength to overpower the strong Canaanite cities, particularly those in the plain which could make effective use of their superb battle chariots, the Israelite tribes had no choice but to content themselves in the first stage of their settlement with peripheral or internal areas where they faced opposition only from the forces of nature. This situation is reflected clearly in Joshua's advice to the people of his own tribe in answer to their complaints: "And the tribe of Joseph spoke to Joshua, saying, 'Why have you given me but one lot and one portion as an inheritance, although I am a numerous people, since hitherto the LORD has blessed me?' And Joshua said to them, 'If you are a numerous people, go up to the forest, and there clear ground for yourselves in the land of the Perizzites and the Rephaim, since the hill country of Ephraim is too narrow for you.' The tribe of Joseph said, 'The hill country is not enough for us, yet all the Canaanites who dwell in the plain have chariots of iron, both those in Beth-shean and its villages and those in the Valley of Jezreel.' Then Joshua said to the house of Joseph . . . , 'You are a numerous people, and have great power; you shall not have one lot only, but the hill country shall be yours, for though it is a forest, you shall clear it and possess it to its farthest borders . . .' " (Josh. 17:14–18.)

Today, many of these initial conquest settlements are known by virtue of archaeological surveys conducted in various areas, but only a few have been excavated thus far. There is no doubt that more detailed answers to questions about the character of the conquest and its dates will be obtained from intensified research in these settlements rather than excavations in the large tells where most digging is concentrated.

A considerable number of conquest settlements have been found in Gilead and southern Transjordan, especially owing to the surveys by Glueck. These sites were founded by the Transjordanian Israelite tribes on one hand and by Ammon, Moab, and Edom on the other, and they bear witness to the rapid and intensive settlement process that took place in those regions. There are still no details concerning the nature of the settlement and its dates, because at the only two sites excavated in Edom—Tuweilan and Buseirah—there were not found any remains from Early Israelite I except for isolated sherds. These two communities may have been founded at a later stage, or the later structures could have simply obliterated the earlier occupation debris in the areas excavated. Of special interest is a line of forts built along the border of Ammon, some of them rectangular and others round, e.g., Rujm Malfouf. It would appear that they were built in Early Israelite I, but their exact date has not been clarified.

An illuminating picture of Early Israelite settlements was revealed in southern Upper Galilee, the highest area of the Galilee ridges. This territory was not occupied at all prior to Israelite I except for a few sites from Middle Canaanite I that appeared here and there. In the survey conducted there a dense network of conquest settlements was discovered; these were founded over a short period of time at small distances from one another. There is no later period in which the density of communities reached such proportions. Pottery from Early Israelite I also exceeds that of Israelite II in its wide distribution. A trial excavation was carried out at one of the most prominent sites of this period, Tel Harashim (Khirbet et-Tuleil) beside Peqi'in. Above a cave containing remains from Middle Canaanite I was found, sitting on bedrock, the occupational debris from the period of the conquest. In the small excavated area a room was uncovered with remains of a kiln, ovens, benches, and vessels, which proved that it served as a workshop for a metalsmith in copper and bronze. Above this stratum was the debris of a settlement of Israelite II protected by a casemate wall. It is worthy of note that according to the survey, the sites from Israelite I are more numerous, and their locations along with the excavation results from Tel Harashim show that they were unfortified, in contrast to the increase of fortified communities during Israelite II.

At one site in Kibbutz Sasa a bit farther north, there were found traces of houses of Israelite I with the same simple, homogeneous pottery typical of Tel Harashim. However, just as at that other site there appeared suddenly an isolated vessel of unusual form, a bowl with a unique incised decoration, so also among the repertoire of Sasa there was a kernos, a libation ring ornamented with animal figures, a vessel widespread in Canaan which certainly had arrived here by trade.

A similar situation was found in the hill country of Ephraim and Judah. In particular, along the slopes somewhat farther removed from the spine of the hill country, there were discovered many small settlements that had their beginnings with the conquest, and many of which were not occupied at a later period even in Israelite II. Excavations have been carried out at a few of these places, viz., Shiloh, Ai, Khirbet Raddana (Ataroth?), Mizpah (Tell en-Nasbeh) and Gibeah of Benjamin (Tell el-Ful). In all of them, occupation was actually established with the Israelite conquest, and there is a gap of hundreds of years between it and the earlier occupations found at some of them (in Shiloh from Middle Canaanite IIA, at Ai from Early Canaanite, and at Mizpah from Early Canaanite I). Most of them were destroyed before the end of Israelite I, in the middle of the eleventh century at the latest. Some of them were never reoccupied (Ai, Raddana) and others only after a certain gap: Gibeah of Benjamin at the end of the eleventh century and Shiloh only in Israelite II. Again, extensive settlement was prominent only precisely in the period of the conquest.

Some concept of architecture in these communities was gained from Ai and Raddana. The houses generally include a courtyard and two or three rooms, and they are especially characterized by squared orthostat pillars for supporting the roof beams. The use of stone pillars, both monoliths and those comprised of flat slabs, is henceforth a characteristic feature of the Israelite house from the conquest to the end of the First Temple. The use of pillars is rare in Canaanite settlements and is almost never found in common houses. The early period of the pillars and their wide diffusion support the theory that this is an architectural practice brought by the tribes when they came into the land. The source of this architecture is still unknown. It is interesting to note that the use of stone pillars made of links and of slabs for beams has recently been discovered at Jawa in northeastern Transjordan, on the border of the basalt wilderness (the Leja). A very similar technique was revealed in Israelite settlements in the Negeb at Tel Masos and Atar ha-Ro'eh beside Sede Boqer. In any case, this technical knowledge of architecture is evidence that the tribes were not completely nomadic when they arrived in the country.

In the courtyards of these houses, there were plastered water cisterns hewn out of the rock both at Ai and at Raddana. They were intended for collecting rainwater from the roofs of the houses and from the courtyards and served as the main water source throughout most of the year. Water cisterns were also found here and there in Canaanite settlements, but now they have become a widespread phenomenon. These cisterns were essential for the maintenance of unwalled communities in the hill regions far from a spring or other source of living water. The tribes adapted themselves with amazing swiftness to the technological means prerequisite to settlement in the areas available to them.

Most illuminating of all is the settlement picture in the Negeb. The reference is to the biblical Negeb, in the limited sense of that term, viz., the transition zone between the settled area and the southern wastes, north and southeast of Beer-sheba. This area was not occupied at all in Late Canaanite. Only in Middle Canaanite II did there arise a pair of fortified centers, Tel Masos and Tel Malhata, and after the destruction of the latter in the mid-sixteenth century there was no community in the entire area. This would appear to contradict the biblical tradition that speaks of the Canaanite king of Arad who smote the Israelites at nearby Hormah. It would seem that this story revolves around the two Hyksos fortifications, which can evidently be identified with Arad and Hormah (in the Israelite period there were two forts named Arad!). If there is a historical background, then it precedes by some centuries the Israelite settlement, back when these two forts actually blocked the way to Canaan against desert marauders. In any case, it is certain that during the conquest there was no settlement here to interfere with the Israelite occupation.

In this arid district, conquest settlements were established at every possible site. As usual, only the main tells have been excavated, and all of them were occupied during this period: Beer-sheba for the first time in its history and the other three, Arad, Tel Malhata, and Tel Masos, after a long period of abandonment (Photos 26, 27). The clearest information about one of the conquest settlements is derived from the excavations at Tel Masos. The reason is twofold: this is the largest settlement in the Negeb discovered thus far, and it was not founded on the older Middle Canaanite enclosure but on a flat hill on the opposite side of the wadi; thus, a typical tell was not created. Since the community was finally destroyed at the end of Israelite I, the building remains are immediately beneath the surface, and it was quite easy to uncover them. The Israelite occupation of Tel Masos was in an unfortified village spread over an area of forty to fifty dunams; it had three strata.

The latest stratum, which came to an end, as mentioned above, at the end of Israelite I, made use in large measure of earlier structures, and it is badly damaged by surface cultivation, the clearing of stones, and erosion. The second stratum is the best preserved, and modifications in the house plans testify to its length. The oldest stratum was only exposed in small measure, but even there pillared houses were found having pillars made of flat stones. It was preceded by seminomadic settlement from which only cisterns and granaries have been preserved. Remains of the three strata were found in every one of the widely distributed excavation areas, a fact which means that already in the earliest phase the village had reached its greatest proportions.

In the second stratum—the best preserved—there was discovered house after house, most of them pillared houses of the typical "four-room" plan. At an early phase of the Israelite period, a definite architectural type of house is widely dispersed throughout the land, which remained in extensive use down to the end of the First Temple. The entry was to a central courtyard with rooms on three sides, usually with two rows of columns delineating the two side units from the courtyard. This type of house did not change, in fact, during the entire Israelite period, except for the addition of a second story. At Tel Masos, no staircases were found, such as were commonly used in the "four-room" houses of the monarchical period (Fig. 48).

It is obvious that this house plan was not originated at Tel Masos, as evidenced by its distribution throughout the country. At Tirzah (Tell el-Far'ah [North]), for example, there were houses identical to those found at Tel Masos. It is still not known how this type developed or from whence it was brought. However, this is clearly a well-defined architectural feature which may be considered a characteristic Israelite house, a real trademark of Israelite occupation.

At Tel Masos a few public buildings were also found which also served as a sort of stockade in times of need. Their size and excellent construction testify to the highly developed public organization of the settlement. Especially interesting is a building with a large silo in its courtyard, the walls of which were strengthened by a series of salients at fixed intervals. This technique is quite rare in Eretz-Israel, and the best example is the fort at Ashdod-yam (Tel Mor) of the thirteenth century, the finds of which indicate that it was under Egyptian control. This technique is widespread in the New Kingdom, so perhaps one may view the building at Tel Masos as the first evidence for such

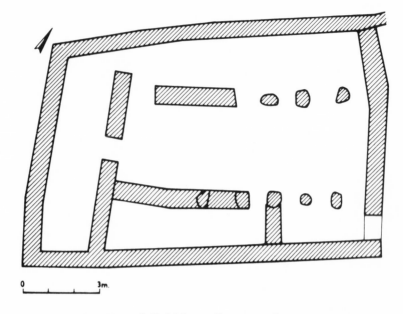

FIG. 48. Tel Masos. Four-room house

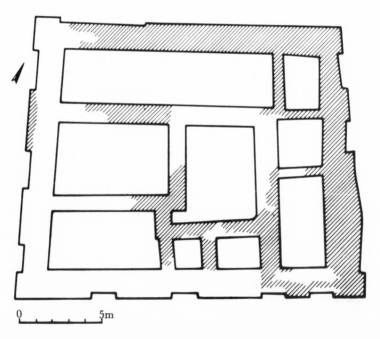

FIG. 49. Tel Masos. Public building

PLATE 24. Pottery of Israelite I

influence in one of the conquest settlements (Fig. 49). No less surprising are the finds discovered in the various houses. Besides the regular local wares there were also lovely vessels with geometric bichrome decoration known up to now mainly from tells in the northern coastal region (Tell Abu Huwam IV; Megiddo VI). Fragments of Philistine ware were also found, also originating from the coast, and others of the decorated "Midianite ware" known from the thirteenth-twelfth centuries around the Gulf of Elath. These finds bear evidence that the trade routes in the Negeb between the Mediterranean shore and the Gulf of Elath were open in this period, and Tel Masos played a part in this commerce. This fact is also demonstrated by various luxury items, in particular a lion's head carved from ivory in the best Canaanite tradition (Plate 24).

The settlement at Tel Masos existed for at least two hundred years. The latest stratum came to an end, as stated above, in about 1000 B.C.E. In the second stratum, quite long-lived, the Philistine pottery

PLATE 24A. Decorated Midianite sherds

was discovered. The earliest stratum belongs to the first half of the twelfth century (Tell Beit Mirsim B$_1$), and apparently it had its beginning toward the end of the thirteenth century. This conclusion is evidenced by fragments of pottery from the end of Late Canaanite, and especially an Egyptian scarab from the Nineteenth Dynasty that evidently bears the name of Seti II.

Investigation of the Israelite settlement at Tel Masos makes it necessary to modify one's views of the Israelite conquest to a large degree. This is not a military conquest, but rather, as in the internal areas of the country and the other peripheral zones, this is a clear picture of penetration into a hitherto unoccupied region. The tribes were not deterred by the special difficulties of settling in the arid Negeb, which was possible only with the help of appreciable technological skill and in the utilization of water sources. More than anything else, the movement testifies to the great hunger for land on the part of the tribes who were compelled to settle down. Concomitantly, this situation indicates that the political and security conditions were different from what one had expected in a period when "there was no king in Israel and every man did what was right in his own eyes." If a large, well-established settlement like this could exist for more than two centuries without the need for real fortifications, the implication is that no serious force threatened its pacific way of life. After the decline of Canaan and the Egyptian authority during the thirteenth century, there was no serious force in the country capable of competing with the Israelite tribes settling down in their areas until the ominous rise of Philistine military power in the mid-eleventh century.

This settlement picture at Tel Masos is clearly reflected in a narrative about one of the settlements of Simeon preserved in the book of Chronicles, although it does not concern Hormah, but rather Gedor (Gerar, according to LXX): "They journeyed to the entrance of Gedor (Gerar, LXX) to the east side of the valley, to seek pasture for their flocks, where they found rich, good pasture, and the land was very broad, quiet, and peaceful; for the former inhabitants there belonged to Ham" (I Chron. 4:39–40). "The sons of Ham" is a general concept covering Egyptians, Canaanites, and Philistines together. It would appear that the reminiscence of the earlier communities in the area was already blurred (Middle Canaanite II!) and would explain the general designation of the former inhabitants as sons of Ham.

The picture at Beer-sheba is similar to that at Tel Masos, but since the earlier remains are hidden under the fortifications of the city from the monarchical period, the information is meager and fragmented. Here there were also found three strata from Israelite I (VIII–VI), preceded by a phase during which cisterns and silos were carved out of the bedrock. Yet even here there were pillared houses (Fig. 50), and in the latest stratum (VI) there was a staircase proving the existence of an upper story. Two discoveries are especially worthy of note, viz., the well and the fortress. A well associated with the earlier strata was found hewn in the bedrock to a depth of more than forty meters. This is a technical achievement since all of the other wells are found in the vicinity of the wadi, where the upper water table is no more than eight to ten meters deep. The excavating of this well on the top of the hill was, therefore, a unique project. Inasmuch as the excavations have demonstrated that the sacred cult place was on the height of this hill, it is probable that the well was somehow associated with it. Thus one may establish with considerable certainty that this is the well, the digging of which is ascribed to the patriarchs in the Bible (Gen. 21:25; 26:25). This identification makes it the first installation discovered in an archaeological excavation that can be associated with the Patriarchal period (Photo 44). Since the well was dug during the period of the conquest and there are no earlier remains in the vicinity, there is no avoiding the conclusion that the patriarchal narratives associated

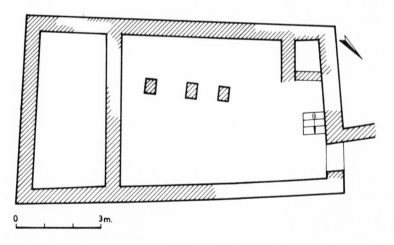

0 _____ 3m.

FIG. 50. Beer-sheba. Pillared house (Stratum VI)

with Beer-sheba are no older than the period of the conquest.

The fort discovered at Beer-sheba belongs to Stratum VII; it was destroyed in the second half of the eleventh century. Its length was about fifty meters, and it was surrounded by a double fortification wall. The fortress at Beer-sheba dominates the well and the buildings spread out over the entire hill. It indicates that Beer-sheba was already a military, administrative, and ritual center. Truly, it is stated that the sons of Samuel judged the people at Beer-sheba (I Sam. 8:2; Fig. 51).

Apparently the fortress at Beer-sheba was not alone but stood at the head of a network of forts built during the eleventh century in the Negeb highlands down to the vicinity of Kadesh-barnea. Today it is clear that the great fortress at the latter site is much later, belonging to the last two centuries of the First Temple period. However, in the entire region there have been found much earlier forts. Outstanding among them is the large fort, approximately 20 by 20 meters (Fig. 52), surrounded by a casemate wall without towers; there were also oval-shaped and rectangular forts. The overwhelming majority of the sherds found in them are not later than the eleventh or the beginning of the tenth century. Especially prominent is a primitive type of local "Negeb ware," pots with straight sides made by hand and very uniformly fired, having flat bases which usually show cloth imprints. It would seem that this Negeb ware was made on the spot by nomadic potters who had only the most primitive of portable implements. It is widespread only in the southern Negeb from the Gulf of Elath and Kadesh-barnea to the vicinity of Yeroham in the north. From the Timna excavations it is clear that the ware has its beginning in the thirteenth-twelfth centuries (Plate 23:11–14), and it is doubtful whether it was used after the tenth. Does this pottery testify to a seminomadic population of different ethnic origin that had settled in the southern Negeb, or could wandering potters from the south have provided some of the needs of the distant Israelite settlements? The second possibility seems more probable in the light of the fortress found at Beer-sheba and the excavations at Tell el-Kheleifeh near the center of the bay of Elath, evidently Ezion-geber, and Ramat Matred in the center of the Negeb highlands. At Tell el-Kheleifeh there was an abundance of Negeb pots mistakenly interpreted at first as smelting pots. This situation occurred in an Israelite fort that controlled the bay and the neighboring Edomite Elath. At Ramat Matred, one of the typical settlements of the Negeb highlands was excavated; the settle-

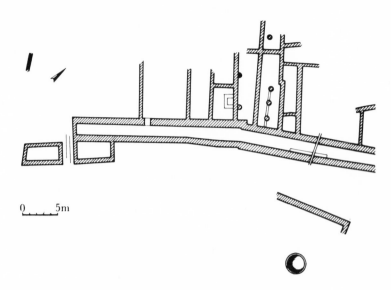

FIG. 51. Beer-sheba. The fort (Stratum VII)

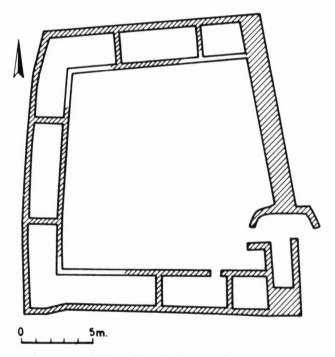

FIG. 52. Mishor Haruah. Fort, 20 by 20 meters

ments had been founded in the vicinity of the fortresses, sometimes at a distance of several kilometers. This settlement was comprised of seven houses adjacent to a flat ravine, the soil of which was cultivated, as indicated by the terraces and the stone fences that connected them. To this area was collected the scanty rainwater from an appreciable area by means of water channels dug along the slopes. This method of desert agriculture, which reached its zenith in the Negeb during the Roman-Byzantine period, had its beginning in settlements from the Israelite period.

The three houses excavated at Ramat Matred were pillared buildings, and along with the Negeb ware there was pottery similar to that from the latest stratum at Tel Masos. The same picture emerges from Atar ha-Ro'eh (Fig. 53), where a typical pillared house was excavated reminiscent in every way of the structures at Tel Masos and also containing the same pottery alongside Negeb ware. At Tel Esdar, on the other hand, a more northerly settlement near Aroer, no Negeb ware was found, but there were pillared buildings and ceramics dating no later than the eleventh century. All of this evidence shows that already in the eleventh century the Israelite occupation had spread out to the

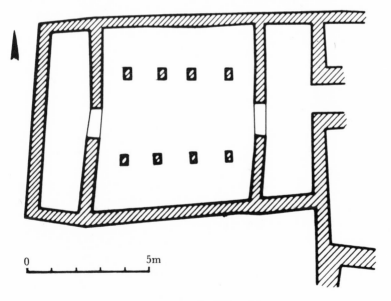

FIG. 53. Atar ha-Ro'eh. Pillared house

more southerly regions of the Negeb. Security for the settlements and the roads was maintained by means of a network of forts. In the more southerly areas people made more use of cheap local pottery supplied by nomadic potters who surely came from the south. This evidence gives an instructive picture of occupation pressure and the spreading out of population surpluses to more remote and difficult areas. The beginning of the Israelite settlement in the northern Negeb was toward the end of the thirteenth century, and by the end of the eleventh century it reached the most southerly corners of the Negeb that could be developed for occupation (Fig. 54). It would seem that the conquest settlements in the northern hill regions were earlier, beginning in the

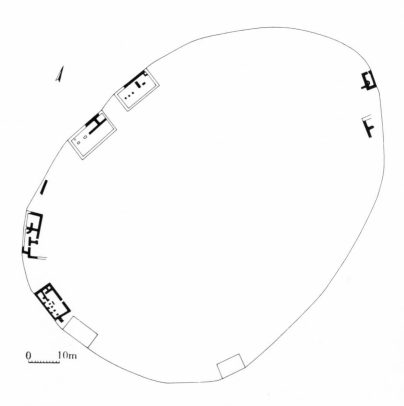

0 ┄┄┄ 10m

FIG. 54. Tel Esdar. Plan of the settlement

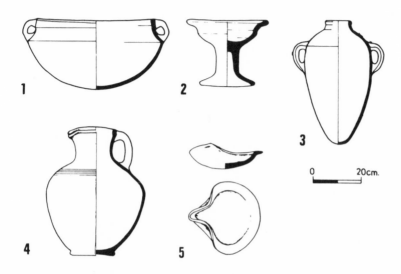

PLATE 25. Pottery of Israelite I

fourteenth century B.C.E. The data are still sparse but it is apparent that the archaeological discoveries support the historical sources, which point in this direction.

In the el-'Amarna period, one hears a great deal about the *'apiru* who have penetrated into the internal areas of the country and are threatening the security of the settlements and their roads. The settlement of the tribe of Issachar on the periphery of the Jezreel Valley may be intimated by a letter from the king of Megiddo, who cultivated the fields of Shunam by means of corvée workers after the destruction of this latter town. A further allusion may be inferred in the stele of Seti I found at Beth-shean. The tribe of Asher is known from Egyptian sources beginning at the end of the fourteenth century, and clan names from that tribe have associations with the southern hill country of Ephraim even though the tribe finally located in western Galilee. In the Bible there are various hints of two main waves of penetration. The later wave, associated with the exodus, came in the mid-thirteenth century, as indicated by the construction of Ramses, the city of Ramses II in the Bible, and the mention of Israel as a consolidated force in the country by the victory song of Merneptah by 1220 B.C.E. It is possible, therefore, to assume that the earlier wave took place during the second half of the fourteenth century, and various tribes probably had come in even earlier.

It is still quite difficult to fix the date for the founding of the various conquest settlements. The widely accepted date, the beginning of the twelfth century, is influenced by the identification of the Israelite period with the Iron Age and has no archaeological basis. It should be noted that at no less than three of the conquest settlements pottery has been found from the Late Canaanite II, viz., Shiloh, Mizpah, and Gibeah of Saul. Of special importance is an incised inscription having three letters ('hr[m]) discovered on a jar handle from Khirbet Raddana. The form of the letters is clear testimony to an intermediate stage between the Proto-Sinaitic script in the middle of the second millennium and the Proto-Canaanite of the fourteenth century. Therefore, it would be hard to associate that inscription with a date later than the fourteenth century.

In the conquest settlements there is a special type of ware worthy of the designation "conquest ware." This is a simple, homogeneous pottery indistinguishable in its basic forms from that of Late Canaanite II, having, nevertheless, some easily discernible characteristics of its own. There is a noticeable decline in the pottery technique: the clay is gritty, the side is thick and the nonuniform firing leaves a black interior. Two vessels are particularly widespread: a cooking pot with an elongated and triangular rim and the "collared rim jar" (Plate 26:3–4). The flat cooking pot with the carinated side and the rounded base resembles in its form the Canaanite pot with one difference: the latter has its rim inclined outward, and the short fold creates a triangular cross-section, while the conquest pot has a vertical rim with a long fold rounding out in the form of an ax. The jar also resembles in form the Canaanite storage jar, but its rim is greatly thickened, and under it there has been added a prominent ridge, the "collar," according to Albright's definition. In this pottery, the fundamental characteristics of the conquest settlements in their consolidated elements are prominent. The settlers borrowed from the basic technology of the neighboring Canaanite community but quickly developed special features surprising in their diffusion and absolute dominance in their settlements. Only with great slowness did changes take place during the ensuing generations. The exclusive appearance of these features in conquest settlements over

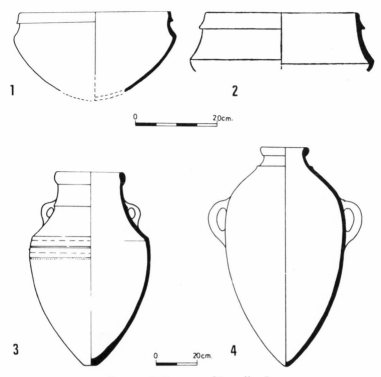

PLATE 26. Pottery of Israelite I

against their rare and sporadic occurrence at Canaanite tells of the same period is thorough justification for recognizing them as a trademark of the ethnic identity of the settlement.

Throughout Israelite I there was virtually no change in the cooking pot in the north and center of the country. On the other hand there is a development in the "collared rim" of the storage jars. This was principally noted at Ai and is discernible in the other sites of the central hill country: the earlier jars have a long neck with a thick and rectangular rim and the ridge around the bottom of the neck; on the later jars, the neck is shortened, the rim is rounded, and the ridge is closer to the rim. In the settlements of Upper Galilee only the earlier type appears, and it is still difficult to ascertain if this change did not occur

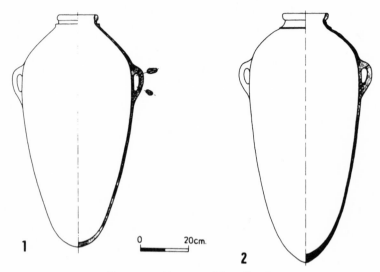

PLATE 27. Pottery of Israelite I

in Galilee, or whether these settlements were already destroyed in an early phase of Israelite I. In the destruction level at Shiloh dating to the mid-eleventh century, there was found a series of jars of the later type (Plate 27). On the other hand, in the fortress of Saul at Gibeah of Saul at the end of the eleventh century, there are no more jars with the collared rim; they are replaced by an entirely new type without the ridge ("collar"). Thus, it would seem that the "collared rim" jars went out of use during the second half of the eleventh century. The same chronological conclusion is imperative from the Megiddo excavations: the early jar appears sporadically in Stratum VIIB (fourteenth-thirteenth centuries), the later is profuse in Stratum VI (end of twelfth, first half of eleventh century), and there is no reminiscence of the "collared rim" jars in Stratum V.

In spite of this uniformity in the ceramic repertoire of the conquest settlement in the northern and central hill country, the situation in the Negeb is appreciably different. There the "collared rim" jars do not occur except for a few sporadic examples which were certainly brought in from the north. In their place, there appear some egg-shaped jars with thick bases and a straight rim, more reminiscent of the Late

Canaanite jars. The cooking pots are similar in the first stage to those with the "hatchet-shaped" rim in the north, although the fold of the rim is generally shorter. However, they undergo a rapid development: at first the "hatchet shape" disappears to be replaced by a straight rim, later followed by a folded and ridged rim, the prototype of the cooking pots in Israelite II. Even more prominent is the appearance of the handles. In the northern parts of the country, cooking pots do not have handles during the entire Israelite I; but in the Negeb the cooking pots are furnished with two handles already in the eleventh century, whence this practice continues to spread northward. In view of the uniformity of architecture, the obvious ceramic differences between the north and south are surprising.

Even in decoration of the vessels, a new characteristic takes over in Israelite I which seems to originate in the Israelite settlements. In Late Canaanite, painted decorations are common, and burnished vessels are proportionately rare. In the twelfth century there are still suggestions of these decorations, which gradually disappear. Then during the course of the eleventh century the burnishing technique begins to expand until it becomes dominant and remains so until the end of the Israelite period. The eleventh century is characterized by irregular hand burnishing in various directions, giving a peculiar impression of variegated flashes. After a short transition period of more continuous and regular burnishing, still done by hand although with closely crowded, contiguous parallel lines, the Israelite potter goes over during the tenth century to standardized spiral wheel burnishing, which remained almost the only kind of decoration to hold the field during the Israelite period.

The conquest settlements in various parts of the country manifest with great clarity the general character of the Israelite penetration and settlement. These mainly took place in unoccupied or sparsely settled areas, a picture that corresponds to the description in The Book of Judges, in contrast to that of a unified conquest in Joshua. At the same time a great uniformity is descernible in the material culture of the conquest settlements in the different regions, testifying to a strong tie between the tribes.

It should not be assumed that certain Canaanite settlements failed to fall into the hands of the tribes when the opportunity presented itself. It is also not impossible that the fort of Jericho was conquered with the arrival of the early wave of tribes in the second half of the fourteenth century, and perhaps Bethel also was reduced by the same group. However, in general, there is no way of establishing whether a particular Canaanite city was taken at the beginning of the invasion or whether it fell to the tribes at some later stage. For the most part the second possibility would seem to be correct. The various tells in the Shephelah were taken, as mentioned above, toward the end of the thirteenth or the beginning of the twelfth century, and even the invasion by the later Israelite wave apparently took place in approximately the mid-thirteenth century. It is evident that in the wake of this wave the Negeb settlements were founded, the beginning of which falls in the second half of the thirteenth century.

This is the case with regard to Hazor, the only place in the north concerning which there is information about its destruction by Israel. The Israelite conquest and settlement in the hill regions began, as previously mentioned, about one hundred or more years prior to this, and there is no reason to assume that Hazor was conquered by new tribes that came from the desert. On the contrary, in the temporary Israelite settlement established on the ruins of the Canaanite city, the ceramics were typical of the usual conquest settlements in Galilee. If these new occupants were party to the conquest, one must assume that they came from the Galilean mountains.

It would seem, therefore, that the diffusion of the tribes in the more densely populated Canaanite areas and the reduction of most of the Canaanite cities belong to the second phase of the period of the judges, and this happened at various stages. Most of the cities of the Shephelah and Hazor had already fallen by about the end of the thirteenth century; Shechem only succumbed in approximately the mid-twelfth century as a result of the quarrel with Abimelech, son of Gideon. In the first chapter of Judges there is a detailed list of Canaanite towns that withstood the pressure of the various tribes. Some towns held out during the entire period of the judges and only fell at the hands of David; these included Jerusalem and Gezer and apparently also Beth-shean and the towns in the Plain of Acco. At Gezer and Beth-shean the excavations have confirmed the biblical tradition, and these Canaanite cities maintained their existence until the end of Israelite I. However, this conclusion is not true with regard to all the towns in the Valley of Jezreel. Taanach and Megiddo were conquered in the third quarter of the twelfth century. Both of them were destroyed about 1125 B.C.E. Taanach remained unoccupied until the founding of a new Israelite city at the end of the eleventh century. The last Canaanite city at Megiddo was, as noted above, Stratum VIIA, and, as already seen, the date of its destruction is fixed with great certainty to about 1125 by Egyptian inscriptions. On top of it was built a new settlement (Stratum VI) entirely different from the Canaanite city. This was an open village without fortifications. All the Canaanite public buildings that had stood for centuries disappeared, including the royal palace, the gate, and the temple tower which had been erected back in Middle Canaanite II. In their stead were built simple private structures, of which the pillared buildings are immediately prominent. The fate of the temple is clear evidence of the radical change and can only be interpreted as the arrival of a new population. It has been shown how temples and high places in the "sacred area" were built and rebuilt in Megiddo during nearly two thousand years from the beginning of Early Bronze down to Stratum VIIA in spite of all the destructions and alterations that took place in the city. This tradition was thoroughly broken with the destruction of Stratum VIIA, and henceforth no shrine is found in that area.

In the light of all this evidence, can it be doubted that Stratum VI is the first Israelite settlement that replaces the Canaanite city whose venerable features have entirely disappeared? Originally, this was also Albright's opinion, since an amazing quantity of typical conquest pottery suddenly appeared in the town just as it is known from the hill regions. Afterward, Albright accepted the opinion of various scholars that the population of Stratum VI remained Canaanite. This conclusion was due to the variety of vessels, which does not match that of the hill settlements but follows rather the Canaanite ceramic tradition. The marvelous bichrome vessels are certainly a Canaanite product from the coastal plain (see Plate 24). All of this evidence is true, but it does not lead to his conclusions concerning the ethnic composition of the settlers. As shown earlier, particularly at the Negeb settlements of the same period, commerce between various parts of the country had already begun to flourish. There is no reason why the occupants of Megiddo would not trade with the Canaanite cities in the neighboring coastal area, especially since similar bichrome vessels were discovered in the Israelite settlements in the Negeb. On the other hand, the many conquest types so profuse in Megiddo VI argue against a continuation of the Canaanite population since it is incomprehensible why they would suddenly introduce these crude and simple vessels in place of the finer ware to which they were accustomed. In the final analysis, the decisive factor is the typical Israelite nature of this village, in contrast to the Canaanite city with its fortifications and public buildings. This theory is supported by the unequivocal testimony of Taanach, which was destroyed along with Megiddo VIIA and abandoned for a long period of time. It is clear that the list in Judges 1 is older than that date, and the central area of the Jezreel Valley had become Israelite by the end of the twelfth century. By that date most of the Canaanite regions had been conquered; the only area that held out in the face of the pressure by the Israelite tribes was the coastal plain, where the Philistines were located in the south and the Canaanites remained in the north.

This was a process of settlement and expansion that had been continuing for more than two hundred years, and in its wake a mighty population revolution was brought about, unparalleled in the history of the country. With the dense settlement of the hill regions and the frontier, the number of settlements increased appreciably and the occupation gaps between the various parts of the country were closed in large measure. For the first time in the life of the country, the occupational center of gravity passed from the valleys to the hill country, which was henceforth the center of Israelite life down to the end of the monarchy. The increase in settlement potential, the closing of the occupation gaps, and the transfer of weight to the hill regions, which changed completely the population map of Eretz-Israel, explain the ever-increasing power of the young tribes and provide a background for the first national unification of the country in its long history, with the establishment of the Israelite monarchy. The peculiar nature of the tribal settlement process led to the result that the Israelite conquest was more than simply a new ethnic wave that settled in place of the local population. Eretz-Israel and Canaan are different from each other in an essential way, not only from the ethnic but also from the geographic and communal standpoint; this fact helps in understanding the deep and decisive break in the history of the land from that time on.

The chief rival that arose against the Israelite settlement during the period of the judges was the Philistine nation, another people that had arrived only recently, bringing with it some outstanding innovations in material culture. The Philistines are one of the "sea peoples," about the coming of whom there is detailed information in Egyptian sources.

Some of them, such as the Sherdanu, already appear in the el-'Amarna Age as mercenaries in the armies of the big powers. But one reads about the Philistines for the first time only in the inscriptions of Ramses III. Their massive invasion, which rocked the foundations of Egypt and the neighboring countries, is described in his inscriptions and his reliefs from his temple at Medinet Habu, dated to his eighth year (about 1190 B.C.E.). The sea peoples are described in their campaign as coming from "their islands," that is, the isles of the Aegean Sea, Cyprus, and the coasts of Asia Minor with the Philistines and the Sikkels *(tj-k-r)* at their head. According to the reliefs they came from the sea in warships, on one hand, and by land with their wives and children in ox-drawn wagons, on the other. The accompanying text says that they obliterated in their wake the cities and kingdoms in Cilicia and northern Syria and reached Amurru, the kingdom in northern Lebanon which had served in that period as the southern border of the Hittite empire on the boundary of the Egyptian province of Canaan. Ramses III claims to have delivered a decisive blow against them. This is not just empty bragging, as proven by the continuation of his rule in the land of Canaan, particularly indicated by his inscriptions and those of Ramses VI at Beth-shean and Megiddo.

This situation raises two questions: If Ramses smote them on the border of Canaan in the area of Lebanon, how did the Philistines reach the territory where they finally settled on the southern coastal plain of Eretz-Israel, and when did they take over that region? Was it already in the reign of Ramses II or only after some time had elapsed? One must not forget that the southern coastal plain was a center of Egyptian rule in Canaan, and that Gaza, which became one of the Philistine capitals, was the administrative center of the province.

The generally accepted opinion is that Philistines reached this area a short time after the battle and were settled there at first as mercenaries in Egyptian service. This assumption is based upon another inscription from the reign of Ramses III (Papyrus Harris I) which summarizes his activities. After the narrative of the victory Ramses adds that he brought many prisoners to Egypt, settled them in fortresses under an oath of allegiance to him and allotted them food rations. The theory is that some of them were also settled in Egyptian fortresses in Canaan, and that with the disintegration of the Egyptian authority they became the masters of the country.

Archaeological researches have not confirmed this assumption, and

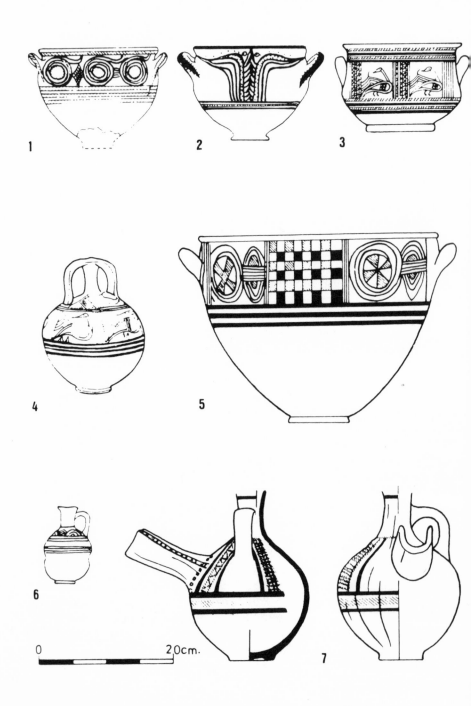

PLATE 28. Philistine pottery from Israelite I

this is another example of how difficult it is for scholars to abandon an accepted theory even when new discoveries contradict it unequivocally.

First of all, it is obvious today that in the Egyptian capitals, there is no continuity between the Canaanite and the Philistine cities as one would expect to find when a garrison force located at a certain place became the masters with the disappearance of Egyptian authority. In a section that was made at Ashkelon by Phythian-Adams, there was discovered a thick burnt layer between the last Canaanite settlement and the stratum containing Philistine ware. This condition is even more certain at Ashdod, where extensive excavations were conducted by Dothan and others. Here also, the last city of the Late Canaanite period concludes with a burnt level; then follows an intermediate phase from the beginning of Israelite I, where Mycenaean and Cypriot imports have ceased but where there is still no Philistine ware (Plate 28).

However, the decisive chronological testimony derives from Philistine pottery. This is a very homogeneous ware, most of the forms and decorations of which are borrowed from the Mycenaean world. The vessels include three Mycenaean forms and a bowl with horizontal handles, a stirrup jar with a closed mouth and an open spout (cf. Plate 28:4), and a pyxis with small horizontal handles, which is somewhat rare. They are characterized by a white slip upon which there is decoration, generally bichrome red and black, with geometric forms such as the spiral, semicircles, crosses, lozenges, and checkerboards. A bird motif with the head usually turned backward, pecking among its feathers, is commonplace. These themes are borrowed from Mycenaean ware, and except for the definitely Mycenaean vessels such ornamentation is also found on vessels of local form, especially jugs with a strainer, which have been interpreted as vessels for drinking beer.

This ware is so homogeneous in quality and material, in forms and decorative patterns, that one must assume it was manufactured in a limited number of workshops in one area. There is no doubt that these workshops were Philistine because of the sudden appearance of this pottery right at the time of their settling down, their obviously Mycenaean origin and their geographical distribution in Philistia. It is quite ubiquitous in all of the sites from Israelite I in that area, and it becomes more and more rare as one moves away from that territory. At Tel 'Eton (Tell 'Aitun), east of Lachish, it was demonstrated by petrographic tests that in contrast to the other types of pottery made there, the Philistine ware was brought in from the coast.

With regard to the stage in the development of Mycenaean pottery from which Philistine ware was derived, there is complete agreement among scholars. This is not the classic Mycenaean which existed down to the end of the Mycenaean kingdom (Mycenaean IIIB). It belongs rather to the second phase (second rather than first) of sub-Mycenaean pottery, a degenerate ware that had lost its classical uniformity and standard quality (Mycenaean IIIC 1b). The best comparison is found on Cyprus, which the Philistines may have passed through on their way.

It would appear that the fact that Philistine ware does not belong to the first stage of the sub-Mycenaean repertoire should require a clear chronological assumption. However, this would contradict the accepted theory concerning their immediate occupation in Philistia after the battles in the reign of Ramses III, and the theory seems more probable than the facts.

Desborough sums up in the third edition of *The Cambridge Ancient History* as follows: "Either, then, Ugarit and Alalakh had been destroyed at some earlier date, or the pottery called 'Philistine' became a characteristic of the Philistines at some time after they first settled in south Palestine." The simple conclusion that a certain period of time separates the battles with Ramses III and their settlement in Philistia is never, for some reason, given consideration.

Therefore, one must cut the Gordian knot and admit that today this is the only possible conclusion. Now there is no doubt that Ugarit and Alalakh were destroyed with the first invasion of sea people in the twelfth century, and that is approximately the date of the end of the Mycenaean kingdom and the end of classical Mycenaean ware (Mycenaean IIIB). The excavation results from Ashkelon and Ashdod, and the intermediate period at Ashdod between the stratum with Mycenaean ware and that with Philistine pottery, indicate that a somewhat later date must be fixed for the appearance of the Philistines.

The same sequence was established by Albright at Tell Beit Mirsim: after the last Canaanite stratum with Mycenaean pottery (C_2) there is a period of temporary occupation which has no major impact (B_1), and only after that is there a phase having Philistine ware (B_2). It is obvious, therefore, that the Philistine pottery does not arrive in the country before the middle of the twelfth century, and if one does not accept the forced assumption that the Philistines came first, only to be followed later by a family of potters who brought with them their particular vessels, then the middle of the twelfth century must be the date of the Philistines' arrival in the land. Hence, it is clear that they were not settled by the Egyptians but actually replaced them with the collapse of Egyptian authority. And this event must have taken place about thirty to forty years after they were beaten by Ramses III.

There is no information about the form of the Philistines' invasion, but since they first seized the harbor cities on the southern coast of Eretz-Israel, one may conjecture that they came in ships. That they had a fleet and that their crews dominated the coast is recorded for us in the narrative of Wen-amon. This is an Egyptian document from the beginning of the eleventh century describing the journey of a priest from the temple of Amon in Karnak to Byblos in order to purchase lumber for the god's sacred bark. One is surprised to find in that scroll that another of the sea peoples had taken over one of the coastal cities of Eretz-Israel, viz., the Sikkels (tj-k-r) who settled at Dor on the Carmel coast. They had at their disposal a fleet of ships whose business took them to the cities of Phoenicia, Tyre, Sidon, and Byblos, and eleven of them pursued Wen-amon as far as Byblos. In another Egyptian document, the Onomasticon of Amenemope, from about the same time, there is a list of names: Ashkelon, Ashdod, Gaza, and then Asher . . . , Sherdan, Sikkel, and Phileshet. The three main Philistine coastal cities are mentioned here, the Israelite tribe of Asher which had settled in the Plain of Acco, and three of the sea peoples. From this it would seem that the Sherdanu had also taken over a certain section of the Palestinian coast.

Of course, one cannot say with certainty where that segment would have been located, but since the Philistines took the southern coast and the Sikkels were in the northern Sharon, it is most probable that the Sherdanu had entered into the southern Plain of Acco. Indeed, at Tell Abu Huwam, an ancient harbor city at the mouth of the Kishon north of the Carmel excavated by Hamilton, there was discovered a stratum which confirms this assumption. The settlement at Tell Abu Huwam (its ancient name is unknown; suggestions are Salmona, known from much later sources, or Libnah, mentioned on the border of Asher in Josh. 19:26), was founded in Late Canaanite. With the increase in coastal shipping, it is a testimony to Egyptian domination (Stratum V). This stratum, very rich in Mycenaean and Cypriot imports, was destroyed at the end of Late Canaanite in about 1200 B.C.E. On its ruins was established a new settlement (Stratum IVA) with a unique type of architecture unparalleled in Eretz-Israel, rectangular houses divided symmetrically into three or four rooms. It is clear that these are new occupants, strangers to the country, who have lived there only a short time. In the following settlement (Strata IVB–III), which was established there after the destruction of those houses, there is an entirely different architecture, viz., the typical Israelite pillared houses. Its pottery is that typical of the coastal region in the eleventh century. It is interesting that in the limited excavations conducted at Dor and the extensive excavations at Tell Abu Huwam, there was no Philistine pottery. From this evidence it is also probable that these were not Philistines. The entire absence of Philistine sherds at Tell Abu Huwam evidently shows that there is a certain gap in the peak period of Philistine ware in the last quarter of the twelfth century. As for that intermediate, foreign stratum, which existed at Tell Abu Huwam between the Canaanite and the later (Israelite?) town during the twelfth century and which was destroyed before the end of that century, could it be the harbor town of the Sherdanu mentioned in the Egyptian Onomasticon? The dominant force among the sea peoples that gained a foothold in Eretz-Israel was the Philistines, who eventually were privileged to give their name to the entire country: *Palaestina,* Palestine. They settled on the southern coastal plain, one of the most fertile and well-developed regions, where the center of Egyptian authority in Canaan had also been located. The three main coastal cities were Gaza, Ashkelon, and Ashdod, which served as important seaports earlier in the Late Canaanite period. When the alliance of Philistine lords confronted the Israelite tribes in the mid-eleventh century, it was led not only by the three coastal cities but also by two more cities farther east in the Shephelah—Gath and Ekron. One does not know if the founding of these five capitals took place all at the same time, or whether the Shephelah cities may have been slightly later. Inasmuch as all of the Philistine capitals were large, well-populated metropolises that covered hundreds of dunams, there is no longer any doubt today about the identity of the two easternmost towns. In the Shephelah, there are two sites with a prominent settlement in Israelite I containing an abundance of Philistine ware and encompassing a surface area unrivaled by any of the other sites, Tel Zafit (Tell es-Safi) and Tel Miqne (Khirbet Muqanna'). Their identification with Gath and Ekron, respectively, seems certain now, and this leads to an important conclusion concerning the circumstances of their founding. Tel Zafit (Gath) was an important Canaanite city and, as in the three coastal towns, the Philistines settled there on an ancient tell. On the other hand, Middle and Late Canaanite sherds have never been found at Tel Miqne (Ekron), and the lesser elevation of the mound shows that it was a settlement founded only at the beginning of the Israelite period on a previously unoccupied site. The Philistines founded, therefore, some new settlements, among them one of their five capitals, in contradiction to the commonly held assumption that they only overpowered existing populations. Another settlement founded by the Philistines was Tel Qasila, a small harbor town near the mouth of the Yarkon north of Joppa, excavated by B. Mazar. In its two earliest strata (XII–XI) was found an abundance of Philistine ware, and the identity of its occupants is confirmed by the first Philistine temple of its type to be discovered on the spot by A. Mazar (Fig. 55). From a building comprised of a single broad room with a central platform, the temple was expanded during the course of time to a rectangular room with an additional vestibule and the notable introduction of two pillars in the center of the holy place which are reminiscent of the story about Samson's demise. In the shrine, there was a large repertoire of cult vessels having distinctly Aegean and Philistine decorations, e.g., a bird-shaped bowl (the standard design for Philistine ware; Photo 45) and an incense stand, the windows of which are comprised of pillars alternating with human figures spreading the hands, and also other vessels with figures of lions and mythical reliefs (Photo 45).

Additional details about the character of Philistine ritual may be deduced from the excavations at Ashdod. In the houses and also in two

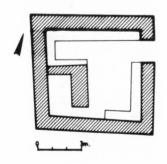

FIG. 55. Tel Qasila. Philistine temple

small shrines, one on the acropolis and the other (the later in date) in the lower city, was a plethora of clay figurines in human form, both male and female, which surely represent a pair of deities. Especially prominent is a combination of a woman and a four-legged chair. The back of the couch terminates with the upper part of a naked female body with a triangular head and a flat cap, eyes and nose, a long neck, breasts, and sometimes arms resting on the armrests. Some of the figurines have a decoration of stripes and triangles in red and black on a white background in the style of Philistine ornamentation. The "Ash-dodas" are reminiscent of mythological figurines from Mycenaean culture. Also well represented are kernoi, libation vessels made in the form of a hollow ring with miniature vessels and figurine heads of animals and birds affixed to it. They also have their origin in the Aegean world, and although they appear in Eretz-Israel as early as Late Canaanite with the Mycenaean imports, their ubiquitousness at Ashdod testifies that they were brought by the Philistines from their country of origin.

If one may judge according to the influence of Mycenaean material culture on the Philistine cult vessels, it is practically certain that their pantheon originated in the Aegean world. However, it would seem that these deities were very soon assimilated to the great Semitic divinities of Canaan, whose names and characteristics were applied to them. All of the names that we know from the Bible are of familiar Canaanite deities, e.g., Dagon, the god of grain and agricultural fertility or Baal-zebub, a transparent corruption of Baal-zebul. This feature is characteristic of the Philistines in general: In spite of their strong military force and their efficient organization in the pentapolis alliance, they were rapidly assimilated into the material and cultural milieu of Canaan, leaving only a residual of their Aegean origins. The same is noticeable in Philistine pottery. That ware disappeared after not too long a time, except for a few Aegean types, principally bowls which preserved their horizontal handles and their ornamentation for a while, but which do not have a continuation. Philistine ware appears, as already mentioned, at Megiddo in Stratum VIB (third quarter of the twelfth century), and only isolated vessels in the beginning of Stratum VIA (first half of the eleventh century). Not even one Philistine vessel was found in Tell Abu Huwam III, which dates mainly to the eleventh century. At Tel Qasila, the Philistine settlement, Philistine ware is only found in Strata XII–XI. In Stratum X, parallel to Megiddo VI, one only finds some degenerate bowls and beer jugs. From all this evidence it is obvious that the Philistine ware actually ceased to exist before the middle of the eleventh century. It was produced for only a few generations from the middle of the twelfth to the beginning of the eleventh century, and its brief existence makes it an excellent chronological indicator.

The Philistines brought with them burial customs from the Aegean world, as manifested mainly in the cemetery at Tel Sharuhen. Five burials are of distinctly Mycenaean type, with a descent by stairs in a narrow corridor (dromos) to a rectangular room with a depression in the center, on the two sides of which the dead and their implements were laid. The pottery found in them is local, but it is influenced in form and decoration by Philistine ware and also by Egyptian styles. In two of the burials, there were anthropoid coffins (with humanoid covers), a practice known mainly from Egypt. It is obvious today—in the light of a rich discovery of anthropoid coffins at Deir el-Balah, south of Gaza, with distinctly Egyptian objects—that even in Eretz-Israel, burial in such coffins was basically an Egyptian practice. But it is now clear that the practice was widely adopted by the sea-people mercenaries who served in the Egyptian fortresses. This conclusion is made especially probable by the anthropoid burials at Beth-shean, the grotesque faces of which are far removed from their Egyptian prototypes, and whose headband ornamentations are reminiscent of the feathered helmets of the Philistines, the Sikkels, and the Danuna on the reliefs from Medinet Habu. In one of the Beth-shean tombs there was found a mouthpiece made of gold, an oval plate attached to the mouth of the deceased, like the well-known examples from Mycenae. The fact that the anthropoid coffins discovered at Beth-shean, Tel Sharuhen, and perhaps also at Lachish (where one coffin was found with a hieratic inscription) evidently belonged to mercenaries from among the sea peoples stationed at Egyptian forts does not contradict the assumption that this was not the way the Philistines came to occupy their territories. Beth-shean in particular and also the other two sites were distinctly Egyptian strong points, and it also seems apparent that the burials at Beth-shean and Lachish precede in time the Philistine occupation. The size of the Philistine towns, the density of population in their areas, and the appreciable diffusions of Philistine ware leave no room for doubt about the great intensity of Philistine influx, even though some of the former Canaanite population may nevertheless have remained, under the yoke of the new rulers. It is also clear that the Philistines brought with them a well-developed tradition of urban society, an efficient confederated organization, and a highly military technology on sea and land. It is no wonder, therefore, that their territory soon became too confining, a fact which led to their expansion into the Shephelah, where they encountered the Hebrew tribes. This encounter is expressed both in conflicts and clashes and also in commercial and familial relationships that are clearly manifest in the narratives about Samson from the beginning of the eleventh century. However, it is erroneous to assume that, at this early stage, the Philistines had already gained domination over appreciable parts of the country, establishing a sort of *pax philistina* (as defined by some scholars) lasting several generations. There is no basis for such an assumption, and conclusions about such a period may be derived from later sources dating from the mid-eleventh century on. In the Bible there is no information about war with the Philistines prior to the battle of Ebenezer; and the scarcity of Philistine ware, both in the Israelite hill country and in the tells on the plain, testifies that the Philistines only reached these areas in a time when that pottery had already gone out of use.

The fateful conflict between Israel and the Philistines began only in the mid-eleventh century and continued for about fifty years to the beginning of David's reign. These two vigorous peoples were now like coiled springs planted in their respective areas and seeking additional territories for their surplus population. Initially the Philistines had the upper hand, thanks to their superior military and administrative organization. But as soon as the Israelite monarchy was established—in particular, when it was headed by a military and political leader of David's stature—the balance was quickly tipped in favor of Israel. There was no comparison between the population potential of Israel and that of the Philistines in their limited territories. So from this standpoint alone, there was no doubt who would be victorious in the struggle for the inheritance of the land of Canaan. Henceforth, the Philistines had to content themselves with their restricted albeit important area, from which they never again tried to break out.

It is possible that during the period of Philistine ascendancy in the second half of the eleventh century, the Israelites borrowed from them certain achievements in material technology and in military and administrative organization. However, this possibility should not be exaggerated, and thus far one cannot point to any substantial evidence. The revolutionary change in Israelite material culture began only during the tenth century, and the predominant sources of influence seem to be Syria and Phoenicia. Until the end of the eleventh century the Israelite population continued with its simple, homogeneous culture with very few innovations. Reference has already been made to the discovery at Gibeah of Saul (Tell el-Ful) of a substantial fort surrounded by a casemate wall. The assumption that this fort was built originally by Philistines for their commissioners located at Gibeath-elohim (I Sam. 10:5; 13:3) has no basis, especially since no pottery or any other small finds indicated an influence there from the coastal region. Today it is clear that Saul built his fort according to a standard Israelite plan, as demonstrated by the Negeb forts (Fig. 56).

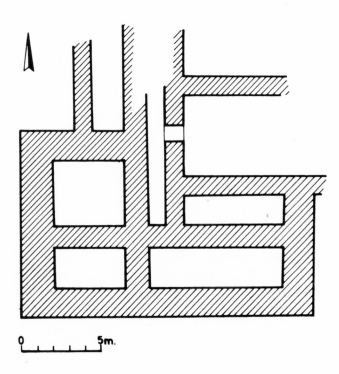

FIG. 56. Tell el-Ful. Israelite fort

THE UNITED MONARCHY—ISRAELITE IIA

David rose to power in about 1000 B.C.E., and during the first ten or fifteen years of his reign he established his mighty kingdom. He not only united the tribes and annexed the Canaanite enclaves remaining in the land but he also conquered the neighboring kingdoms in Transjordan, especially the Aramaean principalities in the Damascene and the Lebanese Beqa', so that he extended the direct sphere of his authority from central Syria to the border of Egypt. Furthermore, some of the Neo-Hittite kingdoms in northern Syria recognized his superiority, as may be deduced from the gifts sent to him by Toi, king of Hamath, through his son Joram (Hadoram; II Sam. 8:10; I Chron. 18:10). What is said about the beginning of Solomon's reign actually corresponds to the second half of David's: "For he had dominion over all the region beyond the river [west of the Euphrates] from Tiphsah to Gaza, over all the kings beyond the river, and he had peace on all sides round about him" (I Kings 4:24 [Heb., 5:4]). This was still a time of weakness for Egypt on one side and Assyria on the other, so there was no serious contender who could interfere with David's progress in Eretz-Israel and in Syria from Tiphsah (Thapsakos at the bend in the Euphrates south of Carchemish) down to the southernmost Philistine principality.

One of David's first and most decisive steps was the conquest of Jebusite Jerusalem and its conversion into the royal capital (Photo 55). It was a choice of genius. This foreign city, which stood between Israel and Judah, was elevated above the two main segments of the nation, and the city of Zion became the city of David. The new capital was located in the heart of the tribal areas, and the small, ancient city whose influence had not exceeded the limits of the southern hill country and its adjacent slopes henceforth became a metropolis, the first and only capital of the entire Eretz-Israel. The drastic changes that took place in Israel at that time are certainly represented first and foremost in Jerusalem, but regrettably the archaeological information about biblical Jerusalem is still quite scanty in spite of the extensive excavations conducted over more than a century. For this situation there are three reasons: (1) In the entire hill region, preservation of the ancient structures is poor because of the widespread use of stone, which was convenient for reuse in later periods. In most of the later walls, there are many more ancient stones appropriated, dug up, or dismantled from earlier structures. (2) In Jerusalem there existed an almost complete occupational continuity down to modern times, which accounts for the destruction of the earlier buildings and the scanty remains hidden under deep piles of debris and dump. (3) Considerable parts of the city are not open to the excavator's spade because of their sanctity, both cemeteries and modern religious structures (Fig. 57).

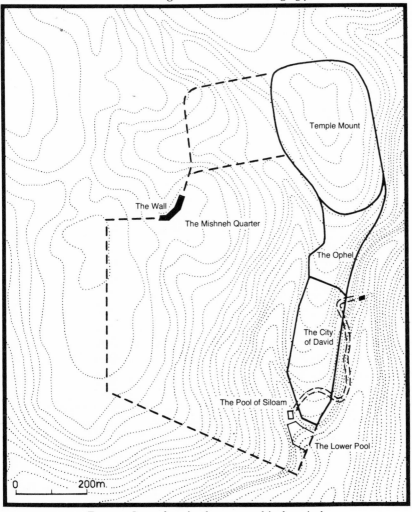

FIG. 57. Jerusalem in the monarchical period

Therefore, practically nothing is known about the Canaanite city and about Jerusalem from the age of the monarchy except for the fact of their existence. The ancient city was located on a relatively low ridge, projecting southeastward from the Old City of our day, sloping steeply to the south. This ridge was convenient for fortification because of its steep slopes above the Kidron Valley on the east and the Tyropoeon on the west. The name of this latter valley is known only from Josephus (Greek, "Valley of the Cheesemakers"), and most of it has been filled in today by later debris. The strategic weak point of the city was to the north, and there one finds the strongest fortifications in all periods. On the highest and northernmost point on the ridge, there was a sort of acropolis, the Ophel, the fortifications of which were strengthened by various kings (II Chron. 27:3; 33:14). Some of its fortifications were evidently included in the Millo, constructed as early as the reign of David and Solomon (II Sam. 5:9; I Kings 9:15). An additional reason, no less important, for locating the ancient city on this spot was the spring of Gihon, the only rich water source in the area, which breaks forth at the foot of the eastern slope above the Kidron Valley. Its course in the descent of the valley was outside the city walls; therefore, great efforts were expended in various periods to ensure the inclusion of its waters within the town.

The area of the ancient city was no more than thirty or forty dunams. Kenyon proved that in the area of the Gihon spring there was a city wall about midway down the slope intended to include the ancient shaft that brought the spring into the city. However, it is doubtful if the course of the wall was so far down elsewhere. Therefore, it is probable that the city area did not greatly exceed about thirty dunams. This was about the size of a village of medium rank, and it cannot compete with important centers such as Lachish, Gezer, or Megiddo. That small area was insufficient for a royal capital, so the city was expanded rapidly northward to the area of the temple mount, where Solomon erected his elaborate royal buildings. With the course of time the city grew westward to a large and loftier hill, the natural defense of which on the west was the Valley of Ben Hinnom. The upper city spread out during the ensuing generations toward the west. Only these general lines of development are known, and from Jerusalem in the monarchical period one is not familiar with even one building. For the detailed biblical descriptions of the palaces and the temple in Jerusalem, one must seek parallels elsewhere.

The expansive united monarchy, the wealth that flowed into the royal court from all directions, and the flourishing commerce dominated by the crown brought about a rapid and noticeable revolution in every aspect of material culture. Today it is clear that the revolution was extreme and much more rapid than had been thought; therefore, the decisive break in the Israelite period is at the beginning of the Israelite monarchy. It is justified, therefore, to begin Israelite II in about 1000 B.C.E. rather than at the time of the division of the monarchy, as was formerly done.

One of the most far-reaching innovations was the construction of public buildings, which began in Israel on a large scale in the reign of David. This is not extensively documented in the Bible because of the selective nature of the sources, which emphasize the prominent features in the personalities of the various kings. It is difficult to assume that David did not busy himself with public construction during the twenty or thirty years of his rule after his great kingdom was firmly established. In fact, one does hear at least about his fortifications in Jerusalem, and likewise about his palace, which he built with the help of materials and craftsmen from Phoenicia, the "house of cedar" (II Sam. 5:9, 11; 7:2). At first glance it is quite difficult to distinguish from an archaeological standpoint between the middle of David's and the beginning of Solomon's reign, time periods separated by more than twenty or thirty years, since one does not have datable inscriptions. Fortunately, however, a most unusual correspondence, with a fair degree of certainty, has been discovered between one of the sources from the reign of Solomon and archaeological structures of his reign. Consequently certain others that are earlier may be assigned to the reign of David. The resultant picture corresponds nicely with the historical events and sheds light on other sources in the reigns of David and Solomon.

The Solomonic gates discovered at Gezer, Megiddo, and Hazor have been mentioned. In the biblical account of the building projects of Solomon, the construction of these three cities is referred to directly after a survey of the great building projects in Jerusalem (I Kings 9:15). In the excavations conducted at the three places, gates identical in plan were discovered in strata from the tenth century B.C.E. In fact, the gate of Gezer was the first one uncovered early in this century by Macalister. Since part of it was in use down to Hasmonaean times, Macalister erroneously assigned its original construction to that period, and it was

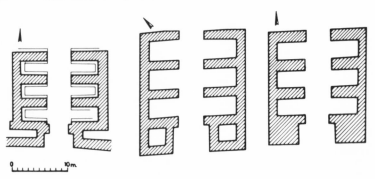

FIG. 58. Solomonic gates: Gezer, Hazor, and Megiddo

only later that Yadin pointed out its resemblance to the other Solomonic gates, which was made more probable by the excavations of Dever. The Megiddo gate was uncovered in the 1930's and the gate at Hazor during the 1950's; not only their plans but even their measurements were practically identical. Of course the building technique was different: those at Megiddo and Gezer were constructed from their foundations up by finely shaped ashlar blocks, in contrast to the gate at Hazor built of unhewn fieldstones. However, it is clear that the three gates were built according to the same plan (Fig. 58). Furthermore, the plan is different from the one common in the gates of Eretz-Israel and Syria in Israelite II. The gate of the Israelite period is a direct development from gates in vogue in Eretz-Israel and in Syria since Middle Canaanite II; the gate is a direct passage between two towers protected by three prominent piers on each side, with two doors attached to the inner and outer sets of piers. This plan was not altered essentially, but the space between the piers was deepened and converted to real rooms on both sides of the passageway, which certainly served as guardrooms when necessary but also as courtrooms and commercial offices in times of peace (Fig. 59).

The Solomonic gates maintain this basic plan but have an additional guardroom and set of piers. Gates like these, with three guardrooms and four sets of piers on each side of the passageway, have been discovered thus far only in two other places: the one at Philistine Ashdod and the other at Lachish. The Lachish gate was evidently built by Rehoboam, son of Solomon (II Chron. 11:9), and it is probable that he still continued building according to the specifications used by his

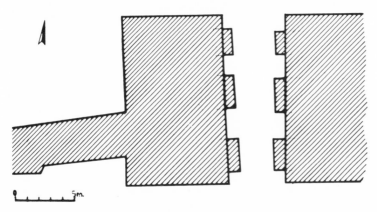

FIG. 59. Gezer. Gate from Middle Canaanite II

predecessor. The gate at Ashdod is also related to the tenth century B.C.E., and one is still unable to establish if the Philistines were imitating the Solomonic gates or vice versa, or whether both of these peoples had borrowed this special plan from somewhere else. As Albright discerned, the gates leading to the courtyard of the Solomonic Temple as described by Ezekiel were also built according to the same plan: "And there were three side rooms on either side . . . ; the three were of the same size" (Ezek. 40:10).

Therefore, there is virtually complete agreement among scholars that the gates of Hazor, Megiddo, and Gezer with their triple chambers belong to the reign of Solomon. Hence it is obvious that the strata of the respective cities associated with them must also be Solomonic in date, so that everything preceding them cannot be later than David. The picture is most unequivocal at Hazor. The city in Solomon's days (Stratum X) is preceded by an occupational gap of at least 150 years: Stratum XII is a short-lived and temporary settlement from the conquest period, which terminated before the end of the twelfth century. Stratum XI is only a small high place on the crown of the tell, and the few implements discovered in it suggest a date close to the Late Canaanite. There is no possibility of considering a settlement that preceded the Solomonic gate, and the site was abandoned for a long time.

Not a great deal has been excavated from the Solomonic city at

Hazor, and, in fact, all that is known about its public buildings pertains to the wall connected with that gate. This is a casemate wall scrupulously constructed with great uniformity. Throughout the monarchical period, there are two types of walls discovered in various places: the casemate and the solid wall. A casemate wall is built from two parallel lines, the outer one thicker than the inner, with rooms and partitions between them. Except for the early forts in the Negeb and some later walls in outlying towns, casemate walls have standard measurements: the outer line is about 1.60 m. and the inner about 1.05 m., i.e., three and two cubits respectively. The space between the two lines varies from 1.40 m. to more than 3 m. The minimal thickness of a casemate wall reaches, therefore, about four meters, and there are some with a general thickness of about six meters. The casemate wall at Hazor was constructed in a straight line, but there are others built in a zigzag plan, having corners and salients to a depth of thirty to fifty centimeters in order to break the straight line and give the wall more stability.

The solid wall, on the other hand, is one massive wall with a thickness of three to four meters without hollow spaces inside, although occasionally it is actually built of two outer lines with a nonuniform fill in between. It is usually furnished with salients and recesses at fixed intervals, thrust forward for nearly a meter from the main line, but on occasion there are only angles made by zigzag lines like some of the casemate walls (Fig. 60). Today it is obvious that the two types of walls served contemporaneously during the entire monarchical period. Casemate walls are known from the tenth century from Hazor, Beth-shemesh, Tell Beit Mirsim, Arad, and perhaps also from Mizpah and Gezer, from the ninth and eighth centuries at Samaria and Beer-sheba, and from the seventh century at Ramat Rahel, Arad, and Kadesh-barnea. Solid walls are known from the tenth century at Megiddo, Lachish, and Beer-sheba and from the ninth and eighth centuries at Hazor, Mizpah, and Arad, while in some of these places the walls continued to exist to the end of the First Temple period.

Solid walls, some having salients and recesses, are known in Eretz-Israel from earlier periods. On the other hand, the casemate wall is not found in the land before the Israelite period, with the exception actually made of two parallel lines with heavy fill between them. It seems certain today that the source of the casemate wall is the Hittite kingdom, where it was widely used during the fourteenth and thirteenth centuries B.C.E. From there, it was transmitted to the Neo-Hittite king-

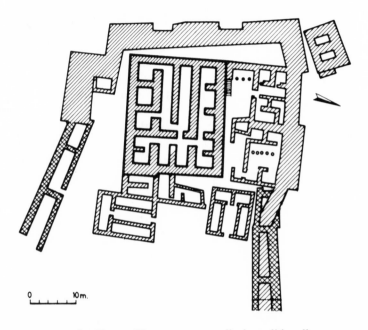

FIG. 60. Hazor. The casemate wall, the solid wall,
and the Israelite fortress

doms of northern Syria and hence it reached Eretz-Israel in the period
under discussion. Inasmuch as one also finds solid walls, it is probable
that the two types were imported at the same time from northern Syria.
At Carchemish, for example, the city wall is comprised partly of a solid
wall and partly of casemates, and at Zinjirli (Sam'al), a line of casemate
rooms was built on the solid wall, which also had salient buttresses at
fixed intervals.

It is clear that each of these types of walls has its own advantages and
disadvantages; therefore, it is no wonder that neither enjoyed absolute
preference over the other. The solid wall is stronger and more stable,
and thus more able to withstand the battering ram and sapping under
its foundation. However, the casemate wall was less expensive in its
construction and it afforded maximum strength with minimum invest-
ment, a consideration that was always an important factor in small
kingdoms with limited territories and poor financial resources, such as
Israel and Judah. At the same time the casemate wall also added many

rooms for storage and for dwelling to the limited area of the city, both
an economic and a functional advantage. The thickness of the casemate wall was also generally more than that of the solid wall, and thus
permitted the stationing of more defenders and more weaponry on
top. This fact explains why in the final analysis the casemate walls were
more popular, especially in little Judah, and more numerous than solid
walls mainly in the later stages of Israelite II.

The various types of walls have been described in considerable
detail since this has a direct bearing on the distinction between the
building projects of David and those of Solomon. At Hazor, as previously mentioned, there was discovered a casemate wall, the Solomonic
date of which is beyond doubt. At Gezer, the picture is insufficiently
clear. According to the biblical description, the city was destroyed
before it was constructed by Solomon (I Kings 9:16), but it would
appear that the older wall was restored. In the vicinity of the gate, one
finds a segment of a casemate wall, albeit without the standard measurements. In the continuation there was found only a single wall with
a thickness of about two meters, and there is no basis for the excavators' assumption that this is the inner line of a casemate wall. There
is no trace of the conjectured outer line, and no original casemate wall
is known, the inner line of which reached such a thickness.

The basic argument revolves around the stratigraphy of Megiddo,
and this is the decisive factor. At Megiddo a solid wall was found with
salients and recesses built partially of ashlar blocks like the gate, and
connected to the Solomonic gate. This wall had associated with it the
city of storehouses (erroneously called stables) and one of the palaces
(building 338—numbered in accordance with the system adopted by
the excavators of Megiddo and published in their report). Two other
palaces, on the other hand (1723 and 6000), were destroyed before the
erection of this wall, which passes over their foundations. Therefore,
if the excavators' conclusion is valid, viz., that the wall was built in the
reign of Solomon along with the gate, it is most probable that the two
palaces are prior to his time and that their construction should be
assigned to David.

Yadin has challenged these conclusions on the basis of his assumption that Solomon could not possibly have built different kinds of walls
at Hazor and at Megiddo, especially with the identical gates. He assumed that even at Megiddo a casemate wall was hidden under the
solid wall or that the excavators simply did not notice that in fact the

casemate rooms had been filled up in a later period, as had happened
in certain segments of the wall at Hazor.

In order to prove his theory, Yadin conducted limited trial excavations in the northeastern corner of the city at a distance of about 50
m. to the east of the gate. At that spot he found, under the solid wall
and the storehouses (the so-called stables) adjacent to it, palace 6000
with building segments on each side of it that he interpreted as a
casemate wall. In the light of this discovery he concluded that his was
the sought-for casemate wall connected with the Solomonic gate, and
that the solid wall was later (from the reign of Ahab). According to this
theory the Solomonic city was comprised of the Solomonic gate, a
casemate wall, and the two earlier palaces (1723 and 6000). The storehouse city, palace 338, the solid wall, and a later gate with two guardrooms were assigned to the reign of Ahab. The Davidic city (Stratum
VB), which preceded these structures, was an unfortified village without any significant public buildings (Fig. 61). These conclusions do not
stand up under critique and more careful scrutiny; it will suffice to
present here two decisive arguments:

1. The so-called casemate wall is no such thing. It is entirely different
on the two sides of the palace. To the west were discovered three
successive rectangular rooms built with ashlar masonry like the palace,
and they evidently belong to a large fortified courtyard surrounding
the palace, like that of palace 1723. Actually its continuation and the
corner closing it off before the gate were discovered in area DD. To
the east of what Yadin actually found was a continuous line of houses
and walls of construction identical to that also found underneath the
palace. These houses are constructed of thin walls, the outer ones
being less than a meter in thickness, and they are not strictly aligned
so that one could claim that they were two basic parallel lines, but
rather they were a series of walls forming one line for about seven or
eight meters along the periphery of the town. There is not the slightest
resemblance between this alleged city wall and the casemate wall at
Hazor; what does exist in fact is a row of adjacent houses, the back
walls of which served as a kind of defense line around the edge of the
mound. The previous excavators had already noted this practice of
erecting a continuous line of houses around the periphery of the tell
in Stratum V, and it is this same row of buildings that has been uncovered in the recent excavations.

2. In the gate area itself, no traces whatever of a casemate wall have

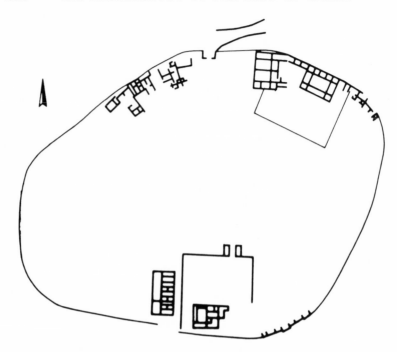

FIG. 61. Megiddo. Plan of the settlement (Stratum V)

ever been found, and Z. Herzog has proved that there is no place for such a wall according to the absolute levels in the houses of Stratum V. Furthermore, there is no possibility of separating the solid wall from the Solomonic gate. The later gate, with only two guardrooms, which evidently has been correctly assigned to the reign of Ahab, is wider than the Solomonic gate, and the solid wall on both sides of it runs under it and is joined to the Solomonic gate. It is obvious, therefore, that the solid wall precedes the bipartite gate. A modified proposal to date the solid wall somewhere between Solomon and Ahab, perhaps to the reign of Jeroboam, certainly has nothing to commend it. First of all, it would leave the Solomonic gate without a wall, and then it would result in Jeroboam's having built an elaborate new wall surrounding a ruined city, restored only in the reign of Ahab. In contrast to the general destruction of the city by Shishak, documented both in his victory list and by the fragment of a stele with his name on it found in the excavations, it is probable that the gate was not damaged, since it shows no sign of repair. Afterward the gate was suddenly destroyed, and on top of it was built the bipartite gate along with the new buildings in the city. All of these forced conjectures have been put forth on the basis of the assumption that Solomon could not possibly have built walls of different types in his various cities. But today there is actually no doubt that the two types of walls served one beside the other throughout the entire monarchical period.

Long before Yadin's excavation other doubts had been expressed about the dating of the city with the storehouses and everything related to them (Stratum IV) to the reign of Solomon by Crowfoot and Kenyon, the excavators of Samaria. They based their conclusions on a comparison of the architecture and the ceramics at Samaria, and claimed that the great resemblance proved that they belonged to the ninth century. This date is founded on the biblical narrative about Omri, king of Israel, having purchased the "hill of Samaria from Shemer for two talents of silver; and he fortified the hill, and called the name of the city which he built, Samaria, after the name of Shemer, the owner of the hill" (I Kings 16:24; Photo 51).

This is a common occurrence, that first-class archaeologists deduce more from a biblical verse than it actually contains and then establish their dates on that basis. The passage in question says that Omri purchased the place and began to build the new capital there, just as David had acquired the Jebusite city by conquest and Mt. Moriah by purchase. Of course, there were no royal buildings at Samaria prior to Omri, and it is doubtful whether the place was even fortified. However, it is in no way stated that the place was not occupied before the reign of Omri. On the contrary, the very act of purchase and the preservation of a name related to an older period can be interpreted in just the opposite manner. In such a case, only the archaeological findings can give an answer, and one must not start out with a preconceived notion that at Samaria everything begins in the reign of Omri and his son Ahab in the second quarter of the ninth century.

Today, there is no doubt that pottery from the tenth century is found at Samaria, and perhaps even from the eleventh, including bowls with irregular hand burnishing and other transition types from early Israelite I to Israelite II. On the other hand, the wall associated with the earliest stratum (Stratum I, except for the pottery from the Early Canaanite) is built of magnificent ashlar masonry and certainly does not predate the reign of Omri. However, therefore, could it happen that Kenyon associated pottery from the tenth century with architecture of the ninth?

Kenyon herself clarifies this beautifully in the report on Samaria. She claims correctly that it is a rule in archaeological excavation that most of the finds in the destruction debris of a particular building belong to the last stages of that structure. On the basis of this correct assumption, she commits two methodological errors.

1. In order to fix the date of the foundation of a building, she publishes the sherd found in the fill *under* the floors instead of the vessels found *in situ*—*on* the floor in the destruction debris (thus, she is undoubtedly influenced by the scarcity of stratified finds in a hill-country site like Samaria). It is true that the sherds (and here one has to do only with sherds and not with vessels) of the latest date may be from a time close to the foundation of a building, but most of the sherds are certainly older and belong to all of the previous occupation levels on the site. The use of such a mixture in a stratigraphic discussion is extremely dangerous and vitiates sound stratigraphic analysis.

2. Even Kenyon later agreed, of course, that the tripartite gates of Hazor, Megiddo, and Gezer belong to the reign of Solomon, but she claimed that the pottery found in these strata, which resembles that of Stratum I at Samaria, does not belong to the tenth century but to the destruction in the ninth century. Thus she completely ignored the clear information about the destruction at Megiddo by Shishak in about 920 B.C.E. and the fact that at Hazor three distinct building phases have been discerned (Strata XA, IXB, IXA) between the Solomonic city (Stratum XA) and that of Ahab (Stratum VIII).

Comparison of the pottery proves, therefore, not that one must lower the date of Stratum IVB at Megiddo to the ninth century, but rather that there was a certain occupation at Samaria when Omri bought the hill. And what about the similarity of architecture? First of all, Kenyon herself admitted later that the two early palaces at Megiddo (1723 and 6000) belong to the tenth century, in spite of the similarity of the ashlar to that at Samaria. On the other hand, today similar construction is recognized throughout the entire monarchical period from the building of the palace at Ramat Rahel near Jerusalem, which was constructed toward the end of the First Temple period, with a technique very similar to that of Samaria. This type of ashlar construction served in Israel and Judah only for royal buildings, and the building method does not show any internal chronological development. It is thoroughly erroneous to use it as a criterion for precise dating.

In the light of all these considerations, which have been reiterated in detail because of their importance for the correct dating of structures and various strata in the monarchical period, one may define the nature of Megiddo during the reign of David and Solomon with great certainty. Stratum VIA at Megiddo was destroyed by a great conflagration at the latest by the middle of the eleventh century. There is no historical information about the circumstances of this destruction, unlike most of the destruction levels in the various cities. But one must remember that the mid-eleventh century is a period of conflicts in which towns and apparently also many small settlements in the hill country were destroyed. There exists a certain gap in the occupation of Megiddo after that destruction and the ensuing settlement (Stratum VB), which was founded only toward the end of the eleventh century, evidently during the reign of Saul. This was an open settlement in which no public construction has been discovered. Stratum VB was destroyed near the end of the eleventh century (at the end of Saul's reign?) and, in its stead, the Davidic city (Stratum VA) was built after a short time.

This town continues, in its essence, the character of Stratum VB, and nowhere did the excavators succeed in distinguishing between the buildings of these two closely related strata. In this town there were also mainly private buildings, not arranged in an orderly fashion, and only on the edge of the mound were the structures aligned in parallel with the slope to form an outer defense perimeter. At the same time the gate area was restored. The ascent to the tell was always along the same path, which was now paved with a layer of chalk. Two structures came into existence in front of the gate itself: a long room with benches on the right-hand side, and a raised platform with two stone steps in front of it on the left, perhaps a ritual *bamah* ("high place"; cf. II Kings 23:8). The new gate was built slightly to the east of the site of the previous gate, on the spot where the Solomonic gate was later constructed, but it consisted of only one pier on each side. In spite of the simplicity and small dimensions of this gate, it should be noted that it is built of ashlar blocks just like the Solomonic gate, and it has two recesses on the inside against which the doors were hung.

The main innovation of David at Megiddo consisted of the two palaces, one east of the gate (6000) and the other on the southern side of the town (1723). Both are built of ashlars, and in front of the southern palace, and perhaps also of the northern, there was a large courtyard surrounded by a wall with a gate on the north which made that palace a fortified enclosure. The gate and the wall are also built of ashlars, the wall constructed in a special manner with ashlar piers at intervals that were filled with fieldstones. The gate has a regular form with two guardrooms, one on each side of the passage. In that area were found two large volute capitals which, in the opinion of the excavators, must have ornamented the entrance to the gate and perhaps the entrance to the palace itself (Fig. 62).

Although there is a certain difference in plan between the two palaces, it is obvious now that both were built according to the basic pattern of the so-called "Hilani house." The origin of this term is from Hittite (*hilamer* = "pillared portico") and, in the ninth-eighth centuries, it is known from Assyrian sources as a designation for the porticoed building which was imported to Assyria from northern Syria (Fig. 63).

This structure, the prototype of which was discovered in a fifteenth-century stratum from Alalakh, is well known in the period under discussion in the Neo-Hittite kingdoms in northern Syria, in excavations at Zinjirli, Tell Halaf, and Tell Ta'yinat. Its basic plan is a portico of pillars usually approached by a row of steps leading to a distinct broad room, the throne room, with service and dwelling rooms in the back. Beside the portico there was usually found a staircase room which must

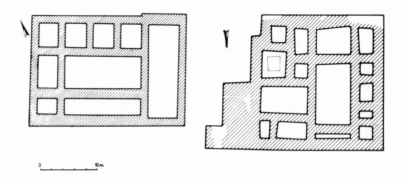

FIG. 62. Megiddo. Palaces 6000 and 1723

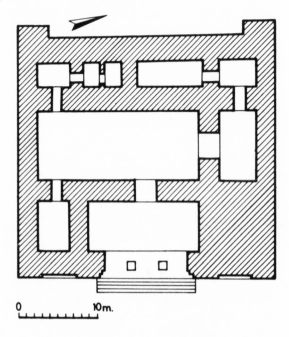

FIG. 63. Zinjirli. "Hilani" house

have led to an upper story. Of course, the pillars of the portico were not discovered at Megiddo, but only the bases of the walls were preserved, and the courses above ground have disappeared. It has already been mentioned that near palace 1723 there were found two volute capitals that permit the conjecture that they were ornamentations for the building's entryway. Three of the additional capitals found at Megiddo were carved on both sides, indicating that they had stood on freestanding pillars, perhaps on those of a Hilani house.

Therefore, the situation at Davidic Megiddo is quite clear: Most of the town consisted of private houses, the backs of which formed a defense line around the perimeter. Constructions of a public nature included a gate beautifully built, though small, and two palaces of the Hilani type, at least one of which had an associated enclosure protected by a wall and gate. Beside it was a large rectangular building with a courtyard and a long row of rooms around its length, which evidently served for storage and administration. Since the entire area of the tell was not uncovered in Stratum VA, it is possible that there were additional public buildings, as seemingly indicated by a gate similar to that of palace 1723, discovered in the area between the two palaces. Apparently this latter gate was older than the storehouses of Stratum IVB, the foundations of which crossed over its line. There was also a drainage canal passing through it.

Solomonic Megiddo (IVB) is entirely different. Nearly the entire southern and eastern half of the city was taken up by public buildings, most prominently by the blocks of storehouses that occupy a great deal of space. The two palaces from the reign of David were destroyed, and the new fortification wall passed over them. Palace 6000 was covered by the northern complex of storehouses, and beside the enclosure of palace 1723 the southern complex of storehouses was built. On the

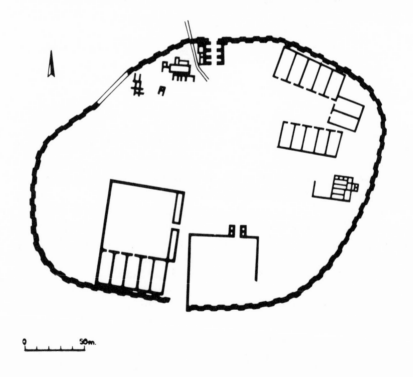

FIG. 64. Megiddo. General plan (Stratum IVB)

eastern side of the tell between the two storehouse complexes, a new palace (338) was built, having a large courtyard in front of it. Its plan is different, and, in accordance with the wide set of stairs on its northern side, it would appear that the main rooms were in the upper story. What remains is only the ground floor, which must have served for storage, as indicated by its oblong rooms. This plan is reminiscent of the palace at Hazor which, in R. Amiran's opinion, was built only in the reign of Ahab (Stratum VIII). However, beneath that building no remains of Stratum X were found, and it is hard to believe that Solomon would not have exploited the top of the mound, thus leaving it empty. Since that building has very deep foundations, and it was in existence throughout the entire period of the monarchy, the question arises as to whether its beginning was not actually under Solomon (Stratum X), like palace 338 at Megiddo (Fig. 64).

Of course, the tripartite gate must also belong to the Solomonic city at Megiddo, as well as the solid wall connected to it. This was an administrative city, well fortified, at least half the area of which was taken up by extensive storehouse complexes and the palace. According to this stratigraphic analysis, which can hardly be cast in doubt in the light of the numerous data from Megiddo, it is reasonable to assume that the city had suffered some destruction between the reigns of David and Solomon. Is such a thing possible, since there is no information about an event such as that? One must be aware of the paucity of source material available and the selectivity of biblical historiography, which make an *argumentum ex silentio* extremely risky. The transition from the rule of David to that of Solomon did not take place without some frictions and clashes, and it is only incidentally that one is told about an Egyptian campaign at the beginning of Solomon's reign during which Gezer was destroyed (I Kings 9:16). One does not find even another word about this campaign, when other towns certainly must have been destroyed, and it is not impossible that Megiddo also fell victim, as it did about a generation later in the campaign by Shishak. Solomon, the builder of Hazor, Megiddo, and Gezer, truly built all of them from scratch. In the rest of the places where structures from the tenth century have been discovered, and concerning which there is no historical information, it is most difficult to distinguish between the reigns of David and Solomon. However, it would seem that the special plan of the Solomonic gate may be of some assistance even in this matter, on the assumption that at least gates in key cities were

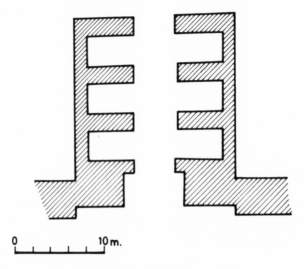

FIG. 65. Megiddo. The Solomonic gate

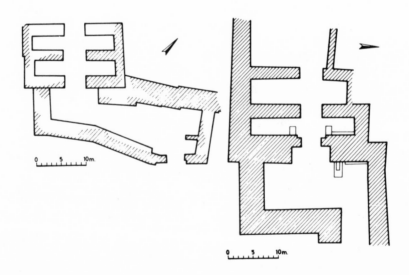

FIG. 66. Beer-sheba and Dan. Gates from the tenth century B.C.E

constructed according to the same layout (Fig. 65).

Two massive gates from the tenth century have been discovered at Dan and at Beer-sheba. That at Dan, which was recently uncovered by Biran, is the largest of the gates in the country from that period and even larger than the Solomonic gates. Both at Beer-sheba and at Dan the gates have a similar plan with two guardrooms between three piers on both sides of the entryway. Likewise, both are furnished with an outer gate having only one pier, with a similar approach way between the two gates protected by a massive wall (Fig. 66).

This similarity between the two gates indicates that both were constructed at the same time, and that was surely during the united monarchy when the two cities were part of the same royal establishment. The regular plan of the bipartite gate, in contrast to the tripartite Solomonic gate, inclines one to the assumption that the gates at Dan and Beer-sheba were built during the reign of David, a conclusion supported by some biblical evidence—"from Dan to Beer-sheba" being the classical concept defining the borders of Israel. This concept appears, of course, in the Bible in two narratives which are older than David's reign but, in his day, there is an administrative source which refers to the two towns, viz., the census carried out by Joab (II Sam. 24:2ff.). It is probable that this is a reference to the two fortified cities which dominated the borders. Furthermore, in the list of towns fortified by Solomon which, as mentioned above, includes Jerusalem, Hazor, Megiddo, and Gezer (I Kings 9:15–17), only those cities are mentioned which are on the strategic road junctions, all of them (except perhaps the last) internal strong points; border towns are not included, neither is Dan or Beer-sheba. It is probable, therefore, that David fortified the main border cities while Solomon continued and expanded the network of fortified cities within the country.

What was the origin of the architectural and ornamental traditions that penetrated the country so rapidly in the second or third decade of the tenth century b.c.e.? It has been shown that the plan of the palaces, the Hilani, originated in the Neo-Hittite sphere of northern Syria. This is also the case with regard to the two types of walls, at least as far as the casemate is concerned. One can add to that the gates: gates very similar to those from Dan and Beer-sheba were discovered at Carchemish on the Euphrates, from approximately the same period. Furthermore, outside of the inner gate at Dan there was found a raised platform, apparently a ritual "high place" (cf. the platform at Megiddo from Stratum VA) which was surrounded by four pillars. The pillar bases were found to be ornamented with a decoration of calyx leaves, and quite similar bases were found at Carchemish.

It is a commonly accepted idea that architectural influences came to Israel from Phoenicia because of the close ties with Hiram, king of Tyre, and the statements that Hiram sent both to David and to Solomon not only cedar wood, juniper, and sandalwood, but also master woodworkers and stonemasons (II Sam. 5:11; II Chron. 2:2ff., etc.). In no way is it intended to cast doubt on these references, but thus far they have not been confirmed by archaeological research. It is true that in Phoenicia only a few excavations have been conducted, but one of the most important Phoenician cities, Byblos, was largely excavated, and even without committing oneself about precise dates, one would have expected some good architectural comparisons there. On the other hand, all of the striking parallels come from northern Syria, including fortifications, gates, palaces, and ornamentation. One may even add here the Solomonic Temple as discussed below, for which the only architectural comparison comes from northern Syria. Does this northern influence, which arrives in Israel so suddenly, have to surprise anyone? David, who annexed to his kingdom both Aram-Damascus and Aram-Zobah in the Lebanese Beqa', reached the Euphrates in his campaigns (II Sam. 8:3; Psalm 60 superscription [Heb., v. 2]), and at the beginning of his reign, Solomon ruled over "all of Beyond the River [Euphrates!] from Tiphsah to Gaza" (I Kings 4:24 [Heb., 5:4]). Tiphsah (classical Thapsakos, today Khirbet Dibseh) was located at the bend of the Euphrates south of Carchemish. This northern influence is probable, therefore, in particular during David's reign and at the beginning of Solomon's. Not only did David come into close contact with the Neo-Hittite kingdoms of northern Syria, but for a time he even must have imposed his governmental seniority over them, as can be deduced from the valuable gifts sent to him by Toi, king of Hamath, and by Joram (Hadoram), his son (II Sam. 8:10; I Chron. 18:10). During this period there flourished in those kingdoms a well-developed culture of monumental architecture partially inherited from the Hittite empire, under whose aegis they had been until its fall in the thirteenth century. So it is no wonder that David took from there his plans for royal building projects.

Along with monumental construction, two other elements also appear which continue throughout the period of the monarchy: ashlar masonry and volute capitals.

The art of building achieved one of its apogees in ashlar construction. The stones were cut into oblong, rectangular blocks, fitted together with precision, and usually laid as alternating headers and stretchers (across the length and width of the wall). For this a relatively soft limestone, easy to quarry and to work, was chosen. It is a dry masonry; that is, the stones touch one another for their full length without any kind of mortar between them. The final smoothing and fitting were done on the spot, and if a corner on some stone was broken during the process, the hole was repaired by means of a small, rectangular patch of stone. The faces of the stones were actually smoothed in part to form a smooth and impressive front. The best examples of this type are in the inner wall of Samaria and the inner casemate wall at Ramat Rahel. On some of the stones the center was left unsmoothed (Photo 46), sometimes with borders smoothed around all four sides but usually only on three or two. These raised areas, "bosses," were not for ornamentation as in later periods, but for preparing the margins of each stone to fit its partner, and such stones were usually below ground level. The foundations usually were also built of ashlar, even though they were not visible above the surface. This practice was intended to give the wall maximum strength. Thus, one finds walls such as the enclosure wall of palace 1723 at Megiddo, where ashlar masonry was used in alternation with fieldstones, so that the ashlar formed a kind of pier at the corners and at fixed distances. It is clear that this method was not intended for decoration but only for strength.

Ashlar masonry is no innovation; there are many examples from other ancient Near Eastern countries including Eretz-Israel throughout the third and second millennia. However, walls were seldom built entirely of ashlar, but only their lower segments, which were faced with orthostats, smoothed and sometimes decorated stone slabs, more often of hard stone such as basalt. From Phoenicia, one is familiar thus far with true ashlar masonry only from the later periods and in northern Syria. The use of orthostats was much more extensive during the period under discussion, while the inner and upper parts of walls were made of brick and wood.

One has instinctive reservations against admitting any impressive achievement for the material culture of Eretz-Israel, which borrowed so much from the surrounding nations that generally overshadowed it. But one must grant that thus far true ashlar masonry, in contrast to orthostats, has not been discovered in any one of the neighboring countries during or preceding the Iron Age, as Y. Shiloh has demonstrated. In the technique of stoneworking, there is a great deal in common between the preparation of orthostats and ashlar blocks, so it is probable that this method was learned by the Davidic and Solomonic stonemasons from Syrian or Phoenician craftsmen. But there is no escaping the conclusion that the accomplished technique of ashlar construction was developed at this time in Eretz-Israel. One may suggest that the impulse for this development derives from the different building material. Eretz-Israel is poor in lumber, a principal building material in Syria and Phoenicia, but on the other hand there is an abundance of soft limestone, which is very easy to quarry and to carve. The almost exclusive use of stone for monumental constructions, while doing without the wooden superstructure, required the replacement of the system of facing with stone orthostats by complete ashlar construction. The same may be said for the main ornamental decoration that accompanied this type of construction from the very beginning, viz., the volute capital. This designation is preferred for such capitals instead of the accepted term, "Proto-Aeolic," or "Proto-Ionic." It is true that there is an appreciable influence in the motifs from the early capitals to the classical Aeolic and Ionic capitals of Greece, but there is no other instance in which it is customary to denote artistic or cultural forms from the ancient East by the features of classical art that were influenced by them. For example, one does not call the Phoenician script "Proto-Ionic."

The motif of the capital, two volutes with a sort of blossom between them, generally in the schematic form of a triangle, is known from the region of Mesopotamia, Syria, and Eretz-Israel beginning with the third and extending to the end of the first millennium B.C.E. It occurs on art objects of many and various types, e.g., cylinder seals, ivories, Neo-Hittite orthostats and reliefs, Assyrian and Babylonian reliefs and wall paintings, and various cult objects. From them, it is obvious that the palm tree is intended, frequently chosen as the symbol of the "tree of life" with mythological forms on both sides of it. In the difficult description of the Temple, one reads a great deal about palm figures and one sees from Ezekiel that this type of ornamentation decorated the gates of the Temple: "And there were seven steps leading up to it, and its vestibule was on the inside; and it had palm trees on its jambs, one on either side" (Ezek. 40:26, etc.). Since most of the capitals were carved only on one side, it is obvious that these stood on square piers against the wall and supported the gate roof, but some are ornamented on both sides and evidently decorated freestanding pillars placed in the center of the passageway. The various comparisons and the biblical description leave no room for doubt that this is a palm decoration. Yet since this opinion is not commonly accepted, others supposing that it derives from the lotus or the Egyptian lily, the designation "palm capitals" is not proposed here but rather a more neutral term: "volute capitals" (Fig. 67). Thus, this is an ancient and widespread motif and clearly came to Israel with the other architectural influences from Phoenicia or perhaps more correctly from the Neo-Hittite kingdoms of northern Syria. However, stone capitals serving in monumental construction have not been discovered in any of the neighboring countries; only on Cyprus does one find similar capitals beginning approximately in the seventh century. Their appearance in Eretz-Israel starting with the tenth century is thus far unique. One can hardly believe it coincidental that in comparison to thirty-four capitals discovered up to now in Israel, all of them from the monarchical period, not even one has been found in some adjacent land. Here as well one must accept, therefore, Shiloh's suggestion that the volute capitals of stone were first created in Eretz-Israel, along with the ashlar masonry, perhaps in place of wooden capitals of a similar design which were evidently widespread in northern Syria during that period.

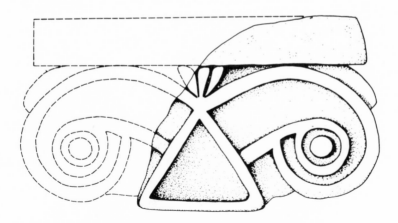

FIG. 67. Megiddo. Proto-Aeolic capital

The volute capitals, like ashlar construction, have only been discovered in royal centers of the first rank. In Israel, two have been found at Hazor, thirteen at Megiddo, and seven in Samaria, to which must be added one found in Transjordan in the fortress of Medeibi, in Moab. In Judah, ten capitals were found at Ramat Rahel and one at Jerusalem; eleven derive from Jerusalem and its immediate vicinity. Their dates are from the tenth century at Megiddo and perhaps Hazor, the ninth at Samaria, and down to the end of the seventh at Ramat Rahel. During that long period of about 400 years there is actually no change in the motif of the capital except for two circles between the volutes and a triangle on those from Judah and Transjordan. Inasmuch as those from Ramat Rahel are the latest, one may possibly see here a technical, chronological development (Photo 47).

Only five capitals are slightly different in their ornamentation: on the two from Hazor, there are no volutes coming out from the triangle, but only the upper portion is seen between them in the form of a sort of blossom. On two particularly large capitals from Megiddo found beside the gate of palace 1723, only one face was carved, and on it the volutes and the triangle come out from the same place. An additional capital was also found at Megiddo with a decoration of palm fronds above the triangle, but its provenance is unknown. All of these capitals, like most of the others, were found in secondary use in later strata. Yet if the palace at Hazor and certainly palace 1723 at Megiddo truly belong to the tenth century, then one may assume that from the beginning there were still certain variations in motif until the early ninth century. Then the schematic form became crystallized and continued unchanged in fact down to the end of the First Temple. To this evidence may be added now the pillar bases from Dan, the likes of which have not appeared elsewhere in the country.

Another detail in the palaces built of ashlar construction is the ornamented windows. The banister of such windows was discovered at Ramat Rahel, comprised of a row of miniature palmette pillars decorated with stylized volute capitals touching one another (Photo 50).

These windows ornamented the front of the building beside the volute capitals that decorated the doorways. The motif of the woman/queen looking out of a palace window is frequent in the Bible, e.g., the mother of Sisera (Judg. 5:28); Michal, the daughter of Saul, in the reign of David (II Sam. 6:16); and Jezebel, the wife of Ahab (II

Kings 9:30). The "woman at the window" theme is widely known from ivories in northern Syria, Phoenicia, and Eretz-Israel, on which a similar banister is also carved. It would appear that these window banisters were generally made of wood, and their first appearance in stone was in Eretz-Israel. Of course the palace at Ramat Rahel belongs to the end of the First Temple (Stratum VA). From approximately the same time, remains of similar ornamented windows are known from Umm el-'Amad, on the Phoenician coast south of Tyre, and from Cyprus. In a burial cave near Ramat Rahel, there was even found a stone slab bearing the relief of a window banister in a slightly different style. It probably originated in an earlier stratum (VB) from about the eighth century.

There is another aspect of architecture that is surprising for its outstanding achievements already in the tenth century, viz., city planning. Of course, an area is seldom excavated sufficient to permit a full grasp of the city plan; one usually is familiar only with the fortifications and some isolated buildings. Among the northern towns, the general plan of only one city is known—that of Megiddo as it was laid out in the tenth century and continued to exist until the destruction of the Israelite town by Tiglath-pileser III in 732 B.C.E. During the reign of David, most of the town area was taken up by regular private houses with only two or three palaces and their large courtyards built against the wall in the north, in the south, and perhaps in the east. One does not discern here a general plan; the town seems to have developed on its own with only certain areas being cleared of private structures to make way for the palaces.

The city received an entirely new form during the reign of Solomon; about half of it was now taken up by public buildings, first and foremost of which were the storehouse complexes. They were built in the area formerly occupied by the palaces and administrative buildings, but special principles for town planning are not discernible.

The picture in Judah is different. Here one finds a city plan first of all in the excavations at Beer-sheba. Of course, the strata there from the ninth and eighth centuries (III–II) were the main ones excavated, and the extensive city plan is that of the town destroyed by Sennacherib in 701 B.C.E. However, in every place where one went down to the older strata (V–IV), it was obvious that both the courses of the streets and the main building complexes had their beginnings in the tenth century (V), and the later changes are insignificant with regard to the city plan. Therefore, one may accept this city plan as a creation originating from David's region (Photo 40).

It is clear that Beer-sheba was built in the tenth century according to a predetermined design based on definite principles. All of the streets follow constant lines, something that was possible only if they were laid out before the buildings were constructed. The circular street that encompassed the entire town parallel to the city wall went forth from the gate plaza, and the structures in the outer circle were built against the wall. From the two sides of the gate plaza, there went forth two additional streets dividing the entire town into two almost equal parts. The left path is slightly rounded and ascends to a public building located on the highest spot in the tell, where the temple seems to have stood originally. The other public buildings were sited around the city plaza. To the left of the gate was an administrative building and behind it, across the circular street, the palace of the city governor, with three monumental entryways built of ashlar (Photo 41). On the other side of the plaza there were two large courtyards evidently serving to entertain transient visitors. To the right of the gate were three contiguous storehouses similar to those at Megiddo. The continuation of the circular street leads from here to the central water installation carved out of the northeastern corner of the town on a slightly lower step (Fig. 68).

It would appear that these fundamental principles are also found in other towns of Judah, although the picture elsewhere is not as clear and regular as at Beer-sheba, e.g., Tell Beit Mirsim. Only two of the city quarters at this latter site were excavated by Albright, and even here the town of the ninth-eighth centuries (Stratum A) is clearer than the one first fortified by a casemate wall in the tenth century (Stratum B_3). In the two excavated areas, the line of houses built against the wall and the circular street originating at the gate plaza and continuing around behind them are most prominent. Of course, the street is not straight and continuous like that at Beer-sheba. Between it and the city wall one finds now one, now two houses, so it would appear that in this case the city plan was imposed upon a settlement that was already partially in existence.

Also at Beth-shemesh, a town similar to that at Tell Beit Mirsim in area (about 30 dunams) and character, a comparable plan may be discerned. In the western quarter of the city, which was entirely excavated, a circular street at a distance of about 12 m. from the casemate

FIG. 68. Beer-sheba. General plan

wall is clearly discernible, and to the left of the city gate a large store-house structure was uncovered having three elongated rooms. Two pillar bases still remaining in the internal walls make it probable that there were two rows of pillars in the stores of Beer-sheba. One is also struck by the same picture that emerges from Mizpah (Tell en-Nasbeh). In the plan, which is not stratified, one finds a casemate wall which preceded the solid wall, and beyond the line of houses built against the wall is the outline of a circular street, the course of which was distorted with the passage of time by later construction. One may, therefore, point today to four towns in Judah built according to the same fundamental plan in the tenth century: Beer-sheba, Tell Beit Mirsim, Beth-shemesh, and Mizpah. The rapidity and consistency of urban planning in the young kingdom is most surprising.

Houses within the town were usually built on the pattern of the "four-room house," with two rows of pillars, that had become standard as early as Israelite I. Throughout the monarchy this was the typical house in the entire country from Hazor in the north to Beer-sheba in the south. One would be hard pressed to find another time in the history of Eretz-Israel when there was such a standard and clearly defined domestic architecture (Fig. 69). The main public buildings within the town were the governor's palace, the storehouses, and sometimes the temple. It has already been seen that in the first stage the palace was of the Bit Hilani type borrowed from northern Syria (the palaces of Davidic Megiddo, Stratum VA). It would seem that the Solomonic palace in Jerusalem also was built according to the same plan, although there is no certainty about the brief technical description. At the front, there is described a "Hall of Pillars," and at the back "the Hall of the Chair" (I Kings 7:6–7), which corresponds well with the Bit Hilani. Afterward is mentioned "his own house where he was to dwell, the other court back of the hall" (v. 8), which could well be the internal compartment of the Bit Hilani. However, this plan gave place quite soon to another layout, and all of the later palaces discovered are not of the Hilani type. This fact is most conspicuous in palace 338 at Megiddo, which evidently was established in the reign of Solo-

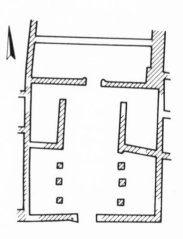

FIG. 69. Tell el-Far‘ah (North).
Plan of a
"four-room house"

0   4 m.

mon, although it has clearly discernible repairs and additions. The same is true for the palace at Hazor (Stratum X), also probably Solomonic in origin. In both of these buildings the main floor was the upper, and the ground floor preserved in the excavations contained storehouses and basements. It cannot be supposed that the plan of the second story was identical to that of the ground floor with its elongated rooms suitable for storage, so one actually does not know the form of the palace apartment(s). On the other hand, in the Bit Hilani the ground floor with its staircase, portico, and throne room is the main one, and the reception and judgment room have now been transferred to the upper floor, requiring a fundamental change in the plan. Perhaps the "House of the Forest of Lebanon," one of the Solomonic buildings in Jerusalem (I Kings 7:2–5), belonged to this latter type since it was characterized by four rows of cedar pillars (three according to LXX) which may have been on the second floor.

One is not familiar with many later palaces. At Samaria and Ramat Rahel, the remains are too fragmented to permit a delineation of their ground plans, and at Lachish, only the high podium was actually discovered upon which the palace had been erected. The governor's palace at Beer-sheba belongs to the eighth century, and the plan of the earlier buildings, evidently somewhat different, is not clear to us. The building was comprised of two parts separated by an entry passage. The dwelling and services wing were on the north and west, mainly on the ground floor. The public wing, which occupied the northeastern corner of the building, looked out toward the gate and must have been located mainly on the second floor. This part had a monumental entrance with three openings built of ashlar, while the rest of the building was constructed of bricks on a foundation of fieldstones. From here an open court in the center of the building led to a staircase, and according to the thickness of the walls, the upper part of the palace consisted of two long halls (Fig. 70; Photo 41).

At Mizpah, several four-room houses were discovered at various places in the town, always near the city wall. Their special size indicated that they were for public use, perhaps houses of the commanders associated with them. A large four-room house was likewise discovered in the fortress in Tell el-Kheleifeh; it was the principal building in the fort and probably served as the governor's house. It would seem, therefore, that during the course of time the typical Israelite house was also adopted as the plan for large public buildings in the town.

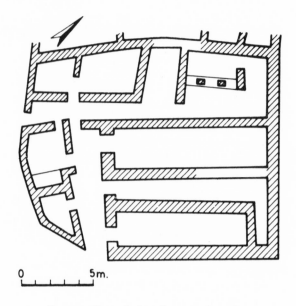

FIG. 70. Beer-sheba. Governor's palace

One of the major elements in the royal Israelite city was the store-house unit. A typical plan of a storehouse is an elongated hall divided by two rows of pillars—made of stones or sometimes comprised of one huge stone block—with small chambers between them. The two side hallways were paved and served for storage, while the middle corridor, unpaved, and generally narrow and slightly raised, served as a passage and work space for preparing the food, as indicated by the grindstones and basins found there. In some but not all of the pillars there were holes bored through the corners of the monolith that faced toward the center aisle. Herzog's suggestion is quite reasonable that these holes were used for tethering pack animals, asses and mules, which had brought the commodities. Usually there was only one entry at one end leading to the center aisle between the two rows of pillars, but at Beer-sheba there were sometimes three, one for each corridor. At Hazor and Tel Qasila the entry was from the side, in the corner (Fig. 71).

Isolated buildings of this type have been discovered at Hazor, Tell

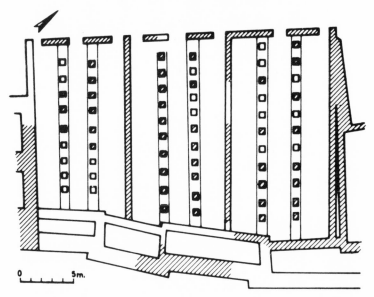

FIG. 71. Beer-sheba. The storehouses

Abu Huwam, Tel Qasila, Beth-shemesh, and Tell el-Hesi, and blocks
of contiguous storehouses have been discovered at Beer-sheba and at
Megiddo. In Beer-sheba there were three contiguous storehouse units
on the right of the gate, and at Megiddo there were two complexes,
one with five store units in the south and the other with twelve on the
northeast, consisting of two groups with five storehouses each and one
with two more. This is an impressive number and shows that the royal
administrative cities ("store-cities," I Kings 9:19; "fortified cities," II
Chron. 14:6 [Heb., v. 5]) were centers where the "stores of food, oil,
and wine" (II Chron. 11:11, etc.) might be concentrated. An illuminating example of the contents and the administrative practices can be
drawn from Beer-sheba and from Arad. At Beer-sheba one found
many storage vessels in every one of the two side chambers of each
storehouse and also a Hebrew ostracon recording the shipment of
quantities of a certain commodity (wine?) from two places near Beer-
sheba, (El)tolad and (Beth-)amam (Josh. 15:26, 30; 19:4; I Chron.
4:29). From the ostraca of Arad, there is detailed information about
the contents of the storehouses and the administrative practices. In the

various epistles allusion is made to wheat, wine, and oil which were issued to military units and to transients in the service of the central authority. The types of commodities, the quantities, and the dates of their issuance were recorded precisely, and they were tallied and checked once a month. The commodities were brought to Arad from districts in the Negeb and the southern hill country, e.g., from Maon and Anim (Josh. 15:50, 55), and Arad was also responsible for the current provisioning of the various forts in the Negeb. In some ostraca, there is a reference to the production of flour, the shipment of dough, and the issuance of bread, all of which indicate that some of the actual preparations were carried out at the storehouse. A similar picture is reflected in the ostraca from Samaria dealing with shipments of oil and wine from different places in the vicinity. Of course, these have to do with shipments to the capital city, but it is possible that in this instance it was also functioning as the district capital. The shipments were dated by the king's reign (nine, ten, fifteen, and perhaps seventeen) and listed under the names of various officials, each of which was evidently responsible for a certain place. The origin of the shipment and frequently also the senders are indicated precisely, and on some of the ostraca the name of the clan unit from Manasseh is also indicated since these seem to be subject to a certain tax quota.

The excavators at Megiddo interpreted the complexes of storehouses there as stables, and this has become the generally accepted opinion. The main support for their interpretation was the "mangers" (the stone compartments) and the holes in the pillars. But these are found, as mentioned above, in other storehouses as well, and there is no doubt about their function. In fact, the only difference is that the compartments at Megiddo are monolithic in contrast to the bins built of smaller stones which one finds elsewhere. But it is hardly likely that this one difference could justify defining the Megiddo structures as stables.

The assumption that Megiddo is described in the Bible as a chariot city is erroneous. The Bible adds only a general statement at the end of the list of Solomon's building projects in which Megiddo is also mentioned "and all the store-cities that Solomon had, and the cities for his chariots, and the cities for his horses . . ." (I Kings 9:19). It is not specified here which cities were for chariotry, and since it may not be supposed that there were separate cities for chariots and for horses, such terminology can only be taken as a general definition.

Pritchard pointed out the difficulty of trying to use these storehouse buildings as stables: There were no horse accouterments whatever found in them, and introduction of horses through the one central opening and then over or around the "mangers" to the side chambers was an impossible feat. In order to take out one horse, it would have been necessary to remove the entire row. As a minimum, one would have expected that the side halls would have been considerably wider at the expense of the central corridor, and that there would be a convenient entryway to every one of the halls as found at Beer-sheba. Actually, there is not the slightest foundation for the "stable" interpretation, and the almost complete identification with the storehouses at other sites proves today what their real function was.

It is possible, of course, to ask where the horses were kept, since they were an important and expensive element in the military armory beginning with the reign of Solomon. To this there is no clear answer, and, except for small stables of an entirely different form for accommodating individual horses, units of stables have not been discovered anywhere. It is otherwise with units of storehouses, typical of all cities in the ancient East. The valuable horses were certainly in need of protection against the rain in the winter and the sun in the summer, but such protection may also be provided by simple, easy-to-service sheds. In the southern part of the town at Megiddo, there were found, as mentioned above, two large corrals, each one occupying a square of more than fifty meters; one remains from the older palace enclosure, and the other—in front of the southern storehouse units—has a large basin made of bricks which, in the opinion of the excavators, served for watering the horses. It is possible that around the walls that enclosed these two areas there were wooden stalls where horses could be kept, and the southern storehouse unit, the smaller one, might have been devoted to rations required by the horses. Therefore, it is also possible that the excavators were right in assuming that the two long halls on the eastern side of the enclosure served for storing chariots. But all of these are pure conjectures in need of concrete proof. The clearly defined architecture of storehouses with two rows of monolithic pillars is unparalleled in the neighboring countries, so it would appear that this was another achievement by the Israelite architects that became crystallized in the tenth century under the influence of the Israelite pillared buildings that had already been in common use for generations.

The crowning achievement of Israelite building in the tenth century was the Temple of Solomon, which receives a detailed description in the Bible and which left a deep impression on the contemporary populace.

The biblical description (I Kings 6–7) includes many technical terms, the meaning of which is not always perfectly clear to us. It is full of precise measurements and technical instructions relating to the building process itself. On the other hand, it is almost entirely lacking in general description pertaining to the completed building and its accouterments, which would have been most helpful for understanding the details and for a general reconstruction. The nature of the biblical description is obvious: it is not that of a visitor and eyewitness but rather a building plan that was surely preserved in the royal archives, a "pattern" or "model" (I Chron. 28:19), in biblical terminology.

Here the various details will not be treated but rather the general plan of the building, with a view to the possible architectural parallels in the country and in neighboring regions, since the Solomonic Temple itself is obviously not available for archaeological research because of the sanctity of the spot. In this discussion one must also remember the nature of an ancient temple and be emancipated from concepts related to the synagogue, church, or mosque. This is not a house of prayer where the public was allowed to enter but rather a structure conceived as the house of the deity where the sacred presence might dwell. The public was not allowed to go into the temple building at all, but only the priests appointed for its service, so the building did not need to have large dimensions. The crowd assembled in the large open courtyard in front of the temple, where the great sacrificial altar for the burning of offerings was also stationed.

According to the description, no opulence was lacking in the Solomonic Temple, but its dimensions were unimposing. The measurements of the building and its accouterments are given in cubits (one cubit = half a meter, between 45 and 52.5 cm.). The entire structure was a rectangular building, twenty cubits wide by seventy cubits long (ten by thirty-five meters). It was divided into three contiguous parts of different sizes: the entry vestibule on the east, ten cubits long; the Holy Place, the main cultic room, forty cubits long; the Holy of Holies on the west, twenty cubits long. In front of the entryway there stood two ornamented, freestanding pillars, Jachin and Boaz, which had no structural function. The most prominent ritual objects in the Holy Place were the different kinds of incense altars, and in the Holy of Holies was the most sacred ritual object, the Ark of the Covenant, situated under the wings of two cherubim. It is worth noting that there is no detailed description of the cherubim except for their measurements and the materials from which they are made (gold-plated olivewood) (I Kings 6:23–28). The only explicit thing said about them is that they had wings.

It must be admitted that so far no temple resembling this description has as yet been discovered in Eretz-Israel in spite of the many Canaanite shrines that have come to light. There are, however, certain lines of similarity which most of the known temples have in common, such as a courtyard, an inner niche (usually elevated), and the holy of holies, which held the most sacred cult object. Neither is there any doubt that most of the ritual artifacts and the general practices are not fundamentally different from the Canaanite cult or that of others; only the significance attached to them was new. Thus, it is possible even to find close parallels to Jachin and Boaz, both in Canaanite shrines such as the orthostat temple at Hazor and in clay models discovered in various excavations. However, the architecture is entirely different. A similar building, with a tripartite division and in similar proportions, is not known from Eretz-Israel.

The only good example leads once again to northern Syria. At Tell Ta'yinat, the capital of a Neo-Hittite kingdom in the Antioch valley, which inherited the former position of Alalakh, there was uncovered a palace and a temple that resemble in great measure the Solomonic buildings in Jerusalem. The palace is a handsomely proportioned building of the Bit Hilani type, and beside it was constructed a much smaller shrine about two thirds the size of the Solomonic Temple. In its general floor plan with three contiguous spaces and its overall proportions it is like the Solomonic Temple. The main cult room, the holy place, is also identical in form to that of the Jerusalem shrine, except that the vestibule and the holy of holies are slightly different and almost reversed: the vestibule at Tell Ta'yinat is a rectangular room like the Holy of Holies in Solomon's Temple, and the holy of holies is a narrow broad room like the vestibule in Jerusalem. Two pillars also stood at the entryway to the vestibule at Tell Ta'yinat. Of course, they were on lion pedestals, and they had the function of supporting the sill above. Therefore, there are certain differences between the two temples, but it is obvious that both belong to the same type. The temple at Ta'yinat is slightly later than that of Solomon (about the ninth century), but it must be supposed that this is a generally accepted type in this region, examples of which may be discovered in the future at other sites (Fig. 72).

The architectural model of the Solomonic Temple was derived, therefore, from the same region whence all the other influences in the field of architecture and the building arts had come. It has been seen

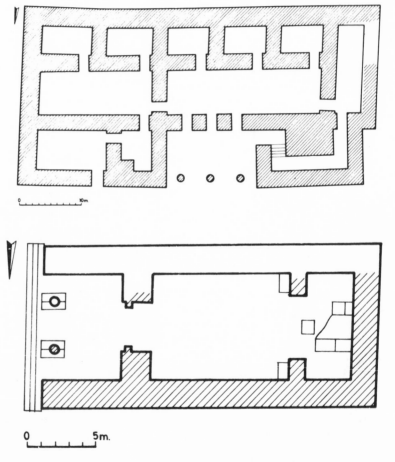

FIG. 72. Tell Ta'yinat. Palace and temple

that this influence reached Israel mainly in the reign of David, and it is not impossible that the plan of the Temple was acquired at the same time. As stated earlier, the description of this shrine is no more than a building plan, a "pattern," in biblical terminology. And in fact, in the book of Chronicles one finds the tradition that David handed over the plan of the Temple and all of its details to Solomon (I Chron. 28:11ff.), all in writing, "all the work to be done according to the plan" (v. 19). The pattern/plan is the source for the biblical description, and there is no reason today not to take seriously the dating from the book of Chronicles, i.e., that it was brought to Israel already toward the end of David's reign.

Today, one Israelite temple is known that is contemporary with Solomon's Temple, to which it can be usefully compared. The excavated temple is at Arad, within the royal fortress on the southeastern border of Solomon's kingdom (Photo 29). There is no doubt that this is an Israelite temple in the full meaning of that word, a house of Yahweh in biblical terms, not just a shrine built during the Israelite period. It was constructed, as mentioned, in the framework of the royal fortress, as one of its most important structures. It was restored and repaired with the fortress in the aftermath of the frequent destructions visited upon it from the tenth to the seventh centuries. Only toward the end of the seventh century was the building put out of commission. This event is surely associated with the cultic reform of Josiah, who concentrated the ritual in Jerusalem, bringing there the priests from the outlying towns. In the various stages of excavation, there was not found even one object relating to idol worship, and all of the accouterments and artifacts discovered in the temple conform nicely to the ritual laws of the Bible. Furthermore, there were found in it some inscriptions with the names of known priestly families, such as Pashhur, Meremoth, and the sons of Korah. There is no doubt, therefore, that this is an Israelite temple, and the question arises—why at Arad, of all places? The answer evidently is that the temple was one of the important permanent public institutions at major centers on the borders, symbolizing the sovereignty of the deity and the king over the land and its people. Therefore, one hears about the erection of temples in the monarchical period both at Dan and at Bethel, on the borders of the northern kingdom, and at Beer-sheba on the southwestern border of the kingdom of Judah. In this light, one can now understand much better the words of Amaziah, the priest at Bethel, to Amos the prophet: "But never again prophesy at Bethel, for it is the king's sanctuary, and it is a temple of the kingdom" (Amos 7:13).

At Arad was found for the first time a king's sanctuary of that type, the like of which was surely to be found at the other royal border centers. If one looks at the temple plan, it becomes obvious that there were certain lines of resemblance between it and the Solomonic Temple, but the difference is greater than the similarities (Photo 30).

The Arad temple has only one cult room, and it is a distinctly broad room in contrast to the strongly emphasized long room of the Holy Place in the Solomonic Temple. In front of the entryway there were two stone slabs, perhaps the bases for pillars like Jachin and Boaz in Jerusalem. In the center of the holy place opposite the entryway, there is a small room with a raised floor reached by three steps (Photo 30). At the entryway to this room, there were found two stone incense altars. In the center of the room there stood a stone stele smoothed on the front and rounded on the top and on its sides. This smoothed stele was the central cult object of the temple and was located in the same relative place as the Ark of the Covenant in the Solomonic shrine. Additional ritual artifacts that were found include two stone offering tables, the fragment of a larger than usual lamp, a pottery incense stand and a large sacrificial altar standing in the courtyard. This altar was constructed of earth and unhewn stones in accordance with the rules of the Pentateuch (Ex. 20:24–25 [Heb., vs. 21–22], et al.). On the top was a large slab of flint, where the sacrifices were offered, and around it were two plastered channels for collecting the blood. The form of the altar was a square of five by five cubits, the measurements of the altar at the Tabernacle (Ex. 27:1), and apparently, also of the original altar at the Solomonic Temple (II Chron. 6:13). The Arad altar was not equipped with horns, but it is possible that horns made of clay and plaster were lopped off when the altar was put out of commission (Fig. 73). The cultic artifacts of the Arad temple are basically identical, therefore, to those of the Solomonic Temple and of the Tabernacle, viz., a sacrificial altar in the courtyard, incense altars, tables for the showbread and lampstand in the holy place. However, the architectural concept is different in the extreme. This temple is actually comprised of only one room, in contrast to the three contiguous rooms of the Solomonic building. It has no vestibule, and the inner room, the holy of holies, does not share the full width of the building, but is rather a sort of raised niche in the center. This one room with

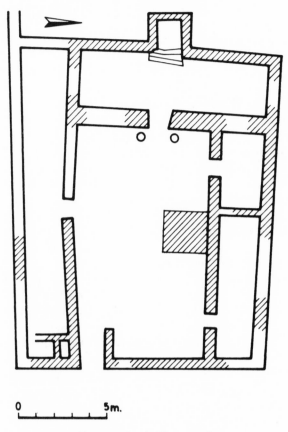

FIG. 73. Arad. The temple

its ritual niche is a definite broad room in contrast to the elongated proportions of the entire Solomonic Temple (70 by 20 cubits) and of the Holy Place in particular (40 by 20 cubits). It would appear, therefore, that only the central Temple in Jerusalem was built according to the "pattern" newly acquired from northern Syria while the other temples were built according to a traditional and venerable plan. And truly, temples with one broad room and a central niche are widespread in Eretz-Israel back in the Canaanite period, e.g., the stele shrine at Hazor, the fosse temple at Lachish, and the temple tower at Megiddo.

One may point out two characteristics shared by the temples of Arad and Jerusalem: the orientation toward the west with the entryway on the east and the general width of the structure, twenty cubits. These two details are not connected with an architectural conception, so there was no problem in maintaining them.

In spite of the difference between the Arad temple and that of Solomon, there is a great resemblance between the former and the description of the Tabernacle, which preserves an ancient architectural tradition. In that portable shrine made of planks and skins there was only one unit, of the size of 20 by 6 planks. The width of every plank was one and one-half cubits, and each was interlocked with the others by means of two "tenons" (Ex. 26:17). If this means that every interlocking connection took up one-half cubit, then the size of the Tabernacle was 20 by 6 cubits, and these are the measurements of the planks. It is hard to imagine that purely by accident the size of the Arad temple is 20 by 6 cubits.

The main cult object in the Tabernacle was, of course, the Ark of Testimony behind the veil. The description does not specify the location of the veil, and since the general idea is the form of a tent, apparently it was in the center like the cultic niche at Arad. The description of the Tabernacle is, therefore, a precise depiction of the Arad shrine in all of its details, including the measurements, with one difference: in contrast to the broad room at Arad, the Tabernacle is described as a long room with its entrance on one of the short sides. It is probable that this detail was influenced by the Solomonic Temple, in the light of which the Tabernacle was now being viewed. This conclusion also clears up a difficulty in the description of the Tabernacle itself. If the building is tripartite like the temple at Tell Ta'yinat, why were only the two inner compartments, the Holy Place and the Holy of Holies, reckoned as the building itself, the general measurements of which, 60 by 20 cubits, are given without taking into account the vestibule (I Kings 6:2–3)? And why, in the continuation of the description, it is emphasized that the Holy of Holies is "in the innermost part of the house" (v. 19), as if it were not a third, independent room, not a sort of internal accouterment, the roof of which was lower than that of the rest of the Temple? This description stressed that, although there were three parts to the house, it was, as it were, one single room—the Holy Place, since the vestibule is not reckoned as part of the house. The Holy of Holies is the sanctified inner compartment within "the house, namely the Holy Place" (v. 17). This complicated description is now comprehensible in the light of the Arad temple. In that shrine, built in the same period, there was only one room with a central cultic niche, and the description of the similar Tabernacle proves that this was the ancient form of a temple. In the opinion of Busink, the Holy of Holies was a wooden cube located inside the "house," emphasizing the continuity of tradition with regard to the "Tent of Meeting." The Solomonic Temple in Jerusalem was built according to a new architecture brought from the north, and these difficult interpolations in the text were inserted to make it more palatable, to adapt the innovations to an accepted pattern. Of course, it does have three contiguous rooms, but actually this is no more than a variant of the same temple with one unit to which people had always been accustomed.

There are two later parallels to the Arad temple, one from Lachish and the other from Beer-sheba. At both places, temples were discovered from the Hellenistic period, resembling in their plans the temple at Arad. Both sites had been royal border centers like Arad, and at both of them there were found evidences of an earlier cultic tradition. At Lachish there were found, under and beside the Hellenistic temple, a cultic worship center and a large stele which had its beginning in the tenth century B.C.E. Beside these was a cultic room with benches and a small platform containing a rich collection of ritual vessels including a stone incense altar, four pottery incense stands, chalice lamps, and other vessels. A very similar repertoire from the same period was also discovered at Megiddo, although it was evidently associated with a local cult place. It should also be noted that in the relief of Sennacherib depicting the conquest of Lachish, two soldiers marching at the head of the column of despoilers are carrying two ornamented incense stands surely taken from the local temple (Photo 52).

Concerning Beer-sheba there is an abundance of information about sanctity and ritual beginning with the patriarchs. In the excavations special evidence was discovered: a large horned altar was found, resembling in size the Arad altar but made of ashlar blocks with horns of ashlar stone (Photo 44). On one of its stones was an incised writhing serpent, a widely known cultic symbol from the days of Moses until Hezekiah. This altar was not found *in situ,* but rather its stones were uncovered, one beside the other, in reuse as a repair to a wall in the storehouse complex, repaired during Hezekiah's reign. They were placed there scrupulously and with care, surely out of reverence.

Three of the horns are complete, but one had been knocked off. This is an instructive confirmation of the cultic reform carried out by Hezekiah, as mentioned by the Assyrian *Rabshakeh* before the walls of Jerusalem: "But if you say to me, 'We rely on the LORD our God,' is it not he whose high places and altars Hezekiah has removed, saying to Judah and to Jerusalem, 'You shall worship before this altar in Jerusalem'?" (II Kings 18:22). It would appear that even the temple in the courtyard of which the altar had originally stood was destroyed and completely dismantled; a new temple was built on that spot only in the Hellenistic period (Photo 44).

All of this evidence strengthens the assumption that the Hellenistic temples at Lachish and Beer-sheba preserved the ancient Israelite cultic tradition on the spot while these two places were still outside the kingdom of Judah during the Second Temple period until the Hasmonaean conquest. Hence, there is further support for the conclusion that the Arad temple was not an isolated phenomenon but represents the Israelite royal border temple, reflecting in its plan an earlier building tradition.

To the public building projects and city planning, which had their beginnings in the united monarchy, one must also add the water installations. The general objective was to assure access to the water source of the city within the walls, in order to maintain a continuous minimum water supply in times of emergency. This was attained within the area of the city by digging a tunnel that led to the water source. Methods of carrying out this procedure varied in accordance with topography and other factors.

The most famous of all of these is the water installation at Jerusalem. The principal source of the city's water was the Gihon spring (or the waters of Shiloah), which flows forth in the Kidron Valley, on the eastern side of the slope of the city of David. In the first stage, a vertical shaft was cut, that is, the Warren Shaft, as it was called after its discoverer, which led from the center of the slope to an underground chamber, where the water springs forth. Actually, there is no date for this shaft, and the conjecture that it is the "water shaft" where David's men went up and surprised the defenders of Jebus (II Sam. 5:8) has no factual basis. It was also quite puzzling that the end of the shaft is about halfway up the slope since, if there was a wall at its top, as was assumed, then the shaft was not very helpful. This problem was solved during Kenyon's excavation when she found the line of a new wall midway down the slope, obviously somewhat below the opening to the shaft. It is doubtful if that wall continued to follow that topographical contour all the way around the hill, a plan which would have enlarged the surface area of the town by at least one third. It is much more likely that there is a connection between the shaft and the line of the wall at that point; that is, the course of the wall was brought lower in that area to permit an access to the spring. The beginning of this wall was established by Kenyon in Middle Canaanite II, whence it was in use until the Israelite period. If such a connection really exists, it turns out that Warren's shaft must have originated in Middle Canaanite II, but both the date of the wall, which was only fixed on the basis of a very narrow section, and the continuation of its course, raised doubts.

In contrast to the Warren Shaft, the date of Hezekiah's channel is quite certain, on the basis of the biblical account: "The rest of the deeds of Hezekiah, and all his might, and how he made the pool and the conduit and brought water into the city, are they not written in the Book of the Chronicles of the Kings of Judah?" (II Kings 20:20). This passage confirms that that water project was carried out by Hezekiah to strengthen Jerusalem during his preparations against the Assyrian threat, that is, in the years preceding Sennacherib's campaign in 701 B.C.E.

This tunnel, the length of which is 533 m. (1,200 cubits according to the inscription), directs the water from the spring at a gentle gradient to the southwestern slope of the hill of the city, where the waters collect in the Pool of Siloam. The tunnel was not hewn in a straight line but in a very winding course, and to this day the reason is not completely clear. It is amazing that in spite of the winding course, the work of quarrying was carried out from both ends, as indicated in the famous Siloam inscription incised on the rock inside the tunnel near the meeting point. Nor has it been proven thus far from an archaeological standpoint that the city included the western ravine (Tyropoeon) and part of the ridge on the western hill (the upper city) at that time, but this seems obvious. It would have made no sense to carry out this mighty project, which made such a strong impression on contemporaries, if the approach to the pool of Siloam had not been protected by the city's fortifications.

Today, water installations are familiar at several of the important tells in the country, and it would appear that at least some of them were in use and perhaps quarried out during the united monarchy. Fixing of dates for them is usually quite difficult since a water installation continued to serve for a long period, and the vessels found in them are usually from the last period of their use. It is also impractical to establish the date for the beginning of the shaft since its upper part cut through earlier strata of the city which then collapsed when the shaft was abandoned.

The date for the water installation at Megiddo seems fairly well founded now. Here a deep shaft was quarried with a winding staircase from which a tunnel led through the rock to the spring outside the city slope. That spring flowed out into a small cave, the outer entrance to which was blocked by an outer wall, certainly at the time that the tunnel was cut. In the tunnel, there was found a sort of guardpost with the skeleton of a man with a few vessels from the end of the Late Canaanite or the beginning of the Early Israelite. It would appear, therefore, that the excavation of the tunnel must be later than that date, and there is an additional argument: on the upper slope of the tell, a covered gallery was discovered built of ashlar masonry about 1 m. wide, which evidently served as a hidden approach to the cave of the spring before the tunnel was cut. This gallery is older than the Solomonic wall, and hence, it must be assigned to the reign of David. It was replaced by the great water shaft in the days of Solomon. Furthermore, one must remember that certain factors have remained hypothetical in this designation, and there are data which suggest that the gallery was only an

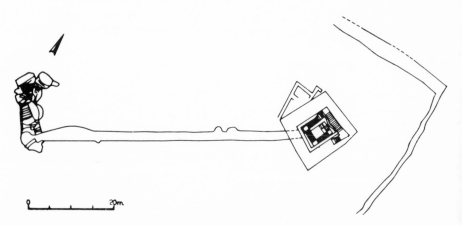

FIG. 74. Megiddo. The water system

intermediate stage during a period when the larger project was abandoned (Fig. 74).

A great water shaft was also dug at Hazor. Like that at Megiddo, it also consists of a wide and deep shaft with a winding staircase, but instead of having a horizontal tunnel, it was continued by a diagonal tunnel with steps leading downward. Surprisingly, that tunnel does not lead to an outside spring but rather to the water table of the springs that were at the same level. If it is not accidental, viz., that they reached the water table during the quarrying, then it would appear that the hydrological engineers at Hazor had an understanding of the geology pertaining to water-bearing strata.

The project at Hazor was dated by its excavators to the ninth century B.C.E. (Stratum VIII). But here one must also entertain doubts as to whether it might not have originated earlier. The tunnel, excavated in the form of a pointed arc, is quite similar to another tunnel discovered in the center of the tell, dating to the fourteenth-thirteenth centuries B.C.E. (Strata XIV–XIII). If the great water project is later, then it is obvious that the builders were imitating the older technique. At Taanach, the beginning of a similar tunnel was also found dating from the Late Canaanite period, and the water tunnel at Gezer leading to the underground water table also seems to have had its beginning in Late Canaanite. Such water installations are also known to us from Mycenae, and it is probable that at least some of the installations of that type made their way to Eretz-Israel in Late Canaanite II.

An additional water installation was discovered at Ibleam, and two adjacent installations were found at Gibeon. One leads through the wall by a slanting tunnel to the spring outside the slope of the hill. The other is a great round shaft with a winding staircase cut into the rock, leading directly to the water table within the city. It is probable that the original intention was to cut a tunnel from the shaft to the same spring, but work was stopped when they reached the water table. This large round shaft with water at the bottom is reminiscent in some sense of a pool, so it might be none other than "the pool at Gibeon" beside which Abner, the son of Ner, and Joab, the son of Zeruiah, had their encounter (II Sam. 2:12–13).

At Beer-sheba a shaft was also found with a winding staircase that evidently led to a similar water installation. Since the fortified city of Beer-sheba is not older than the reign of David, it seems obvious that the water project was part of the urban planning in the Israelite period, which in this case may perhaps be part of the heritage from similar water projects at the end of the Canaanite period.

The Israelite was "gathered to his fathers." This is a continuation of the Canaanite tradition of burial caves serving for generations, where older burials are moved aside in order to accommodate the new. It is interesting that also in this field a crystallized tradition of the form of the burial cave was created beginning in the tenth century and continuing without change to the end of the First Temple. The entry was through a vertical shaft with a few steps at the end leading through a small rectangular entrance (stomium) to a rectangular vestibule (atrium). This opened onto several burial chambers with benches or arcosolia along the sides, the number of which may vary from one to four, with additions being made as needed. The prototype of these burial caves is to be found in the Philistine burials at Tel Sharuhen and Tel 'Eton. It would seem that this is an Aegean practice brought to the country by the Philistines and adopted very quickly by the Israelite tribes. Again, one witnesses an interesting phenomenon in the way that a custom is accepted rapidly and soon becomes a hallmark of Israelite settlement.

In some burial caves from the eighth and seventh centuries, drawings and various reliefs have been found, e.g., human forms, lions, and boats, sometimes accompanied by Hebrew graffiti with names of the deceased, blessings, and prayers. At Jerusalem there was found a unique "city of the dead," doubtless intended for princes and nobles of the city. Most of the tombs known are in the village of Silwan, on the slope opposite the city of David. They are excavated in the rock and have a monumental front. In some of them the remains of Hebrew inscriptions have been preserved, including the names of the deceased and a warning not to open the grave. They have well-carved burial chambers, some with a domed roof, and others with a flat roof, in Phoenician and Egyptian style. Burials of Phoenician style were also discovered in the excavations at the Western Wall, conducted by Mazar. It has turned out that even burials which were considered to be Herodian in date, north of the Old City, are in fact luxurious graves from the First Temple period. It would appear that this is a special custom adopted by the Jerusalem aristocracy (Photo 53).

On the other hand, the practice of burning the dead, cremation, which was common in Phoenicia, was not taken over by Israel. In the Bible there is evidence only of burning for the dead, apparently a ritual that accompanied the burial. It would seem that archaeological testimony to this has been found. West of Jerusalem a group of more than thirty tumuli dotting the landscape have long been known. In an excavation conducted at one of them by R. Amiran, pottery was found from approximately the eighth century with a provisional sort of platform that bore in the center signs of burning. Their temporary nature precluded any possibility that these were "high places" which were defiled. Since tombs were not discovered there, as in the tumuli in Anatolia or Cyprus, the suggestion by Barkay is more probable, viz., that they were associated with impressive ceremonies of burning for the dead conducted in behalf of the Jerusalem aristocracy.

The change in material culture during the tenth century is discernible not only in luxury items but also especially in ceramics. In that century all of the basic forms were actually created, and these changed very little during the course of the monarchical period. The quality of the pottery and its firing improved beyond all recognition. Instead of the homogeneity of the utilitarian, everyday vessels, except for the addition of certain imports in the coastal area which characterized Israelite I, there suddenly appeared a rich repertoire of various types of vessels. The united monarchy also stimulated uniformity so that regional differences gradually disappeared. At the same time the products become more and more mass-produced, and with the passage of time this tendency develops at the expense of the potter's originality. After the tenth century there are not many surprises. Apparently the products become less and less expensive, and they were available to everyone so that the repertoire is almost identical in most of the houses. To this industrial development, one must also associate wheel burnishing, which becomes exclusive from the middle of the tenth century. It also becomes better perfected and cheaper, but the pottery loses its individualistic lines as formerly expressed in the irregular hand burnishing (Plate 29).

THE KINGDOMS OF ISRAEL AND JUDAH—ISRAELITE IIB–C

Although one may discern some differences in material culture between the two kingdoms during the ninth, eighth, and seventh centuries which have led to various proposals for subdividing this long period, there is, in fact, a direct continuity in nearly everything so that the various divisions are more historical than archaeological.

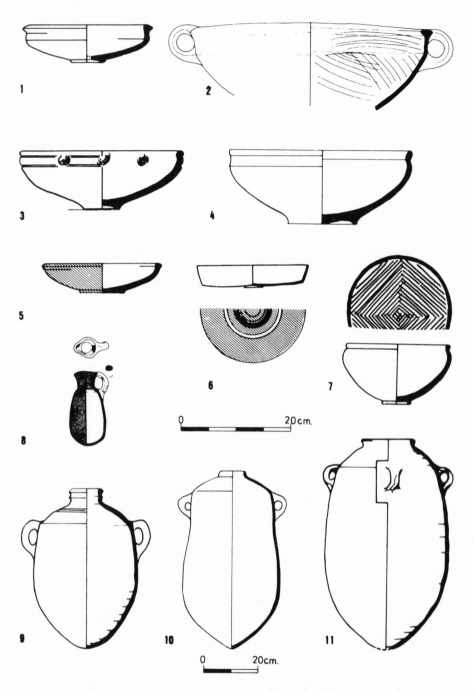

PLATE 29. Pottery of Israelite IIA

It is natural that with the division of the monarchy, differences crystallized between the two kingdoms. It is interesting that although the northern kingdom was always the larger, the richer, and the stronger, Judah exceeded it from the standpoint of a varied material culture. Various forms of vessels that reached Israel from Judah can easily be pointed out, but it is very difficult to find elements of reciprocal influence. Obviously, the two kingdoms were greatly weakened by the division, with the resultant loss of control over areas outside of Eretz-Israel in the restricted sense. With the loss of political influence, they also lost the monopoly on the trade routes and the rich income associated with them. Their military weakness was expressed in the widespread destruction that visited the land only five years after the death of Solomon, as the result of Shishak's campaign. From his relief, one knows that his plundering raid was conducted against both Judah and Israel, and the course of the campaign, which traversed the hill country, the plain, and the Negeb, is more or less clear. Of course, definite testimony exists only with regard to a few towns, in particular Megiddo (Stratum IVB), which not only is mentioned in the Shishak list but also has produced the fragment of a stele bearing his name. Another place referred to in the list is Arad in the Negeb, and there is no doubt that this was the first fortress destroyed there (Stratum XI). But with regard to the remaining towns, one does not have a definite correlation between evidence from excavation and that of the list. However, particularly in towns of the Shephelah, excavations have revealed destruction levels that are no later than the end of the tenth century; therefore, it is logical to make the association. Of course, these towns are not preserved in the list, but one must remember that an entire section of the text has been defaced. One may refer especially to Tell Beit Mirsim B_3, to Lachish V, and to Beer-sheba V. As for Lachish, one reads that it was fortified by Rehoboam, son of Solomon (II Chron. 11:9), certainly after the Shishak campaign if he damaged the city. It has been mentioned that a tripartite gate of the Solomonic type was found there, and although its stratigraphic relationship has yet to be established with certainty, it is probable that it was built in Stratum IV. One would not be surprised if Rehoboam were still trying to imitate the public building projects of his illustrious father. The two kingdoms enjoyed a new period of flourishing after about forty to fifty years, during the reigns of Omri and Ahab in Israel, and of Asa and Jehoshaphat in Judah. Good relations were once again established between the two monarchies, which were strengthened by royal intermarriage. It is obvious that Israel was the stronger of the two, but the close ties were beneficial to both. Ahab is revealed as a great builder, first of all at Samaria, to which the capital had been transferred in the days of Omri, his father. Of course, the remains are most fragmentary, and one does not have definite ground plans; however, the segments of ashlar that have been preserved and the volute capitals discovered there testify to the magnificence of the new kingdom. With that period one must evidently associate some of the ivories found at Samaria (cf. the "ivory houses," Amos 3:15). Some of them perhaps were luxury items imported from Syria and Phoenicia, although others were only partially worked, proving that the ivory workers were practicing their trade at Samaria. At Megiddo, one sees only repair and refurbishing of the Solomonic city, including the storehouses and palace 338. The Solomonic gate was not restored, but in its stead was built a bipartite gate to which the salient and recess wall was also attached.

On the other hand, an essential change is discernible at Hazor (Stratum VIII). The city was expanded to about double its former size and now extended over the entire upper tell. The Solomonic gate, now in the middle of the town, went out of use, and its area remained empty. The new gate (as yet unexcavated) was transferred to the eastern end of the hill. The line of the old casemate wall, which bisected the tell, served now partly for storage while the rest was destroyed and rebuilt. The newly added eastern half of the town was fortified by a new solid wall, and in order to give the city wall a uniform shape the casemate rooms were filled up with rocks and continued to serve as a wall (Fig. 75). In the city of Ahab, at Hazor, only a few buildings have been excavated. The palace on top of the tell continued to fulfill its original function, if one is correct in assuming that it began in Stratum X, and beside it some new structures were built which were attached to it. Beside the old Solomonic gate was built a large storehouse with two rows of monolithic pillars, and adjacent to it there were two additional storage halls with paved floors. At Hazor, one sees the economic prosperity which visited the kingdom, perhaps by virtue of the commercial privileges obtained by Ahab in Damascus during a certain period, "And you may establish bazaars for yourself in Damascus" (I Kings 20:34; Photo 51).

Ahab took particular pains to renew good relations with Tyre, which were strengthened by his marriage with Jezebel, daughter of Ittobaal,

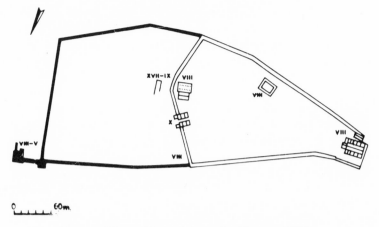

FIG. 75. Hazor. Plan of the walls (Stratum VIII)

king of Tyre. The interest was mutual: Tyre was concerned with the trade routes for marketing her products, and Israel benefited from those revenues and from the luxury items that she obtained. Judah also took part in this commerce, and the kings of Israel and Judah even made an attempt to renew the maritime trade from Ezion-geber (I Kings 22:49) in which Tyrian mariners must have also had a part, as in the days of Solomon.

In Judah as well, the reigns of Asa and Jehoshaphat were a time of prosperity, but there are not many archaeological evidences. In the light of the biblical account about Asa having fortified Mizpah with the stones from Ramah (I Kings 15:22), one may link to this period with considerable certainty the new wall built there outside the line of the older casemate wall. This is a solid wall with an angular course, strengthened by buttresses all around at more or less fixed intervals. At first a gate with two chambers on each side was built, but later a new gate farther to the north was constructed that was strengthened by a massive tower but had only one guardroom on each side. In front of them was an open space with benches on both sides, a clear example of the place of judgment and the council chamber for the elders of the city and its noblemen. In front of the older gate and next to the new wall was built a four-room house, much larger than usual. Other buildings were scattered about in various sectors of the city next to the wall.

These were certainly special public buildings, but their function and the date of their construction are not sufficiently clear (Fig. 76).

Another town whose restoration evidently must be related to the reigns of Asa and Jehoshaphat is Beer-sheba (Stratum III). The city of David and Solomon, which was destroyed by Shishak, was of course restored rather quickly, and with it the solid wall, but it underwent another destruction at the beginning of the ninth century at the latest. This destruction was extensive, and the old wall was no longer restorable. In its place was now built a casemate wall with the classic dimensions and with angles along its course in order to break up the straight line and to give it more stability. On top of the older gate with two guardrooms was built a newer gate, similar to its predecessor in plan; however, the outer gate was dispensed with and the old outer wall was converted to a terrace and covered by a massive rampart.

Inasmuch as the destruction of Stratum IV was heavy and the buildings covered by a thick burnt layer, most of the buildings were rebuilt,

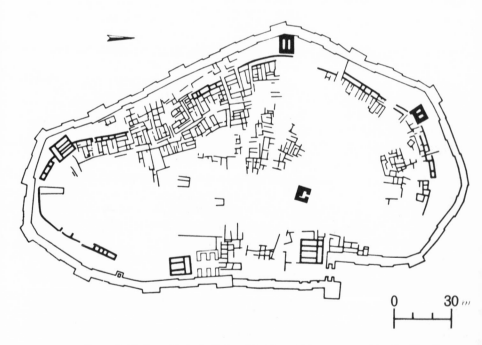

0   30 ₘ

FIG. 76. Tell en-Nasbeh (Mizpah). Plan of the town and its fortification

sometimes on an additional layer of fill. But the builders took pains to preserve the older courses of the streets, thereby preserving the fundamental plan of the city. The new houses were built against the casemate wall, the chambers of which were incorporated in the dwelling units.

The complex of storehouses beside the gate also belongs to this period. It was constructed on a thick layer of fill from the previous stratum, a fact which indicates that a public building had originally stood there, although every trace of the former structure was removed. One cannot establish with certainty what buildings may have been located here in the united monarchy, and only on the basis of the general continuity in plan may one conjecture that the storehouses were not an innovation of Stratum III.

Also the palace, which one was able to date, belongs to this stratum, but, as mentioned above, the plan of the structure that preceded it is uncertain. The gate plaza ("the square at the gate of the city," II Chron. 32:6) just inside the gate was doubled in size at the expense of buildings that had been there, and from it two entryways led to the plastered courtyards that evidently served the needs of visitors.

This city actually existed for about 150 years. As for the changes and alterations between Strata III and II, they must be considered more as essential repairs carried out during the course of a long period rather than as a true destruction level. The city is evidence of a relatively quiet period, during which the towns of Judah in the Negeb flourished unhindered, and to a period of construction and renovation that took place during the first half of the ninth century, after the destructions that visited the kingdom following the initial split.

Two other building projects that must be assigned to the reigns of Asa and Jehoshaphat are the two principal fortresses in the Negeb, Arad and Ezion-geber (Tell el-Kheleifeh). Both were destroyed near the end of the tenth century during the campaign of Shishak—Arad, in accordance with the allusion to it in Shishak's list, and perhaps also Ezion-geber. One must assume that the Egyptian campaign to the Negeb was mainly aimed at disrupting the control over the trade routes that competed with Egypt, especially the sea trade from Ezion-Geber. It would appear that the fortresses were left in ruins for some time, and the evidence for this conclusion is the absence of Arad and the Negeb forts from the list of fortifications built by Rehoboam (II Chron. 11:6–10). It is possible, therefore, that for a certain period the

Egyptians were able to impose their authority over this area, as they had over Philistia; thus, they may not have permitted the restoration of these fortresses.

Arad was refortified as early as the beginning of the ninth century (Stratum X), and at the latest in the reign of Asa. The small fort preserved its basic plan although the fortification system was changed. Instead of a casemate wall with its projecting towers, there was now erected a solid wall with a thickness of three to four meters built in a zigzag line for strength, somewhat different from a salient and recess wall (Photo 28). This was an extremely stable solid wall which lasted for a period of nearly two hundred years until the end of the seventh

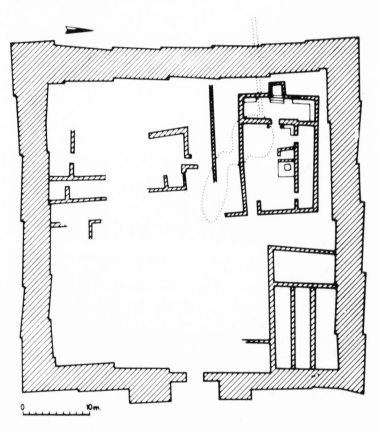

0   10m.

FIG. 77. Arad. The fortress (Stratum X)

century, in spite of the frequent destructions that befell the site during the course of that period (Strata X–VII; Fig. 77).

Down below at the foot of the slope was built a narrower revetment wall but with the same zigzag technique. Between the two walls there was an earthen rampart. At this stage there was also constructed a special installation for storing water. Between the two walls a narrow channel was excavated in the rock, smaller than a human passage, covered with stone slabs but with a wider passage above it, sufficient to permit human ingress through the upper wall (Photo 29). The channel led to large plastered cisterns hewn in the rock under the fortress, mostly beneath the temple courtyard. It is possible, of course, that these cisterns belong to the earlier phase, but it seems that only now were they furnished with a channel through which water could be poured without interrupting the normal course of life in the fortress. In the vicinity of Arad there is no spring or well, and the water supply was founded upon the collection of rainwater in cisterns, most of them naturally on the ridges outside the small fort. It would appear that from there people brought the water and took pains with the day-to-day filling of the cisterns inside the fortress by pouring the water into the channel which conducted it inward. This was a great effort to see that the cisterns were continually full for times of emergency and for everyday living.

The gate was now transferred from the northeastern corner to the center of the eastern wall. In contrast to the older gate with two guard chambers that projected out from the outer wall, the new gate was situated within the solid wall, and it passed between two massive towers. Only their foundations were preserved below floor level, so it might have been furnished with two chambers, although its plan was not clear.

The temple was restored in its traditional place, and most of the walls in the building itself were reconstructed carefully on the original foundations. At the same time a very interesting modification was introduced. The walls were lengthened by 1.5 meters approximately toward the north so that the holy place, which was broad and shallow in any case, now took the form of an even more distinct broad room, and the entryway and the holy of holies lost their symmetrical position in the center. An alteration so strange and, at first glance, without purpose in a sacred building requires an explanation; there must have been a special reason for it. The motivation could only have been a change in the standard of the cubit measurement. And in fact, it turned out that the older measurement (nine meters) and the newer dimension (10.5 m.) correspond respectively to the two standards of the cubit as they are known from Egypt: Nine meters is twenty cubits according to the shorter, common cubit of 45 cm., while 10.5 m. is also twenty cubits according to the larger royal cubit of 52.5 cm. It seems obvious that an intentional modification has been carried out with respect to the dimensions of the building, in accordance with a change in the standard of the cubit. This theory clarifies the statement in II Chronicles, "These are Solomon's foundations [Syriac: measurements] for building the house of God: the length, in cubits of the old standard, was sixty cubits, and the breadth twenty cubits" (II Chron. 3:3). The Solomonic temple at Jerusalem, built in the tenth century according to the "old cubit," still stood with these dimensions to the end of the monarchical period. Since it is now known that in Judah the cubit was changed at the beginning of the ninth century and made to conform to the Egyptian royal cubit, it was necessary to indicate this fact whenever it was desirable to be precise about the measurements of the temple. In the Arad temple, on the other hand, it was deemed proper to correct the measurements and to make them conform to the new standard.

Shifting the site of the gate also required a certain change in the plan of the whole fort. It would appear that the courtyard of the fortress was originally in the northeastern corner. Hence, there was access to the temple on the western side and probably also to the storehouses and dwellings on the south. But now the courtyard was moved to the center of the eastern side of the fortress so the storehouses could be placed in the northeastern corner. Therefore, the fortress was divided henceforth into two distinct areas according to function: north of the central court were the principal public buildings, the storehouses and the temple; to the south was the dwelling area for the commander of the garrison and other officials, while to the west was a series of workshops. That plan remained unchanged in basic outline throughout Strata X–VII, and only with the destruction of the temple and the transfer of the gate to the northern side in Stratum VI was there a new change, with the courtyard being transferred to the area of the ruined temple. Especially worthy of note is a small find from one of the rooms of Stratum IX, viz., a stone seal 6 cm. square incised with a schematic plan of the fortress including the solid wall, the elongated central courtyard, the dwelling quarters to the south, the storehouses to the north, and the temple indicated by a raised hump. One should not assume that the artist intended to represent a dome. It is more probable that the roof of the temple was flat like the rest of the buildings but that the artist wanted to emphasize the special sanctity and importance that emanated from this structure, a sort of radiance. A seal with the plan of a town, quarter, or house is a rare find. In Eretz-Israel one may point to a stone seal from En-gedi bearing the design of the house in which it was found, and there are isolated examples from Mesopotamia.

It would appear that very similar innovations were introduced in the fortress at Ezion-geber, which was certainly restored during the reigns of Asa and Jehoshaphat, with the reconquest of Edom and the renewal of attempts at maritime trade from the coast of Elath (I Kings 22: 48–49). True, one has seen that from air photographs it is most difficult to determine which of the two walls is chronologically older, but by analogy with Arad, it may be permissible to conjecture that here also the casemate wall is the earlier. In the center was placed the large administrative building, and during the course of time the entire area was filled with closely crowded rooms, although their respective phases are not easy to establish (Fig. 78).

The new fortress was greatly expanded, especially toward the south and east, and it was now encompassed by two walls, greatly resembling those at Arad, an inner solid wall and a narrower retaining wall at the edge of the slope. Both of them are built with zigzag lines, and an earthen rampart was built up between them. The old casemate wall remained in the center of the fortress, and its rooms served as stores in addition to all of the other rooms. The gate was located close to the center of the southern side facing the sea, and it had a bipartite plan typical of that period. This obvious resemblance to Arad points to the conclusion that the two fortresses were built according to the same pattern more or less at the same time.

The mid-ninth century brought the kingdom of Israel into direct contact with Assyria for the first time. One knows this fact from Assyrian inscriptions in the reign of Shalmaneser III. At the battle of Qarqar in Syria in 853 B.C.E., Ahab took part with a reputed force of 2,000 chariots, the largest number ascribed to any of the forces in the Syrian alliance. In Na'aman's opinion, this is a scribal error and Ahab only had 200 chariots. On his campaign in 841, Shalmaneser and the

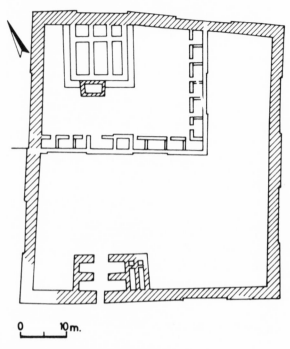

0   10m.

FIG. 78. Ezion-geber. Israelite fortress
(Phase 1, parallel lines unshaded; Phase 2, shaded lines)

Assyrian army passed through the Damascene and the Hauran to "Beli-rasi," i.e., Mt. Carmel, which was now the border between Tyre and Israel. There Shalmaneser received tribute from Jehu, "son of Omri," depicted doing obeisance before the Assyrian king on the Black Obelisk. However, these contacts were brief and have left no trace in the archaeological record. It is probable that Hazor VIII was destroyed at about this time, and in Hazor VII the city had suffered an appreciable decline; but Aram-Damascus may just as well have been the cause of this destruction.

It is obvious that in the second half of the ninth century there is a sharp deterioration in both kingdoms in every sphere with the rise of Aram-Damascus and its domination of the two important trade routes passing through Eretz-Israel, the King's Highway in Transjordan and the Way of the Sea along the coast. Nevertheless, in nearly all of the tells excavated in Israel and Judah, there is a continuous occupation uninterrupted throughout this period, and the economic decline cannot be discerned (Photo 51).

This is also the case with the renewed prosperity during the first half of the eighth century, following the weakening of Damascus in the reign of Adad-nirari III and the revival of strength by Israel and Judah under Jeroboam II and Uzziah. It is natural that one should be inclined to associate rich finds from the various excavations with that period, but the archaeological picture does not add much to the available historical sources (Photos 35, 36, 37, 38, 43). In addition to the conquest by Uzziah in Philistia, on the border with Egypt, and in Transjordan, as well as the construction of Elath—evidently the last Israelite fortress at Ezion-geber (Tell el-Kheleifeh), the fortifications of which were not different from its predecessors—one reads in the book of Chronicles about his ambitious projects in the wilderness: "And he built towers in the wilderness, and hewed out many cisterns, for he had large herds" (II Chron. 26:10). It is most likely that the casemate fortresses at Kadesh-barnea and Horvat 'Uzza (Ramath-negeb) were built during his reign since the earliest pottery collected there belongs to the eighth century. However, when the Bible says simply "wilderness" as a geographical term, it usually means the "Wilderness of Judah" (Josh. 15:61). Here were discovered, on the one hand, fortress towers above En-gedi and on the height of Nahal Se'elim, and on the other, three sites in the Buqei'ah Valley near the northern end of the Dead Sea notable for their elaborate water installations. The pottery discovered in the trial excavations conducted at these sites is also from the eighth century. It is possible, therefore, that the biblical passage refers primarily to those building projects. Further study of this material by Stager indicates that there is also late-seventh-century ware.

Stratum V at Hazor, with all of its structures, was destroyed by fire, and there is no doubt that this catastrophe, like that at Megiddo IV, must be attributed to the campaigns of Tiglath-pileser III in 733/2 B.C.E. Transjordan, Galilee, and the coastal area were converted into three Assyrian provinces (Gilead, Megiddo, and Dor), much of the population was exiled, and the cities were destroyed.

At Megiddo, the Israelite town (Stratum IV) also came to an end, but since this city was chosen to be the seat of an Assyrian governor, a new town was built on a completely different plan (Stratum III). The city was laid out with a network of streets at right angles, and between them there were building complexes most of which reflect a typically Assyrian character. This Assyrian plan is especially prominent in two large buildings near the gate, where the city's palaces had stood in previous periods. These are structures having an enclosed courtyard with rooms all around approached by an internal entryway. One wing is double and served as the governor's chamber with various service rooms behind it (Fig. 79).

These are distinctly Assyrian palaces. By the uncovering of similar structures at other places, a picture emerges in some degree of the Assyrian administrative and military dispositions in the land. The gate at Megiddo now has only one chamber, and the old city wall continues to exist (Fig. 80).

In the north one is familiar thus far with one additional Assyrian fort on the top of Hazor built on the ruins of the Israelite palace. Although Hazor did not continue to exist as a town, its strategic location required its continued maintenance as a military center besides Megiddo (Fig. 81). Samaria itself fell about ten or eleven years later (721 B.C.E.), in the reign of Sargon, and it was also converted now into the capital of a district to which a new population was imported. Since at Samaria it is not possible to ascertain the plan of the town and its buildings, its importance can be observed mainly in the small finds. Even in the

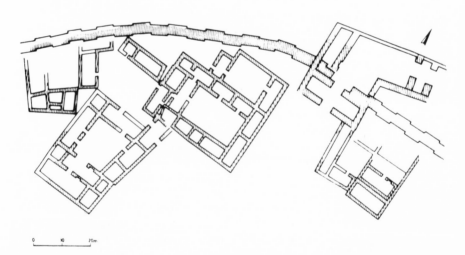

0   10   20m

FIG. 79. Megiddo. The Assyrian town (Stratum III)

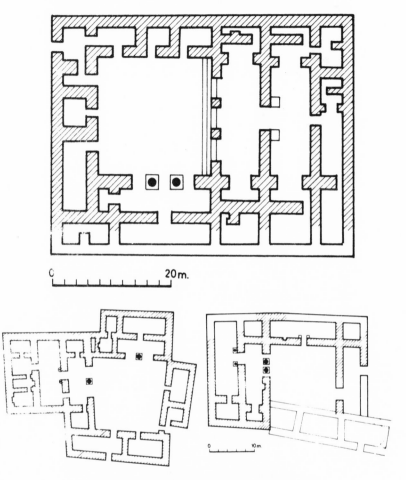

FIG. 80. Assyrian Palaces: Lachish (top),
Zinjirli (left), Megiddo (right)

pottery one notes an imitation of Assyrian forms and distinctly Assyrian imports of "palace ware" which occur now for the first time in
the country (Fig. 82).

Judah managed to preserve itself from these waves of destruction,
but a calamity similar in force befell it twenty years later during the

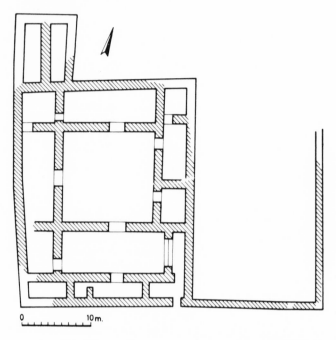

FIG. 81. Hazor. The Assyrian fortress (Stratum III)

campaign by Sennacherib (701 B.C.E.). This destruction was preceded by a time of prosperity and construction clearly discernible in the various excavations. Hezekiah was an active king and developed the trade routes and the economy, and the resultant riches permitted the development of the royal cities including their fortifications. His most famous project was the excavation of the Siloam tunnel at Jerusalem, but his activity is discernible throughout the entire kingdom.

To this period must also be assigned an administrative innovation over which scholars are still sharply divided. From the very beginning of archaeological research in Eretz-Israel, jar handles have been coming to light from the various tells in Judah. These bear seal impressions with a symbol in the center and the inscription *lmlk*, "For the king," above it and one of four place names below it: Hebron, Ziph, Socoh, and *mmst*. The first three are well-known towns in Judah; only the last is still unidentified. The symbols are of two types: a scarab beetle with four wings or a sun disk with two wings. Neither is Israelite in origin

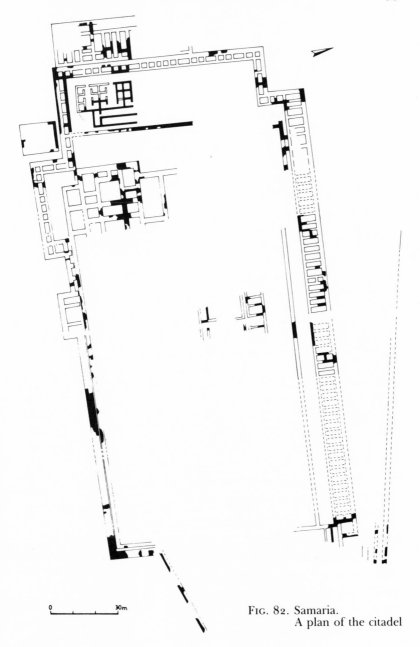

0 _____ 30m.

FIG. 82. Samaria.
A plan of the citadel

or derivation, but they are well known in the art of this period in Syria and in neighboring kingdoms. No one knows why these were chosen to be the royal symbol of Judah at that time or why the symbol was changed during the course of time even though the inscriptions remain constant (Photo 49).

These impressions were stamped on a special type of jar known now as *lmlk* jars. Of course only a few complete jars have been discovered thus far, but the pinkish color of the handles, the fine white grit and the two ridges along the length of the handles testify to the uniformity of the vessels which, according to form and quality, were made in one potter's shop or at least by an identical technique in nearby workshops (cf. I Chron. 4:23). Furthermore, even though no seal has as yet been found, it is obvious from the identical impressions found at the different places that all of the jars were stamped by a very limited number of seals. Naturally, that is an additional testimony to the single or limited number of workshops as well as the the short span of time over which these impressions were in use. If people had continued to use them for a long time, one would expect a much larger number of actual seals due to attrition.

It is also important to note that at the various sites in Judah a great number of jar handles with "private" seal impressions have also been found, i.e., ovoid impressions bearing only the name of a person and his father, frequently omitting the word for "son of." Identical impressions from these seals have been found at tells quite far apart from one another, and it has become clear that they were impressed on handles of jars identical to those bearing the royal seal. Not only that, but there are now two examples on which a royal and a private seal were impressed, one beside the other on the same handle, one from Ramat Rahel (Photo 49) and the other from Lachish. Therefore, there is no escaping the conclusion that the two types of impressions fulfill similar functions, and it may be assumed that the owners of the private seals were not just private citizens but royal officials acting in a certain capacity.

Today one can establish two additional facts that complete the circle of proofs. It has turned out that the measurements of the jars are not identical, and therefore the assumption that the seals were intended to indicate the official measure of the vessel, according to a royal standard, is seriously undermined. At Beer-sheba a jar was discovered, unique thus far, of an entirely different type with a four-winged stamp, the capacity of which was about three times that of the regular *lmlk* jars. Furthermore, with the discovery of several more *lmlk* jars at Lachish, it has been demonstrated that their measurements are 44.5 and 52.25 liters. True, there is not a great difference in their size, and after all, one does have a uniform type of jar, which naturally preserves some degree of standardization, but it is clear that no effort was expended to assure a precise and uniform measurement. Therefore, it is obvious that the impression was not intended for that purpose.

A final detail of great importance is the date of the impressions. This is now based on the archaeological finds at various sites, inasmuch as one cannot distinguish palaeographically between the eighth and seventh centuries B.C.E. on seals of this type. Even the attempt to date the two-winged seals later than the four-winged, from a palaeographic standpoint, does not stand up under critique. Further on, this account will deal with the dating of the strata in the various sites in Judah that require serious revision. Here they will be accepted as established data, and one will point only to the appearance of *lmlk* jars at particular sites and in particular strata.

It is important to stress that no account may be taken of stray seal impressions discovered in later strata. This is a rule in every stratigraphic excavation. Older sherds will always be found in later strata, having been brought up by activities such as construction, filling, and excavation carried out on the tells during all periods. From that standpoint, isolated handles with seals are nothing more than stray sherds, and cannot be taken into account. One may reckon with only three factors: (1) a vessel *in situ,* in other words, a complete jar or a major part of it found on a floor as a vessel in its proper stratum; (2) the earliest appearance of the impressions; sherds may also work their way down among the strata, but this occurrence is rare, and for that reason the earliest appearance of the seals in a particular stratum may generally be accepted as trustworthy; (3) a certain quantitative factor, that is, a large number of impressions found in a particular stratum, while rare in other strata of later date.

If one takes these considerations into account, then today one has sufficient data to establish the date of the seals with great certainty. At Ramat Rahel, only a few seals were found in the last stratum (V), while impressions of both types were discovered in large quantity in the fill under the floors along with pottery that was older than the last palace in Stratum VB. As will be seen subsequently, the construction of palace

VA was established in the reign of Jehoiakim, so at least one conclusion is demanded: the seal impressions do not continue in use until the end of the First Temple, and the latest possible date according to Ramat Rahel would be the reign of Josiah.

In Stratum III at Lachish, all of the complete vessels with *lmlk* impressions were found, both the four-winged, and now, in the recent excavations by Ussishkin, also the two-winged, and the overwhelming majority of the broken handles also come from that stratum. It must be noted that in Stratum II the *lmlk* jars have gone out of use. In the light of the most recent excavations and researches, it has become clear that jars with both types of impressions must be associated with Stratum III, and since it is certain today, as will be seen below, that Stratum III was destroyed in the campaign of Sennacherib in 701 B.C.E., there is no escaping the conclusion that both types of seals were in use prior to that date, i.e., during the reign of Hezekiah. Such a date is also appropriate for the isolated jar found in Beer-sheba having the four-winged seal impression since it also comes from a stratum destroyed during Sennacherib's campaign. At Arad one four-winged impression was found belonging to the fragment of a jar in Stratum VIII, while the other isolated seal impressions cannot be stratigraphically assigned. One may also reckon with the find at Tel 'Erani (information provided by Prof. S. Yeivin) of a complete jar with a four-winged seal impression discovered in the lower of the three latest strata in Israelite II, a stratigraphic sequence identical to Arad.

One astounding detail remains: the vast majority of seal impressions found at Lachish are of the four-winged type (about 80 percent), while in the Judean sites from the hill country (Ramat Rahel, Gibeon, and Mizpah) a similar percentage of two-winged types has been found. Furthermore, there was a larger number of seals used for stamping the two-winged impressions, a fact which would suggest that these were in use for a much longer time. If all this evidence has any chronological significance, and that can hardly be doubted, then perhaps one may suggest the following solution: the four-winged stamps were the earliest and were inaugurated by Hezekiah, but later on in his reign, and prior to Sennacherib's campaign, the decoration was changed to the two-winged symbol. Jars with these impressions remained in use for some time after 701 B.C.E., until the death of Hezekiah, and perhaps also for a certain time into the reign of Manasseh. This situation would explain their smaller number at Lachish, which was restored immediately after its severe destruction.

This date is also decisive with regard to the function of the seal impressions. There are a few hints in the Bible regarding an administrative reform carried out by Hezekiah (II Chron. 31:2ff.). If the seal impressions were instituted during his reign, and this fact seems certain, it is hard to believe that there was no connection. This situation possibly had already begun during the reign of Sargon, with the increase of strong commercial ties, or it may be that this reform was part of the preparations for the campaign by Sennacherib. Therefore, it seems highly probable that *mmst* is not some mysterious and still unknown town but rather an abbreviation for *mms(l)t*, "government," "administration"—referring to Jerusalem, the capital (cf. II Kings 20: 13). Judah had formerly been divided into twelve administrative districts (Josh. 15:20–63), like the twelve Solomonic districts in Northern Israel (I Kings 4:7–19), a traditional division which was surely complex and unwieldy for such a small kingdom. One should not be surprised, therefore, if a king like Hezekiah, desiring to streamline his administration, should unite the twelve former districts, three by three, into four districts with capitals at Socoh in the Shephelah, Ziph in the southern hill country, and Hebron in the center, all of them cities fortified already in the reign of Rehoboam (II Chron. 11:7–10), and in the northern hill country—Jerusalem/*mmst,* which did double duty as the royal and the district capital, a fact which might explain its special designation.

This theory has recently received support from one of the Hebrew ostraca found at Arad. This is a list of commodities brought to Arad, evidently grain, recorded by means of Egyptian symbols, and these are the places mentioned:

> [From] Lower [A]nim . . .
> From Upper . . .
> From Maon . . .

Lower and Upper Anim are Khirbet Ghuwein et-Tahta and el-Foqa respectively, two adjacent ruins. At both of them, sherds from Israelite II have been collected. Eusebius makes reference in the Late Roman period to two neighboring settlements by that name, one of Jews and the other of Christians. Maon is Khirbet Ma'in, 10 km. farther north. The two places are mentioned in the biblical lists of the towns of Judah, Anim in the southern mountain district (Josh. 15:50) and Maon in the southern eastern hill district, the same one to which Ziph also belongs (Josh. 15:55). Arad, on the other hand, is in the Negeb district (Josh. 15:21; Heb. text corrupted to Eder). If commodities were brought to Arad from the two southernmost districts of the hill country, it seems probable that these three districts now comprised one administrative unit, that dominated by Ziph on the *lmlk* jars. The Arad ostracon belongs to the end of the First Temple period, and it seems likely that this division, which was effected in the reign of Hezekiah, remained unchanged down to the end of the Judean monarchy (Photo 33).

Hezekiah's concern for the development of international trade between Assyria and Egypt, which was especially beginning to flourish in the reign of Sargon, also found expression in an interesting standardization of the shekel weights recognized by the merchants. One finds weights of stone and metal in earlier periods as well, some with inscriptions such as *pym* (Photo 39; cf. I Sam. 13:21) and *nsp*, but Hezekiah was the first to inaugurate shekel weights having a fixed numerical marking. These were round shekel weights with a flat base, having the number alongside a symbol representing the shekel incised on the top; the symbol is still without a definite explanation. The weight of one shekel was about 11 gr., as one can deduce from one- and two-shekel weights marked by numerals, but for the others there is a remarkable phenomenon: in line with the regular decimal system used in Israel, the larger units were marked by five and ten shekels, and then twenty and thirty and so forth; however, their weights do not correspond to the numbers—the basic unit was eight, then sixteen, twenty-four, etc. Were numerals on shekel weights different from those in daily use in Israel?

This phenomenon led to considerable deliberation among scholars until its rationale was discovered. Much to one's surprise, the Phoenician numerals were not used in Israel but rather the cursive (hieratic) numerals of Egypt. In everyday life, the hieratic 10 is used for ten in Hebrew, but the same numeral for 10 is used to designate a weight of eight shekels. The solution is that the common, basic unit of weight in Egypt, which was also in use for international trade, the *deben*, was the approximate equivalent of eight shekels and it is divided into units of ten *qedet*'s. The Hebrew system is not thoroughly consistent; one and two shekels were marked according to the Hebrew system with the numerals 1 and 2, but four and eight shekels were designated in conformity with the Egyptian *deben/qedet* and were actually denoted henceforth by the larger values of the Egyptian unit. Thus, the merchant had to be aware of the practice!

The stratigraphy of the tells in Judah is still a subject of fierce debate; there is no doubt that in contrast to the received view, a thoroughgoing revision is required in the light of more recent excavations.

The pioneer work concerning the stratigraphy and chronology of ceramics during the second and first millennia B.C.E. was carried out by Albright at Tell Beit Mirsim. And, as usual with a classic work of that type, it happened that alongside the grand achievement of establishing the chronology on a firm foundation, some errors also became entrenched and very difficult to uproot.

With regard to the entire period of the monarchy (Israelite II), Albright was able to define only two strata, Stratum B_3 from the tenth century and Stratum A, which he assigned to a long period of more than three hundred years (end of the tenth century to the beginning of the sixth century B.C.E.). Albright tried to introduce a subdivision (A_1 and A_2) but Stratum A_1 is in fact a "ghost" stratum, indefinable and having practically no published finds. All of the finds from Israelite IIB belong, in fact, to Stratum A_2. There is no use being overly critical of Albright, who was naturally inclined to fix the end of the settlement at his site, the end of A_2, at the fall of the First Temple, especially since there had been no other excavation in Judah with a stratigraphic distinction between the eighth and seventh centuries. However, Albright with his historical sense and his acute understanding did not ignore certain problems, the solutions of which seem extremely forced. First of all, he expected some destruction level from the campaign of Sennacherib, since in the latter's inscription reference is made to the conquest of forty-six cities in Judah, among them neighboring Lachish. Albright could not point to any trace of that expected destruction.

But a more serious problem arose. The city was surrounded in the tenth century by a casemate wall which continued to exist in Stratum A with a widening of the outer wall. In fact, it became clear to Albright beyond all doubt, even during the course of his excavations, that this wall did not remain in use down to the final phase of the Israelite city's existence. This situation is quite obvious in three places. Near the gate a segment was found broken down and destroyed, which was only repaired by a thin stone fence. Not far away there were very fragmentary remains of a large public building, the preserved walls of which were built of stones very similar to those in the casemate wall. It seemed logical to assume that this fortified building was constructed of stones from the broken-down wall. The entire building was destroyed down below its floor levels, from which no material was retrieved. But a glance at its plan proves that precisely in this area, there are segments of later buildings on top of the regular houses of Stratum A₂. One should also note another archaeological find of special interest in this area: two jar handles with seal impressions bearing the inscription "(Belonging) to Eliakim, the servant of Yawkhin." The very same impression was also found at Beth-shemesh and at Ramat Rahel, and Albright's theory was plausible to the effect that Eliakim was an official who represented the interests of Jehoiachin, king of Judah, perhaps being responsible for the latter's property. That king, it will be remembered, was exiled to Babylon after a three-month rule in Jerusalem in 597 B.C.E., and Albright conjectured that Eliakim was responsible for Jehoiachin's estate after the ruler was removed to Mesopotamia. On the basis of this assumption, the seal impressions would date to the reign of Zedekiah and thus represent an additional proof that a settlement existed at Tell Beit Mirsim down to the end of the First Temple. However, one must remember that these seal impressions were found beside a house built of stones taken from the wall, and there is no ceramic material that can be assigned to it. (Recently, F. M. Cross has argued on palaeographic grounds that the seal of Eliakim belongs to the eighth rather than the seventh century.) Further evidence for the wall's going out of use, in the last stage, is the "Western Tower," which Albright wrongly interpreted as a gate. This is a large fortified building of the standard four-room type that projects outward from the line of the casemate wall and is obviously built over it. Albright indicated that in this building also there were no preserved floors, but he reckoned that it had four phases, on the basis of building repairs. He established its date mainly on the evidence from a pit with vessels typical of Stratum A₂ found in one of the rooms, which, according to the level of its preservation, he associated with the second phase of the building. Here he was caught in an internal contradiction, namely: If this assignment is correct, there are at least two phases of the building after the destruction of the city, since it is much more likely to assume that the pit preceded the building and with the rest of the vessels it concludes the settlement of the city in A₂. (Fig. 83.)

To Albright's credit, it must be said that he was aware of the destruc-

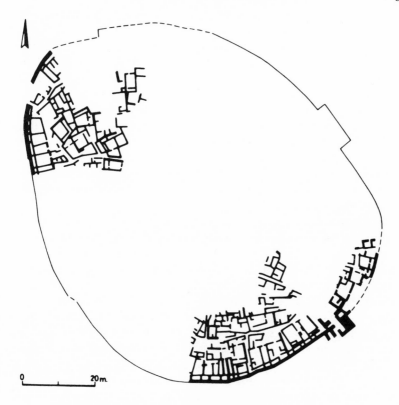

FIG. 83. Tell Beit Mirsim. Plan of the Israelite settlement

tion visited upon the city before its final occupation phase. Albright did
not dare to raise this date by a century, and thus was introduced a
series of alleged destructions supposedly related to the first campaign
of Nebuchadnezzar in 597 B.C.E.; and this was in contradiction to the
written sources.

The same error was repeated by Albright and others at Lachish.
Here, there really were two prominent destruction levels quite distinct
from one another, Strata III and II. The city of Stratum III was far
superior to Stratum II in its fortifications, in its large gate, in its
buildings and its wealth. Furthermore, the gate and the double fortifications are highly reminiscent of the city as depicted on the reliefs of

Sennacherib. In addition, there was no other significant destruction level prior to that of Stratum III which could be assigned to the Sennacherib campaign. But what is so surprising? The ceramic repertoire of Lachish III is thoroughly comparable to that found in Tell Beit Mirsim A$_2$. If so, then both of these destructions must be assigned to Sennacherib! Hence, one can feel the full force of the arguments that became so widely accepted among scholars, according to which the first campaign by Nebuchadnezzar was also introduced as an "historical" factor in the interpretation of Lachish. O. Tufnell, who prepared the material from the Lachish excavations for publication, clearly discerned this absurdity, and pointed out obvious differences between the pottery of Strata III and II; how could this change be within a period of only 11 years?

Today one is familiar with the complex of vessels from the seventh century in other sites as well. Although the vessels are not fundamentally different and sometimes certain types were in use throughout the entire Israelite II period, nevertheless there are some discernible differences, and these are defined. At Ramat Rahel there was discovered, as discussed above, a stratum belonging to the very end of the First Temple, and the *terminus ante quem* was established by the late material buried under the floors. The cooking pots, the bowls, the hole-mouth jars, the decanters, etc., are strikingly different from those of Tell Beit Mirsim A$_2$, but they resemble those of Lachish II (Plate 31: 5, 6, 8).

A clear stratum presenting a similar picture was discovered at Engedi. This is the earliest stratum at Tel Goren, which must be assigned to the reign of Josiah, and its pottery repertoire is absolutely identical to that of Ramat Rahel and Lachish II. A third site of Metzad Hashavyahu, a small fort on the shore between Ashdod and Yavneh-yam, was excavated by Naveh. According to a Hebrew ostracon found there, an epistle directed to the commander of the fortress by a fieldhand claiming that his garment had been taken from him unjustly, the fort must date from the reign of Josiah, when he had gained control for a brief period over most of the coastal region with the collapse of Assyrian rule. The pottery repertoire corresponds to the vessels found in sites from the seventh century referred to above, with the addition of East Greek ware testifying to the presence of Greek mercenaries in the garrison serving there.

One can also add three sites in the Negeb, the pottery of which is unpublished. At Arad, two strata were discovered from close to the end

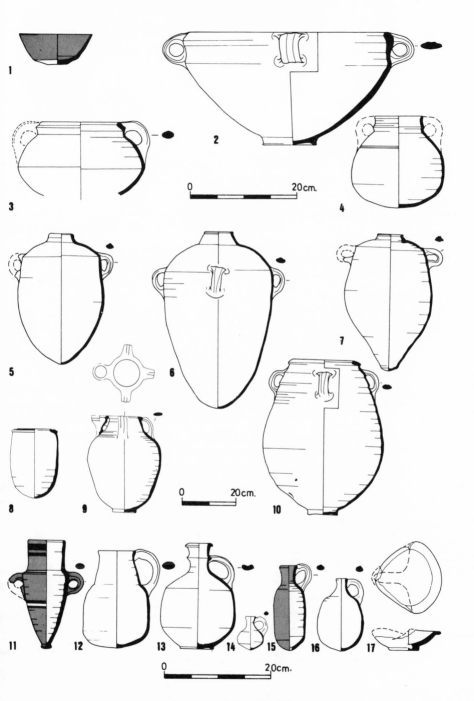

0   20 cm.

0   20 cm.

0   20 cm.

PLATE 30. Pottery of Israelite IIB

of the First Temple (VII and VI), and similar strata were discovered at Tel Malhata and in the occupation of Tel Masos, which was re-founded in the seventh century after a long chronological break. At Arad and also at Tel Masos the strata were dated with great precision thanks to Hebrew ostraca (Plate 31).

Over against these clear repertoires from the second half of the seventh century, one finds a clearly distinct pottery horizon in the complex of materials from the eighth-century Tell Beit Mirsim A_2, Lachish III, Beth-shemesh IIC, Arad VIII, and Beer-sheba II. Today there is no room for doubt that all of these severe destructions must be assigned to the Sennacherib campaign in 701, as should be ex-pected from the historical sources. In fact, the year 701 was the period of greatest disaster in the Shephelah. This is the end of the royal city at Beer-sheba, which was never restored. Also, it is actually the termi-nation of Tell Beit Mirsim and Beth-shemesh as towns, and only near the end of the First Temple period, perhaps during the reign of Josiah, is there a certain measure of renewal at Tell Beit Mirsim, as expressed by two fortified buildings and a few structures surrounding them. Of course, a great decline is noted at Lachish, and even here the town was not rapidly restored, although it did enjoy a certain final period of flourishing right near the end of the Judean monarchy (Plate 31).

The erroneous conception of the strata at Lachish led to an addi-tional error in the dating of one of the most famous and interesting buildings discovered there.

On top of the great podium, at the high point of the tell not far from the gate area, there were found the ruins of the final palace called by the excavators the "Residency." A glance at its plan shows immediately that this was a distinctly Assyrian building. It has an obvious similarity to one of the two Assyrian buildings at Megiddo, with which it shares another architectural feature. Actually, two typical northern Syrian Hilani houses were combined in order to create the two sides of the regular Assyrian courtyard building. This feature is also found in one of the structures at Zinjirli (Sam'al) in northern Syria that was built as the residence of the Assyrian governor during the reign of Esarhad-don. Beginning in the reign of Tiglath-pileser III, but especially under Sennacherib, this style was introduced to Assyria itself, where the Syrian Hilani portico house was joined as a central unit to the Assyrian courtyard building. As in Syria, the pillars of the portico have rectan-gular bases although the pillar itself is round—another special feature

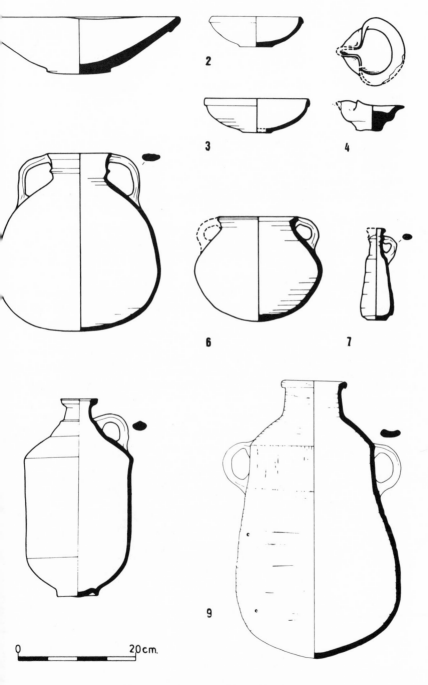

2

3

4

6

7

9

0   20cm.

PLATE 31. Pottery of Israelite IIC

originating in the Assyrian Hilani house, which was carried over in that period to Assyria. All of these features were found in the "Residency" at Lachish. It seems quite obvious that, as in the other places, this palace was built after the Assyrian conquest as the seat of a governor who was stationed there, and hence there is an additional explanation of the special role of Lachish in Assyrian sources, it being built as a center for the Assyrian administration on the border between Philistia and Judah (Fig. 84).

The building was dated, for some reason, to the Persian period, and thus it remains in the literature to this day. If Strata III and II actually belong to the end of the First Temple, then this building must, of course, be later. Vessels of the Persian period were found in it, but these were in a secondary and later level of occupation, when the building was already partially in ruins and the main elements of the palace were in reuse. It should be noted that this is the identical situation in the Assyrian fortress at Hazor. In the building itself there were very few remains from the Israelite period, and the main finds belong to a final, secondary use in the Persian period. Furthermore, Tufnell does not entertain any doubts that the "Residency" was built

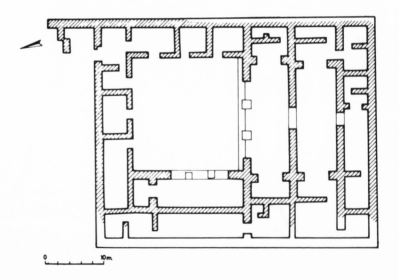

FIG. 84. Lachish. "Residency" (An Assyrian palace)

on the last palace of Stratum III, and she is astounded that the central location remained unoccupied for more than a hundred years until the end of Stratum II. The solution is simple: an elaborate building of obvious Assyrian design was constructed early in the seventh century by the Assyrian authorities, and during the first half of that century it was the one prominent structure dominating the town, like the Assyrian palace at Hazor. Only with the decline of Assyrian authority at that place were conditions created for the development of the last Judean town. Another Assyrian building was discovered in southern Philistia at Tell Jemmeh (misnamed "Gerar" by Petrie; modern Heb. Tel Gamma), apparently to be identified with the ancient Yurza/Arza. According to its plan, this was also a distinctly Assyrian structure, correctly dated by Petrie to the seventh century, but it suffered the similar fate of having its date lowered by scholars to the Persian period. Since the continuation of this building has been recently excavated by Van Beek, it is now obvious beyond doubt that Petrie was correct, because there was found in it an abundance of clearly Assyrian bowls, the identity of which Petrie had already sensed with his characteristic acumen (Fig. 85).

A final period of flourishing was enjoyed by Judah during the reign of Josiah, who shrewdly took advantage of the disintegration of the Assyrian empire to extend Judah's domination once more over all of Eretz-Israel, including the former Assyrian provinces of Samaria, Megiddo, Dor, and Gilead.

Of course, there is unequivocal information about his annexations with regard to only two places: one hears about his conquest of Bethel, the destruction of its temple and the defiling of the cult places of Samaria (II Kings 23:15ff.). Another fate fell to the priests of the Judean towns who were brought to the vicinity of Jerusalem "from Geba to Beer-sheba" (II Kings 23:8). One may not deduce from this passage that Geba became the border town of the kingdom at a certain point during Josiah's reign, but rather that this was the traditional border of Judah (Geba=Jeba'; mentioned already in the reign of Asa, I Kings 15:22). Hence northward, in the kingdom of Israel, he behaved with excessive cruelty toward the remains of the priests and the cult places.

Another piece of information is that concerning the death of Josiah near Megiddo (II Kings 23:29–30). One can hardly assume that Josiah positioned himself for battle against Pharaoh Neco at that place unless

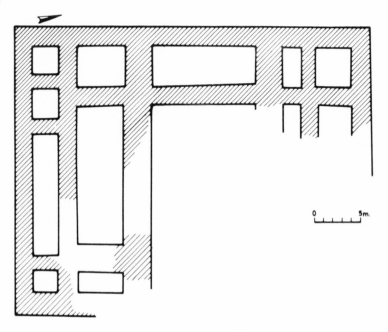

FIG. 85. Tell Jemmeh (Tel Gamma; so-called Gerar).
The Assyrian palace

Megiddo were really in his hands. And sure enough, at Megiddo there
was found a large fortress on the eastern side of the mound (Stratum
II), and nothing prevents its being dated to the reign of Josiah. In its
general outline, this fortress follows the Assyrian style, and it would
appear that Josiah continued to follow this pattern. The tell itself was
no longer fortified in this period, and only the strong fort standing on
the eastern side of the mound dominated the expanse of the valley
below. Using that fort as his base Josiah evidently tried to block the way
of the Egyptian army at this sensitive point but, as is well known,
without success (Fig. 86). To the archaeological evidences for Josiah's
conquests, one must now add the Hashavyahu fort erected on the
seacoast between Yavneh-yam and Ashdod. The Hebrew ostracon discovered there testifies that the place was under Judean control. Since
this is a one-period fort with homogeneous finds limited to the second
half of the seventh century, it is obvious that the fortress was erected

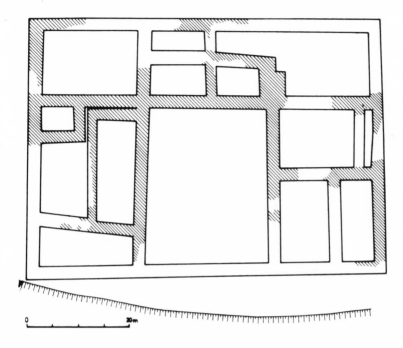

FIG. 86. Megiddo. An Assyrian palace (Stratum II)

during the reign of Josiah as a defensive point on the coast at the border with the kingdom of Ashdod.

The East Greek ware found at Hashavyahu, mentioned earlier, indicates that Greek mercenaries were serving there. There is additional evidence to that effect in the Arad letters. Therefore, one must see the construction of Metzad Hashavyahu as a proof of Josiah's domination of the coastal region, the former province of Dor, and the fortification of his kingdom's borders facing Philistine Ashdod.

Today there are clear testimonies from the sources and from archaeology about Josiah's taking over the provinces of Samaria, Megiddo, and Dor, and only with regard to Gilead (Transjordan) is concrete information lacking.

Some would argue, on the basis of the distribution of the *lmlk* stamps, for a severe limitation of Josiah's kingdom. Their distribution from a Jericho-Mizpah-Gezer line in the north, Shephelah sites such as Tel Zafit and Tel 'Erani in the west, and as far as Aroer in the Negeb, corresponds to the limited kingdom of Judah up to that time. Scholars who begin with the assumption that the *lmlk* seal impressions date to the reign of Josiah are turning the evidence upside down instead of admitting what is obvious from other standpoints, viz., that the date of the seal impressions is not suitable for that period.

Today there is another source of an epigraphic nature. Among the Arad inscriptions, the fragment of a letter was found in which a king of Judah announces to the commander at Arad that he has ascended the throne, as follows:

> I have come to reign in . . .
> Gather strength and . . .
> The king of Egypt to . . .

In spite of the broken nature of this text the general meaning is sufficiently clear. Since it pertains to military preparations ("Gather strength") having something to do with the king of Egypt, it can only refer to the year 609, when Josiah lost his life, and his son Jehoahaz announced to the commander of Arad that he had been crowned in place of his father. In that same year the Egyptian army went to the aid of the Assyrians at Carchemish, and Jehoahaz was trying to take defensive measures in the face of a renewed Egyptian threat. In the author's opinion, the passage in which Jehoahaz alludes to the extent of his kingdom is most important, this being the kingdom of his father, which he was taking over. Only the letters *bk* . . . were preserved, but one can hardly admit of any completion other than *bkl h'rs* = *bᵉkol ha'ares*, "in all the land," or *bkl 'rs ysr'l* = *bᵉkol 'eres Yisra'el*, "in all the land of Israel"; and compare II Chron. 34:7, the narrative about Josiah's cultic reforms, "in all the land of Israel." As in many other instances, the editor of Chronicles is preserving a trustworthy ancient tradition here, and although one may not press this formulation too far, it is obvious that Josiah and his son Jehoahaz considered themselves the legitimate rulers over the entire area of ancient Eretz-Israel including Gilead.

Evidence for Josiah's activities in Judah may be found in some of the tells in the Shephelah, the Negeb, and the Wilderness. As previously stated, there is no doubt today that Stratum II at Lachish belongs to his reign after the awesome destruction during the campaign of Sennacherib (Stratum III) and the intermediate Assyrian phase (the "Residency"). The new fortifications were, of course, quite inferior to the older ones; in place of the massive wall, a new thinner wall was built with fill between two facings, and instead of the older tripartite gate, a new gate was erected with only one pier on each side. However, along with it the outer gate was restored, also with only one pier in a fashion evidently similar to that of the outer gate during Stratum III. In a small room beside the outer gate from Stratum II were discovered the famous Lachish letters to which one will return subsequently.

The city was refortified, therefore, although the fortifications were weaker and less permanent, and at least part of the quarters and houses were restored. In spite of the destruction level separating the two strata, the new walls were built in many instances on the older foundations, which, of course, can make stratigraphic analysis difficult. An illuminating example was found in the new excavations near the Hellenistic "Solar Shrine" (Photo 52). An area of workshops and a substantial building of Stratum III were uncovered on two sides of a street that ascended to the ancient cult place. That quarter was restored in a less permanent fashion during Stratum II, while some of the foundations of the previous house served to support the new walls. In spite of the makeshift nature of the new buildings, which cannot be compared in quality to the older structures, a rich collection of vessels was also found from Stratum II. Particularly worthy of note was a small storage room with a stone-lined silo in the center. On the floor of the silo and also of the room, the following finds were made: a nice repertoire of vessels from Stratum II; six inscribed shekel weights; a Hebrew ostracon with a list of people, each of whose names is preceded by the *lamed* preposition, "to," apparently a ration list of some commodity; a complete juglet containing seventeen clay *bullae* with the impression of papyrus on one side, and that of Hebrew personal stamp seals on the other. One of them bears the inscription "(Belonging) to Shibnayahu [servant/son of] the king"—that is, the seal of a royal official. This is a unique find also indicating that even in this area so remote from the center of the tell there was lively commercial activity, and perhaps the administrative center which was formerly located somewhere else had been transferred here during Stratum II (Photo 52).

Furthermore, there is no reason to assume that the "Residency" was destroyed, as one may conjecture that Josiah took over that central palace from the Assyrian authorities. There is no archaeological evidence for this idea since on the only floor preserved, of later date, only

Persian material was found, as noted earlier. But this is the last phase of the building, when the pillars were no longer standing in their original places, and it may certainly be assumed that this phase came after the destruction of Stratum II. This "Assyrian building" which was under the authority of Josiah makes a useful comparison with the "Assyrian building" at Megiddo that evidently was also built in his reign.

Another example of Josiah's restoration activities is the last stratum at Tell Beit Mirsim, which deserves the designation A_3. If the stratigraphic analysis here is correct, then this phase includes two fortified public buildings constructed over buildings previously destroyed and also over the city wall: the "Western Tower" and the public building on top of the tell.

Another site the establishment of which may be assigned to Josiah is the oldest stratum (V) on Tel Goren at En-gedi. The special character of that settlement is worthy of note: workshops for the production of the expensive perfume, the *apharsimon.* The settlement of En-gedi, the rich desert oasis on the shore of the Dead Sea, flourished throughout the First Temple period, as indicated by the burials, but it would seem that a special phase of prosperity principally based on the expansion of the perfume industry took place in the reign of Josiah (Photo 38).

After the destruction of Beer-sheba in the Sennacherib campaign, the main center of authority passed to the eastern Negeb, particularly to Arad. Its fortifications were repaired after a short time. In that area, a renewed prosperity is observable during Josiah's reign. At Tel Masos, which had been abandoned ever since the beginning of the tenth century when the settlement evidently moved to neighboring Tel 'Ira, occupation was suddenly renewed, and it would seem that a trading station was set up to serve the immediate vicinity. Also at Beer-sheba, one finds that a settlement was located near the wadi but one does not know whether it was surrounded by any kind of fortification.

Josiah's son Jehoiakim ruled only eleven years, four of them under the exploitive dominion of Egypt, and seven under the yoke of Nebuchadnezzar. Nevertheless, it turns out that precisely this king engaged in several unusual building projects. The Arad fortress of Stratum VII was destroyed in 609 B.C.E. The name of its commander is known—Eliashib, son of Ishiahu (Photo 34)—and an inventory list of the fortress made by an Egyptian scribe in hieratic writing explains what happened. This was not warfare or conquest. Egypt was not interested in developing the competitive Negeb routes and the fortresses dominating them; therefore, instructions were given to destroy them, but not before confiscating the stores in the royal warehouses (Photo 33).

The same commander, Eliashib, son of Ishiahu, certainly returned to this fortress after four or five years when the Egyptian rule was replaced by the Babylonian. In the fifth year of Jehoiakim or thereabouts, Arad was thus settled (Stratum VI), and this time the fortifications were rebuilt. The solid wall, which had been erected as early as the ninth century and had remained in use for nearly two hundred years, was not repaired, but in its place a new casemate wall was constructed, partly with ashlar blocks taken from previous buildings. The new fortifications only stood for a few years (Fig. 87).

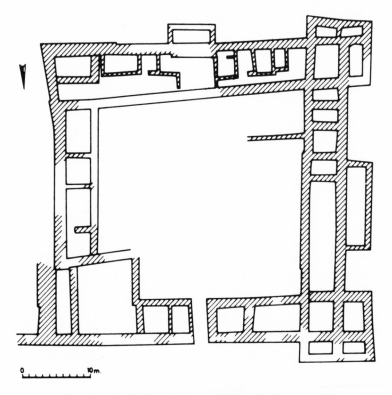

FIG. 87. Arad. The fortress of Eliashib (Stratum VI)

A larger and more elaborate building project was the palace at Ramat Rahel. This prominent hill, halfway down the road between Jerusalem and Bethlehem, was certainly a military strongpoint, but that was not its most important feature. At Ramat Rahel, an impressive palace was built which can compete with the best construction of this era. In fact, there is no preserved example of such construction from Judah in any other period, and the best comparison is with the palace of Omri and Ahab at Samaria, which preceded it by more than two hundred and fifty years (Photo 46). It has been stressed that only royal palaces were built with this technique, and the method had not been forgotten in Judah. With regard to Ramat Rahel, there is an unprecedented description from the mouth of the prophet Jeremiah, a contemporary, in his words to Jehoiakim (Fig. 88):

> Woe to him who builds his house by unrighteousness,
>   and his upper rooms by injustice;
> who makes his neighbor serve him for nothing,
>   and does not give him his wages;
> who says, "I will build myself a great house
>   with spacious upper rooms,"
> and cuts out windows for it,
>   paneling it with cedar,
>   and painting it with vermilion.
>   (Jer. 22:13–14; Photo 46)

Note also the representation of a seated royal figure on a sherd from the palace at Ramat Rahel (Photo 48).

Concerning the last chapter in the history of the First Temple, there is additional information from Hebrew inscriptions. It is clear that scribes and archives and royal administration were in existence throughout the monarchy, but most of the writing was done in ink on perishable materials, such as papyrus and vellum, which normally would not be preserved under regular conditions. Of course, people also wrote most of the time on potsherds (ostraca), but their ink could also be easily defaced. It may be that only in the last phase of the Judean monarchy did the use of that inexpensive writing material become widespread in routine royal administration (Photo 32). From the attractive and uniform script it is obvious that the letters and documents were written by professional scribes, which would explain why the palaeographic changes in the form of letters were general and

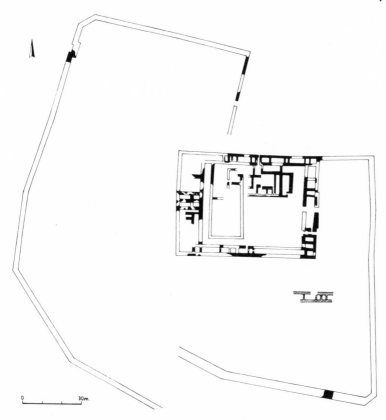

Fig. 88. Ramat Rahel. Plan of the fortress
(Shaded area represents the older stratum)

uniform in that cursive script, and are thus given to precise chronological definition. Nevertheless, there is some basis for the assumption that during the course of the seventh century the fundamental knowledge of reading and writing became common among a larger portion of the population. Private seals with the names of their owners, generally including the father's name, with or without the expression "son of," become widespread beginning with the eighth century. But in that period the name is generally accompanied by some decorative pattern, either of a kind borrowed from mythological decorations in the neighboring countries or of animals. Sometimes the images of animals are depicted in an impressive and realistic manner, as on the famous seal found at Megiddo with a roaring lion and the inscription "(Belonging) to Shema, the servant of Jeroboam"—that is, the seal of one of the ministers under Jeroboam II. In the seventh century the ornamentation disappears almost entirely. It is possible that this development represents the opposition to heathen decorations which grew steadily stronger from the reign of Hezekiah on. But the fact remains that henceforth the seals include only the name of the man and his father; thus, it must be assumed that the average person who saw such an inscription was able to decipher it.

An additional testimony is the increase in jars from the seventh century upon which the owners inscribed their names, usually after the vessel was fired, with the addition of the *lamed* preposition to indicate "(Belonging) to" someone. Not only is the writing style quite individualistic, but it also includes numerous errors. It is obvious, therefore, that these inscriptions were written by the owners of the vessels who had acquired at least a nominal standard of literacy.

The richest treasure of inscriptions was discovered at Arad. From them one learns about the royal storehouse at Arad and how it furnished provisions of bread and wine to various transients (Photo 33). Among those receiving rations are mentioned the Kittim, units of mercenaries of Greek origin who served in the Negeb fortresses. According to the quantities issued to them, these were bands of fifty or one hundred men (their numerical strength was not necessarily complete). Their rations were furnished for a certain number of days' march. From these figures one can deduce that along the Negeb routes in that period there were way stations at fixed distances of a certain number of days that were well known, usually about thirty kilometers, actually according to the contemporary practice in Mesopotamia.

The registration at Arad was precise, including the exact dates. One reads about an additional commodity that was in the warehouses, viz., oil, but it was not issued as travel rations; it was only sent in a sealed vessel to its destination.

The commander of Arad was responsible for the entire region and had to take care of the other fortresses in the vicinity with which he had daily communication. In one of the letters, he is even ordered to bring rations to Beer-sheba with the load of a pair of donkeys. Of course, the unfortified settlement, which seems to have been in some emergency situation, is intended.

A grave emergency is reflected in some of the letters. It turns out that the weakness of Judah in the struggle between Egypt and Babylon was exploited by the Edomites, who had always cast a longing eye on the Negeb in order to open up the trade route for themselves to the Mediterranean coast. One learns about this situation from one of the epistles of which was preserved only the latter part:

> . . . from Arad 50 and from Kinah . . . and you shall send them (to) Ramath-negeb by the hand of Malkiyahu the son of Qerab-'ur, and he shall hand them over to Elisha the son of Jeremiah in Ramath-negeb, lest anything should happen to the city. And the word of the king is incumbent upon you for your very life. Behold, I have sent to warn you today: (Get) the men to Elisha! Lest Edom should come there.

One does not know if the troops from Arad and neighboring Kinah were sent in time. But from the destruction level with which this letter must be associated, it would appear that the Edomites had swarmed into the entire Negeb, so that even Arad did not escape this fate.

No less dramatic are the Lachish letters which precede, only by a short time, the conquest of Jerusalem. In them, one hears about a prophet who went down to Egypt, as recorded in The Book of Jeremiah. A local commander writes in one of the epistles to the commander at Lachish: "We are on the lookout for the fire signals of Lachish because we do not see Azekah . . ." This text must have been written only a short time after the same instance described in the words of Jeremiah: "And the army of the king of Babylon was fighting against Jerusalem and against all of the cities of Judah that were left, Lachish and Azekah, because these were the only fortified cities of Judah that remained" (Jer. 34:7). The destruction in 587/6 B.C.E. was total. No place that has been examined in the Shephelah or in the hill country escaped its fate except Mizpah, to which the seat of government was transferred with the destruction of Jerusalem, a fact that assured its further existence for a number of years.

With this date—the destruction of the First Temple—a historical event and the archaeological break coincide in one clear-cut moment. An era had come to a close.

ABBREVIATIONS

AAA	*Annals of Archaeology and Anthropology*
AASOR	*The Annual of the American Schools of Oriental Research*
Abydos	Petrie, W. M. F. 1902–1903. *Abydos I–II.* London
Adeimeh	Stekelis, M. 1935. *Les Monuments mégalitiques de Palestine (Les Fouilles d'el Adeimeh).* Paris
AG I–IV	Petrie, W. M. F. 1931–1934. *Ancient Gaza I–IV.* London
AHL	Kenyon, Kathleen M. 1970. *Archaeology in the Holy Land.* (3d ed.) London
AJA	*American Journal of Archaeology*
APEF	*Annual of the Palestine Exploration Fund*
'Atiqot	*'Atiqot,* Journal of the Israel Department of Antiquities. (Hebrew and English Series)
'Ay	Marquet-Krause, Judith. 1949. *Les Fouilles de 'Ay (Et Tell), 1933–1935.* Paris
BA	*The Biblical Archaeologist*
BASOR	*Bulletin of the American Schools of Oriental Research*
Beer-Sheba I	Aharoni, Y., ed. 1973. *Beer-Sheba I. Excavations at Tel Beer-Sheba, 1969–1971 Seasons.* Tel Aviv
Beth-Shan I	Rowe, A. 1940. *The Four Canaanite Temples of Beth-Shan, I, The Temples and Cult Objects.* Philadelphia
Beth-Shemesh	Grant, E. 1929. *Beth-Shemesh.* Haverford
CAH	*The Cambridge Ancient History*
Carmel	Garrod, Dorothy A. E., and Bate, D. M. A. 1937. *The Stone Age of Mount Carmel.* Vol. I. Oxford
CPP	Duncan, J. G. 1930. *Corpus of Dated Palestinian Pottery.* London
DMT	Lapp, P. W. 1966. *The Dhahr Mirzbaneh Tombs.* New Haven
EI	*Eretz-Israel,* Archaeological, Historical, and Geographical Studies. Jerusalem. (Hebrew and English)
Enc. Arch. Exc.	*Encyclopaedia of Archaeological Excavations in the Holy Land.* 1975–1978. Jerusalem. (Hebrew and English)

Gezer III	Macalister, R. A. S. 1912. *The Excavation of Gezer III*. London
Gha I	Mallon, A.; Koeppel, R.; and Neuville, R. 1934. *Teleilat Ghassul I*. Rome
Gha II	Koeppel, R. 1940. *Teleilat Ghassul II*. Rome
Haz I–IV	Yadin, Y., *et al.* 1958, 1960, 1961. *Hazor I–IV*. Jerusalem
Hazor 1972	Yadin, Y. *Hazor.* (Schweich Lectures 1970.) London
IEJ	*Israel Exploration Journal*
IDAM	*Israel Department of Antiquities and Museums*
JAOS	*Journal of the American Oriental Society*
JARCE	*Journal of the American Research Center in Egypt*
Jer I	Kenyon, Kathleen M. 1960. *Excavations at Jericho, I: The Tombs Excavated in 1952–4.* London
JNES	*Journal of Near Eastern Studies*
JPOS	*The Journal of the Palestine Oriental Society*
Judée	Neuville, R. 1951. *Le Paléolithique et le Mésolithique du désert de Judée.* Paris
Lach	Tufnell, O.; Inge, C.; and Harding, L. 1940, 1953, 1958. *Lachish (Tell ed-Duweir), II, III, IV.* Oxford
Lach V	Aharoni, Y. 1975. *Lachish V. Investigations at Lachish. The Sanctuary and Residency.* Tel Aviv
Levant	Stubbings, F. H. 1951. *Mycenaean Pottery from the Levant.* Cambridge
Meg I	Lamon, R. S., and Shipton, G. M. 1939. *Megiddo I.* Chicago
Meg II	Loud, G. 1948. *Megiddo II.* Chicago
Meg T	Guy, P. L. O. 1938. *Megiddo Tombs.* Chicago
MJ (BS)	FitzGerald, G. M. 1935. "The Earliest Pottery of Beth-Shan." The Museum, *Journal* 24: 5–22
Munhata	Perrot, J. 1968. "La Préhistoire Palestinienne." *Supplément au Dictionnaire de la Bible.* Paris: 8:416–439
Negev	Rothenberg, B. 1973. *Zefunot Negev.* Ramat-Gan. (Hebrew)
PBI	*Pontifical Biblical Institute.* Jerusalem
PEQ	*Palestine Exploration Quarterly*
PMB	*Palestine Museum Bulletin*
QDAP	*The Quarterly of the Department of Antiquities in Palestine*
RB	*Revue Biblique*
RR I–II	Aharoni, Y. 1962–1964. *Excavations at Ramat Rahel.* Rome
Sam I–III	Crowfoot, J. M.; Kenyon, K. M.; and Sukenik, E. L. 1938, 1942, 1957. *Samaria-Sebaste, I–III.* London
Shiloh	Buhll, Marie-Louise, and Nielson, S. H. *Shiloh.* 1969. Copenhagen
TA	*Journal of the Tel Aviv University Institute of Archaeology*
TAH	Hamilton, R. M. 1935. "Excavations at Tell Abu Hawam." *QDAP* 4:1–69
TBM I–III	Albright, W. F. 1932, 1933, 1938, 1943. *The Excavation of Tell Beit Mirsim,* I, IA, II, III, in *AASOR* XII, XIII (pp. 55–127), XVII, XXIII

Timna	Rothenberg, B. 1972. *Timna.* Aylesbury
Ubeidiya	Stekelis, M.; Bar-Yoseph, O.; and Schick, Tamar. 1969. *Archaeological Excavation at Ubeidiya 1964–1966.* Jerusalem
Upper Galilee	Aharoni, Y. 1957. *The Settlement of the Israelite Tribes in Upper Galilee.* Jerusalem. (Hebrew)
VT	*Vetus Testamentum*
Yarmuk	Stekelis, M. 1972. *The Yarmukian Culture.* Jerusalem
ZDPV	*Zeitschrift des Deutschen Palästina-Vereins*

LIST OF FLINT TOOLS AND POTTERY

DESCRIPTION	SOURCE	REFERENCE

Plate 1. LOWER PALEOLITHIC FLINT TOOLS   Page 15

1. Choppers	'Ubeidiyah	*Ubeidiya*, Pl. 5:4
2–3. Racloirs	Tabun	*Carmel*, Pl. 45:2, 10
4. Hand tool	Tabun	*Carmel*, Pl. 43:1
5. Hand tool	Tabun	*Carmel*, Pl. 43:4
6. Hand tool	Tabun	*Carmel*, Pl. 46:4

Plate 2. MIDDLE PALEOLITHIC FLINT TOOLS   Page 17

1. Mousterian point	Abu Zif	*Judée*, Fig. 22:7
2. Levalloisian point	Abu Zif	*Judée*, Fig. 22:1
3. Mousterian point	Tabun	*Carmel*, Pl. 34:3
4. Levalloisian blade	Tabun	*Carmel*, Pl. 34:4
5. Racloir	Tabun	*Carmel*, Pl. 34:5
6. Double racloir	Tabun	*Carmel*, Pl. 34:7
7. Double racloir	Tabun	*Carmel*, Pl. 34:1

Plate 3. UPPER PALEOLITHIC FLINT TOOLS   Page 19

1–6. Scrapers	el-Wad	*Carmel*, Pl. 24:1, 2, 6, 9, 10, 13
8–9. Burins	el-Wad	*Carmel*, Pl. 20:4, 7, 1

Plate 4. EPIPALEOLITHIC FLINT TOOLS   Page 21

1–6. Crescents	el-Wad	*Carmel*, Pl. 8:14, 19, 15, 16, 17, 18
7–9. Triangles	el-Wad	*Carmel*, Pl. 8:20, 21, 22
10. Triangle	el-Wad	*Carmel*, Pl. 9:30
11. Trapezoid	el-Wad	*Carmel*, Pl. 9:31

DESCRIPTION	SOURCE	REFERENCE
12–14. Awls	el-Wad	*Carmel,* Pl. 8:28, 29, 30
15–21. Bladelets	el-Wad	*Carmel,* Pl. 9:37, 38, 40, 41, 22, 43; Pl. 8:24
22–25. Sickle blades	el-Wad	*Carmel,* Pl.9:15,16,17,18

Plate 5. NEOLITHIC FLINT TOOLS   Page 26

1–3. Crenellated blades	Sha'ar ha-Golan	*Yarmuk,* Pl. 21:23, 7, 12
4–6. Arrowheads	Sha'ar ha-Golan	*Yarmuk,* Pl. 23:4, 18, 3
7. Ax	Sha'ar ha-Golan	*Yarmuk,* Pl. 13:5
8. Borer	Sha'ar ha-Golan	*Yarmuk,* Pl. 32:9

Plate 6. NEOLITHIC POTTERY   Page 33

1. Bowl	Munhata	*Munhata,* Fig. 845
2. Storage jar	Munhata	*Munhata,* Fig. 845
3. Krater	Munhata	*Munhata,* Fig. 845
4. Bowl	Munhata	*Munhata,* Fig. 845
5. Bowl	Munhata	*Munhata,* Fig. 845
6. Bowl	Munhata	*Munhata,* Fig. 845
7. Chalice	Munhata	*Munhata,* Fig. 845
8. Chalice	Munhata	*Munhata,* Fig. 845
9. Bowl	Jericho	*AHL,* Fig. 4:7
10. Bowl	Jericho	*AHL,* Fig. 4:8
11. Bowl	Jericho	*AHL,* Fig. 4:6
12. Hole-mouth jar	Jericho	*AHL,* Fig. 4:10
13. Cup	Munhata	*Munhata,* Fig. 845
14. Storage jar	Munhata	*Munhata,* Fig. 845
15. Hole-mouth jar	Munhata	*Munhata,* Fig. 845

Plate 7. CHALCOLITHIC POTTERY   Page 38

1. Bowl	Teleilat Ghassul	*PBI*
2. Bowl	Teleilat Ghassul	*Gha II,* Pl. 77:3
3. Bowl	Safadi	*IEJ* 6, Fig. 8:17
4. Hole-mouth jar	Abu Matar	*IEJ* 6, Fig. 3:9
5. Bowl	Teleilat Ghassul	*Gha II,* Pl. 96:2
6. Krater	Abu Raqiq	*IEJ* 6, Fig. 7:4
7. Chalice	Teleilat Ghassul	*PBI*
8. Goblet	Adeimeh	*Adeimeh,* Fig. 19:q
9. Goblet	Teleilat Ghassul	*Levant* 1, Fig. 6:9
10. Cornet	Teleilat Ghassul	*Gha II,* Pl. 76:16
11. Spoon	Teleilat Ghassul	*PBI*
12. Storage jar	Teleilat Ghassul	*Levant* 1, Fig. 6:6
13. Churn	Horvat Beter	*'Atiqot* 2, Fig. 16:1

DESCRIPTION　　　　　　　SOURCE　　　　　　REFERENCE

Plate 8. CHALCOLITHIC POTTERY　Page 41

1. Storage jar	Teleilat Ghassul	*Gha II*, Pl. 78:9
2. Storage jar	Safadi	*IEJ* 6, Fig. 11:1
3. Hole-mouth jar	Abu Matar	*IEJ* 6, Fig. 3:8
4. Storage jar	Teleilat Ghassul	*Gha II*, Pl. 77:7
5. Hole-mouth jar	Teleilat Ghassul	*Gha II*, 96:5
6. Storage jar	Teleilat Ghassul	*Gha I*, Fig. 50:5
7. Storage jar	Abu Matar	*IEJ* 6, Fig. 5:4
8. Hole-mouth jar	Abu Raqiq	*IEJ* 6, Fig. 2:10
9. Pithos	Teleilat Ghassul	*Gha I*, Fig. 53

Plate 9. POTTERY OF EARLY CANAANITE I　Page 53

1. Bowl	Far'ah (North)	*RB* 59, Fig. 12:13
2. Bowl	Far'ah (North)	*RB* 59, Fig. 11:11
3. Bowl	Far'ah (North)	*RB* 59, Fig. 12:9
4. Hole-mouth jar	Far'ah (North)	*RB* 59, Fig. 8:6
5. Storage jar, small	Megiddo	*Meg T*, Pl. 3:7
6. Storage jar, small	Far'ah (North)	*RB* 56, Fig. 1:21
7. Bowl	Far'ah (North)	*RB* 52, Fig. 3:1
8. Spouted jug	Asawir	*IDAM*, No. 53–537
9. Storage jar, small	Far'ah (North)	*RB* 56, Fig. 8:28
10. Storage jar, small	Far'ah (North)	*RB* 59, Fig. 11:20
11. Juglet	Asawir	*IDAM*, No. 53–540
12. Storage jar	Far'ah (North)	*RB* 56, Fig. 2:8
13. Chalice	Far'ah (North)	*RB* 56, Fig. 2:4
14. Bowl	'Afula	*JPOS* 21, Pl. 2:1
15. Bowl	Far'ah (North)	*RB* 56, Fig. 2:8
16. Bowl	'Afula	*JPOS* 21, Pl. 12:2
17. Storage jar	Ai	*'Ay*, Pl. 73:927
18. Juglet	Ai	*'Ay*, Pl. 72:870
19. Double juglet	Ophel	*PMB* 3, Pl. 4:10
20. Jug	Ai	*'Ay*, Pl. 67:7.587
21. Bowl	Ai	*'Ay*, Pl. 72:828
22. Storage jar	Ai	*'Ay*, Pl. 73:933
23. Hole-mouth jar	Far'ah (North)	*RB* 54, Fig. 3:1
24. Storage jar	'Afula	*JPOS* 21, Pl. 5:1

Plate 10. POTTERY OF EARLY CANAANITE II–III　Page 68

1. Bowl	Far'ah (North)	*RB* 55, Fig. 8:6
2. Bowl	Beth-yerah	*IDAM*
3. Bowl	Beth-shean	*MJ (BS)*, Pl. 5:22

DESCRIPTION	SOURCE	REFERENCE
4. Bowl	Megiddo	*Meg II*, Pl. 5:19
5. Jug	Jericho	*AAA* 23, Pl. 39:13
6. Jug	Jericho	*Jer I*, Fig. 25:34
7. Jar	Far'ah (North)	*RB* 55, Fig. 8:10
8. Jug	Abydos	*Abydos I*, Pl. 8:4
9. Jug	Megiddo	*Meg II*, Pl. 5:1
10. Jar	Far'ah (North)	*RB* 54, Fig. 6:6
11. Hole-mouth jar	Far'ah (North)	*RB* 54, Fig. 6:8
12. Jar	Beth-yerah	*IDAM*
13. Pithos	Far'ah (North)	*RB* 55, Fig. 7:3

Plate 11. POTTERY OF EARLY CANAANITE II–III   Page 70

1. Bowl	Jericho	*AAA* 19, Pl. 2:25
2. Storage jar	Ai	*'Ay*, Pl. 65:26.1503
3. Hole-mouth jar	Ai	*'Ay*, Pl. 65:23.1510
4. Chalice	Beth-shean	*MJ (BS)*, Pl. 8:6
5. Storage jar	Beth-yerah	*IDAM*
6. Lid	Beth-shean	*MJ (BS)*, Pl. 10:4
7. Goblet	Ai	*'Ay*, Pl. 65:1562
8. Bowl	Beth-shean	*MJ (BS)*, Pl. 8:4
9. Bowl	Ai	*'Ay*, Pl. 65:1519
10. Krater	Beth-shean	*MJ (BS)*, Pl. 7:6
11. Krater	Beth-yerah	*IDAM*

Plate 12. POTTERY OF EARLY CANAANITE IV (After Thomas Schaub)   Page 72

1. Bowl	Bab edh-Dhra'	*BASOR* 210, Fig. 6:12
2. Bowl	Bab edh-Dhra'	*BASOR* 210, Fig. 7:18
3. Bowl	Bab edh-Dhra'	*BASOR* 210, Fig. 7:19
4. Lamp	Bab edh-Dhra'	*BASOR* 210, Fig. 8:26
5. Jug	Bab edh-Dhra'	*BASOR* 210, Fig. 6:5
6. Bowl	Bab edh-Dhra'	*BASOR* 210, Fig. 6:8
7. Bowl	Bab edh-Dhra'	*BASOR* 210, Fig. 7:20
8. Goblet	Bab edh-Dhra'	*BASOR* 210, Fig. 6:9
9. Jug	Bab edh-Dhra'	*BASOR* 210, Fig. 6:10
10. Jug	Bab edh-Dhra'	*BASOR* 210, Fig. 6:11
11. Storage jar	Bab edh-Dhra'	*BASOR* 210, Fig. 7:21

Plate 13. POTTERY OF MIDDLE CANAANITE I   Page 82

1. Teapot	Ma'ayan Barukh	*'Atiqot* 3, Fig. 5:8
2. Teapot	Megiddo	*IDAM*, No. 55-14
3. Teapot	Megiddo	*Meg T*, Pl. 11:30
4. Teapot	Ma'ayan Barukh	*'Atiqot* 3, Fig. 6:4
5. Bowl	Megiddo	*Meg T*, Pl. 22:10

DESCRIPTION	SOURCE	REFERENCE
6. Jug	Megiddo	*Meg T*, Pl. 21:8
7. Teapot	Megiddo	*Meg T*, Pl. 12:3
8. Goblet	Ma'ayan Barukh	*'Atiqot* 3, Fig. 6:7
9. Goblet	Megiddo	*Meg T*, Pl. 22:19
10. Jug	Megiddo	*Meg T*, Pl. 22:7
11. Teapot	Megiddo	*Meg T*, Pl. 10:5
12. Lamp	el-Husn (Transjordan)	*APEF* 6, Fig. 1:1
13. Storage jar	Ma'ayan Barukh	*'Atiqot* 3, Fig. 5:3
14. Storage jar	Megiddo	*Meg T*, Pl. 10:10
15. Storage jar	Megiddo	*'Atiqot* 3, Fig. 7:15
16. Storage jar	Ma'ayan Barukh	*Meg T*, Pl. 21:10
17. Storage jar	Ma'ayan Barukh	*'Atiqot* 3, Fig. 6:2

Plate 14. POTTERY OF MIDDLE CANAANITE I   Page 88

1. Lamp	Dhahr Mirzbaneh	*DMT*, Fig. 15:4
2. Jug	Dhahr Mirzbaneh	*DMT*, Fig. 24:7
3. Storage jar	Dhahr Mirzbaneh	*DMT*, Fig. 6:4
4. Jug	Dhahr Mirzbaneh	*DMT*, Fig. 13:12
5. Bowl	Benaya	*IDAM*, No. 57-542
6. Goblet	el-Kirmil	*EI* 12, Fig. 5:20
7. Goblet	Lachish	*Lach IV*, Pl. 66:409
8. Lamp	Lachish	*Lach IV*, Pl. 66:399
9. Teapot	el-Kirmil	*EI* 12, Fig. 5:1
10. Teapot	Lachish	*Lach IV*, Pl. 67:455
11. Jug	Tell Beit Mirsim	*TBM IA*, Pl. 3:10
12. Storage jar	Lachish	*Lach IV*, Pl. 67:459
13. Storage jar	Lachish	*Lach IV*, Pl. 67:482
14. Storage jar	Tell Beit Mirsim	*TBM IA*, Pl. 2:1

Plate 15. POTTERY OF MIDDLE CANAANITE IIA   Page 96

1. Bowl	Aphek	*TA* 2, Fig. 9:6
2. Bowl	Megiddo	*Meg II*, Pl. 9:3
3. Bowl	Megiddo	*Meg T*, Pl. 31:3
4. Bowl	Aphek	*TA* 2, Fig. 14:5
5. Bowl	Aphek	*TA* 2, Fig. 10:4
6. Cooking pot	Megiddo	*Meg II*, Pl. 9:19
7. Jug	Aphek	*TA* 2, Fig. 15:6
8. Juglet	Aphek	*TA* 2, Fig. 15:7
9. Juglet	Aphek	*TA* 2, Fig. 15:8
10. Jug	Aphek	*TA* 2, Fig. 12:4
11. Jug	Megiddo	*Meg II*, Pl. 23:18
12. Jug	Aphek	*TA* 2, Fig. 10:8
13. Juglet	Aphek	*TA* 2, Fig. 9:4

DESCRIPTION	SOURCE	REFERENCE
14. Juglet	Aphek	*TA* 2, Fig. 14:7
15. Juglet	Aphek	*TA* 2, Fig. 12:7
16. Jug	Megiddo	*Meg II*, Pl. 10:8
17. Jug	Megiddo	*Meg II*, Pl. 13:5
18. Storage jar	Aphek	*TA* 2, Fig. 10:10
19. Storage jar	Aphek	*TA* 2, Fig. 1:4
20. Storage jar	Aphek	*TA* 2, Fig. 15:9
21. Storage jar	Aphek	*TA* 2, Fig. 14:4

Plate 16. POTTERY OF MIDDLE CANAANITE IIB–C   Page 98

1. Bowl	Megiddo	*Meg II*, Pl. 29:25
2. Bowl	Megiddo	*Meg II*, Pl. 36:22
3. Bowl	Megiddo	*Meg II*, Pl. 37:9
4. Cooking pot	Megiddo	*Meg II*, Pl. 30:3
5. Cooking pot	Megiddo	*Meg II*, Pl. 46:6
6. Cooking pot	Tell Beit Mirsim	*TBM IA*, Pl. 13:4
7. Krater	Ginossar	*IDAM*, No. 847
8. Jug	Megiddo	*Meg T*, Pl. 24:10
9. Juglet	Megiddo	*Meg II*, Pl. 26:10
10. Jug	Megiddo	*Meg II*, Pl. 23:2
11. Bowl	Tell Beit Mirsim	*TBM IA*, Pl. 7:13
12. Storage jar	Megiddo	*Meg II*, Pl. 27:3
13. Storage jar	Tell Beit Mirsim	*TBM IA*, Pl. 6:1
14. Storage jar	Megiddo	*Meg II*, Pl. 27:8

Plate 17. TELL EL-YEHUDIYEH WARE FROM MIDDLE CANAANITE IIB   Page 105

1. Zoomorphic vessel	Megiddo	*Meg II*, Pl. 247:1
2. Jug	Lachish	*Lach IV*, Pl. 77:750
3. Jug	Lachish	*Lach IV*, Pl. 77:728
4. Jug	Megiddo	*Meg II*, Pl. 24:32
5. Jug	Megiddo	*Meg II*, Pl. 32:31
6. Jug	Megiddo	*Meg II*, Pl. 32:32
7. Jug	Megiddo	*Meg II*, Pl. 24:31
8. Jug	Megiddo	*Meg T*, Pl. 23:23

Plate 18. CYPRIOT WARE FROM MIDDLE CANAANITE IIC   Page 112

1. Jug	Megiddo	*Meg II*, Pl. 26:14
2. Jug	Megiddo	*Meg II*, Pl. 26:16
3. Jug	Megiddo	*Meg II*, Pl. 34:4

Plate 19. BICHROME WARE FROM LATE CANAANITE I   Page 113

1. Jug	Megiddo	*Meg T*, Pl. 48:3
2. Jug	Tell el-'Ajjul	*AG IV*, Pl. 56:1517

DESCRIPTION	SOURCE	REFERENCE
3. Jug	Megiddo	*Meg II*, Pl. 51:6
4. Krater	Tel Nagila	*IEJ* 14, Fig. 2
5. Krater	Lachish	*Lach II*, Pl. 49:256

Plate 20. POTTERY OF LATE CANAANITE I   Page 116

1. Storage jar	Megiddo	*Meg II*, Pl. 60:2
2. Bowl	Hazor	*Haz II*, Pl. 129:7
3. Cooking pot	Hazor	*Haz I*, Pl. 107:7
4. Lamp	Megiddo	*Meg II*, Pl. 62:4
5. Chalice	Megiddo	*Meg II*, Pl. 72:3
6. Flask	Megiddo	*Meg T*, Pl. 34:13
7. Chalice	Lachish	*Lach II*, Pl. 47:223
8. Jug	Megiddo	*Meg T*, Pl. 134
9. Chalice	Megiddo	*Meg II*, Pl. 62:8

Plate 21. CYPRIOT WARE FROM LATE CANAANITE I   Page 117

1. Cypriot milk bowl	Lachish	*Lach IV*, Pl. 79:835
2. Cypriot milk bowl	Lachish	*Lach IV*, Pl. 79:833
3. Jug	Gezer	*Gezer III*, Pl. 74:3
4. Jug	Lachish	*Lach IV*, Pl. 80:850
5. Jug	Lachish	*Lach IV*, Pl. 80:851
6. Bowl	Lachish	*Lach IV*, Pl. 81:870
7. Jug (bilbil)	Lachish	*Lach IV*, Pl. 80:845
8. Jug (bilbil)	Lachish	*Lach IV*, Pl. 80:866
9. Jug (bilbil)	Lachish	*Lach IV*, Pl. 80:863
10. Jug (bilbil)	Lachish	*Lach IV*, Pl. 80:842

Plate 22. MYCENAEAN WARE FROM LATE CANAANITE I   Page 118

1. Pyxis	Beth-shemesh	*Beth-Shemesh*, 189:508
2. Pyxis	Lachish	*Lach IV*, Pl. 83:947
3. Pyxis	Beth-shemesh	*PMB* 3, Pl. 7:6
4. Mycenaean jug	Lachish	*Lach IV*, Pl. 83:945
5. Jug	Lachish	*Lach IV*, Pl. 83:948
6. Mycenaean jug	Lachish	*Lach IV*, Pl. 83:946

Plate 23. Nos. 1–10, "Midianite" Ware; Nos. 11–14, Negeb Cooking Pots. From the End of the Late Canaanite Period (Thirteenth Century B.C.E.)   Page 138

1. Bowl	Timna	*Negev*, Pl. XII
2. Bowl	Timna	*Negev*, Pl. XII
3. Bowl	Timna	*Negev*, Pl. XII
4. Bowl	Timna	*Negev*, Pl. XII

DESCRIPTION	SOURCE	REFERENCE
5. Bowl	Timna	*Negev*, Pl. XII
6. Small bowl	Timna	*Negev*, Pl. XII
7. Bowl	Timna	*Negev*, Pl. XII
8. Bowl	Timna	*Negev*, Pl. XII
9. Jug	Timna	*Negev*, Pl. XII
10. Jug	Timna	*Negev*, Pl. XII
11. Cooking pot	Timna	*Negev*, Pl. XIV
12. Cooking pot	Timna	*Negev*, Pl. XIV
13. Cooking pot	Timna	*Timna*, Fig. 31:1
14. Cooking pot	Timna	*Timna*, Fig. 31:2

Plate 24. POTTERY OF ISRAELITE I   Page 165

1. Storage jar	Tel Masos	*TA* 2, Pl. 23:1
2. Jug	Tel Masos	*TA* 2, Pl. 23:2
3. Jug	Tell Abu Huwam	*TAH* 4, Pl. 14:152
4. Jug	Tell Abu Huwam	*TAH* 4, Pl. 14:158

Plate 24A. DECORATED MIDIANITE SHERDS   Page 166

Midianite sherds	Tel Masos	*TA* 2, Pl. 23:3

Plate 25. POTTERY OF ISRAELITE I   Page 173

1. Cooking pot	Isdar	*'Atiqot* 5, Fig. 14:1
2. Chalice	Isdar	*'Atiqot* 5, Fig. 12:7
3. Storage jar	Isdar	*'Atiqot* 5, Fig. 13:9
4. Jug	Isdar	*'Atiqot* 5, Fig. 14:4
5. Lamp	Isdar	*'Atiqot* 5, Fig. 12:10

Plate 26. POTTERY OF ISRAELITE I   Page 175

1. Cooking pot	Megiddo	*Meg II*, Pl. 85:16
2. Cooking pot	Tel Harashim	*Upper Galilee*, Fig. 5:19
3. Storage jar	Tel Harashim	*Upper Galilee*, Fig. 4:4
4. Storage jar	Megiddo	*Meg II*, Pl. 83:4

Plate 27. POTTERY OF ISRAELITE I   Page 176

1. Storage jar	Shiloh	*Shiloh*, Pl. 15:186
2. Storage jar	Shiloh	*Shiloh*, Pl. 15:187

Plate 28. PHILISTINE POTTERY FROM ISRAELITE I   Page 182

1. Bowl	Beth-shemesh	*Beth-Shemesh III*, Fig. 2:20
2. Bowl	Ashkelon	*PMB* 4, Pl. 1:3
3. Bowl	Gezer	*Gezer III*, Pl. 163:1

DESCRIPTION	SOURCE	REFERENCE
4. Stirrup jar	Gezer	*CPP* 64 R2
5. Krater	Gezer	*Gezer III*, Pl. 158:1
6. Jug	es-Safi	*PMB* 4, Pl. 2:4
7. Jug	Megiddo	*Meg II*, Pl. 75:22

Plate 29. POTTERY OF ISRAELITE IIA (Tenth–Ninth Centuries B.C.E.)   Page 240

1. Bowl	Hazor	*Haz II*, Pl. 53:17
2. Bowl	Beer-sheba	*TA* 2, Fig. 5:5
3. Bowl	Lachish	*Lach III*, Pl. 99:592
4. Bowl	Megiddo	*Meg II*, Pl. 84:18
5. Bowl	Hazor	*Haz II*, Pl. 51:1
6. Bowl	Samaria	*Sam III*, Fig. 19:3
7. Bowl	Tell Beit Mirsim	*TBM I*, Pl. 51:14
8. Juglet	Beer-sheba	*TA* 2, Fig. 5:12
9. Storage jar	Hazor	*Haz II*, Pl. 60:6
10. Storage jar	Megiddo	*Meg I*, Pl. 20:119
11. Storage jar	Beer-sheba	*TA* 2, Fig. 6:7

Plate 30. POTTERY OF ISRAELITE IIB   Page 265

1. Bowl	Beer-sheba	*BASOR* 224, Fig. 4:1
2. Bowl	Beer-sheba	*Beer-Sheba I*, Pl. 64:8
3. Cooking pot	Beer-sheba	*Beer-Sheba I*, Pl. 70:18
4. Cooking pot	Beer-sheba	*Beer-Sheba I*, Pl. 70:10
5. Storage jar	Beer-sheba	*Beer-Sheba I*, Pl. 74:6
6. Storage jar	Beer-sheba	*BASOR* 224, Fig. 4:6
7. Storage jar	Beer-sheba	*BASOR* 224, Fig. 4:7
8. Hole-mouth jar	Beer-sheba	*Beer-Sheba I*, Pl. 58:26
9. Storage jar	Beer-sheba	*Beer-Sheba I*, Pl. 65:2
10. Storage jar	Beer-sheba	*Beer-Sheba I*, Pl. 58:30
11. Jug	Beer-sheba	*Beer-Sheba I*, Pl. 72:17
12. Jug	Beer-sheba	*Beer-Sheba I*, Pl. 62:17
13. Decanter	Beer-sheba	*Beer-Sheba I*, Pl. 64:17
14. Juglet	Beer-sheba	*Beer-Sheba I*, Pl. 69:17
15. Juglet	Beer-sheba	*BASOR* 224, Fig. 4:15
16. Juglet	Beer-sheba	*Beer-Sheba I*, Pl. 66:15
17. Lamp	Beer-sheba	*BASOR* 224, Fig. 7:14

Plate 31. POTTERY OF ISRAELITE IIC   Page 267

1. Bowl	Arad	*BASOR* 224, Fig. 7:2
2. Bowl	Lachish	*Lach V*, Pl. 47:13
3. Bowl	Lachish	*Lach V*, Pl. 47:14
4. Lamp	Lachish	*Lach V*, Pl. 48:3

DESCRIPTION	SOURCE	REFERENCE
5. Cooking pot	Lachish	*Lach V*, Pl. 47:21
6. Cooking pot	Lachish	*Lach V*, Pl. 47:19
7. Decanter	Lachish	*Lach V*, Pl. 55, Type Dec.
8. Decanter	Lachish	*Lach V*, Pl. 48:13
9. Storage jar	Tel Masos	*BASOR* 224, Fig. 8:5

SOURCES OF FIGURES

1. Map of Neolithic and Chalcolithic sites.
2. Kenyon, Kathleen M. 1960. "Excavation at Jericho." *PEQ* 92: Fig. 2.
3. Garstang, J. 1940. *The Story of Jericho.* London: Fig. 5.
4. Koeppel, R. 1940. *Teleilat Ghassul I.* Rome: Fig. 12.
5. Ussishkin, D. 1971. "The Ghassulian Temple in Ein Gedi and the Origin of the Hoard from Nahal Mishmar." *BA* 34: Fig. 12.
6. Map of sites from the Early Canaanite period.
7. Dothan, M. 1959. "Excavations at Meser." 1957. *IEJ* 9: Fig. 2.
8. Amiran, Ruth. 1975. "Arad." *Enc. Arch. Exc.* 1:77. (English)
9. Y. Aharoni, from plan in the Institute of Archaeology, Tel Aviv University.
10. Mazar, B.; Stekelis, M.; and Avi-Yonah, M. 1952. "The Excavations at Beth Yerah." *IEJ* 2: Fig. 3.
11. de Vaux, A. 1962. "Les Fouilles de Tell el Far'ah." *RB* 69: P. 20.
12. Marquet-Krause, Judith. 1949. *Les Fouilles de 'Ay (Et-Tell), 1933–1935.* Paris: P. 42.
13. *Meg II:* Fig. 390.
14. Ibid.: Fig. 394.
15. Ibid.: Fig. 394.
16. Kochavi, M. 1967. *The Settlement of the Negev in the Middle Bronze (Canaanite) I Age.* Ph.D. Dissertation. Jerusalem: Fig. 3. (Hebrew)
17. Ibid.: Fig. 18.
18. Map of Middle Canaanite sites.
19. *Hazor 1972:* Fig. 3.
20. *Meg II:* Fig. 378.
21. *Hazor 1972:* Fig. 13.
22. *Meg II:* Fig. 378.
23. *Meg II:* Fig. 378.
24. Albright, W. F. 1938. "TBM II. The Bronze Age." *AASOR* 17: Pl. 55.
25. Dothan, M. 1956. "The Sacrificial Mound at Nahariya." *EI* 4: Fig. I. (Hebrew)
26. *Meg II:* Fig. 247.

27. Sellin, E. 1926. "Die Ausgrabung von Sichem." *ZDPV* 49: Pl. 33.
28. Map of Late Canaanite sites.
29. *Beth-Shan I*: Pl. 6.
30. Ibid.: Pl. 8.
31. Ibid.: Pls. 10–12.
32. *Hazor 1972:* Figs. 18–19.
33. *Hazor 1972:* Figs. 20–21.
34. *Haz I:* Fig. 181.
35. *Hazor 1972:* Fig. 26.
36. Tufnell, Olga, et al. 1940. *Lachish II, The Fosse Temple.* London: Pls. 66–68.
37. Fritz, V. 1971. "Erwägungen zu dem spätbronzezeitlichen Quadratbau bei Amman." *ZDPV* 87: Abb. 2.
37a. Hennessy, J. B. 1966. "Excavation of a Late Bronze Age Temple at Amman." *PEQ* 98: Fig. 2.
38. James, Frances W. 1966. *The Iron Age at Beth-Shan.* Philadelphia: Fig. 77.
39. Petrie, W. M. F., and Tufnell, Olga. 1930. *Beth Peleth II.* London: Fig. 69.
40. Rothenberg, B. 1972. *Timna.* Aylesbury: Fig. 41.
41. *Meg II:* Fig. 411.
42. Ibid.: Fig. 381.
43. Ibid.: Fig. 382.
44. *Meg II:* Fig. 383.
45. Ibid.: Fig. 384.
46. Development of the early Hebrew alphabet.
46a. The Ugaritic alphabet, after A. F. Rainey, *Quadmoniot* 1.
46b. Egyptian hieroglyphic signs, after A. Gardiner.
47. Map of sites from the Israelite period.
48. Y. Aharoni, from plans in the Institute of Archaeology, Tel Aviv University.
49. Y. Aharoni, as above.
50. Y. Aharoni, as above.
51. Y. Aharoni, as above.
52. Evenari, M.; Aharoni, Y.; Shanan, L.; and Tadmore, N. H. 1958. "The Ancient Desert Agriculture of the Negev." *IEJ* 8:256: Fig. 5.
53. Cohen, R. 1970. "Atar ha-Ro'eh" *'Atiqot* 6: Fig. 6. (Hebrew)
54. Kochavi, M. 1969. "Excavation at Tell Esdar." *'Atiqot* 5: Fig. 1. (Hebrew)
55. Mazar, A. 1975. "Excavations at Tell Qasile, 1973–1974." *IEJ* 25: Fig. 1.
56. Sinclair, L. A. "An Archaeological Study of Gibea (Tell el-Ful)." *AASOR* 4: Pl. 22.
57. Avigad, N. 1972. "Excavations in the Jewish Quarter of the Old City." *Quadmoniot* 5:94. (Hebrew)
58. Herzog, Z. 1976. *The City Gate in Eretz-Israel and Its Neighboring Countries.* Tel Aviv. Ph.D. Dissertation. Drawings 81, 82, 83.
59. Seger, J. D. 1975. "The MB II Fortifications at Sechem and Gezer," *EI* 12: Fig. 4.

60. Yadin, Y. 1976. "Hazor," *Enc. Arch. Exc.* II:492. (English)
61. Y. Aharoni, from plans in the Institute of Archaeology, Tel Aviv University.
62. As above.
63. Nauman, R. 1971. *Architektur Kleinasiens.* Tübingen: Fig. 553.
64. Y. Aharoni, from plans in the Institute of Archaeology, Tel Aviv University.
65. *Meg II:* Fig. 389.
66. Y. Aharoni. 1974. "The Building Activities of David and Solomon." *IEJ* 24: Fig. 1, p. 14.
67. Shiloh, Y. 1974. *Outside Influences on the Architecture of Eretz-Israel in the Tenth–Ninth Centuries B.C.E.* Jerusalem. Ph.D. Dissertation: 81C.
68. Y. Aharoni, from plans in the Institute of Archaeology, Tel Aviv University.
69. de Vaux, R. 1955. "Les Fouilles de Tell el Far'ah." *RB* 63: Pl. 6.
70. Y. Aharoni, from plans in the Institute of Archaeology, Tel Aviv University.
71. Y. Aharoni, as above.
72. Haines, R. C. 1971. *Excavations in the Plain of Antioch II.* Chicago: Pls. 102–103.
73. Y. Aharoni, from plans in the Institute of Archaeology, Tel Aviv University.
74. Lamon, R. 1935. *The Megiddo Water System.* Chicago: Fig. 2.
75. *Hazor 1972:* Fig. 27.
76. McCown, C. 1947. *Tell en-Nasbeh I:* After the Survey map.
77. Y. Aharoni, from plans in the Institute of Archaeology, Tel Aviv University.
78. Glueck, N. 1965. "Ezion Geber." *BA* 28: Fig. 9.
79. *Meg I:* Fig. 89.
80. *Lach V:* Fig. 9.
81. *Hazor 1972:* Fig. 54.
82. *Sam I:* Pl. 2.
83. *TBM III:* Pl. 47.
84. *Lach III:* Pl. 119.
85. Petrie, W. M. F. 1928. *Gerar.* London: Pl. 11.
86. *Meg I:* Fig. 95.
87. Y. Aharoni, from plans in the Institute of Archaeology, Tel Aviv University.
88. Y. Aharoni. 1964. *RR II:* Pl. 6.

SELECT BIBLIOGRAPHY

Aharoni, Y. 1957. *The Settlement of the Israelite Tribes in Upper Galilee.* Ph.D. Dissertation. Jerusalem. (Hebrew)

Aharoni, Y. 1966. "Entry to Exile." *Apud* Ben Gurion, D., ed. *The Jews in Their Land.* London: 8–67.

Aharoni, Y. 1972. "The Stratification of Israelite Megiddo." *JNES* 31:302–311.

Aharoni, Y. 1979. *The Land of the Bible.* (Revised ed.) Philadelphia.

Aharoni, Y., and Amiran, Ruth. 1958. "A New Scheme for the Sub-Division of the Iron Age in Palestine." *IEJ* 8:171–184.

Aharoni, Y., and Avi-Yonah, M. 1977. *Macmillan Bible Atlas.* (Revised ed.) New York.

Albright, W. F. 1942. "A Case of Lèse-Majesté in Pre-Israelite Lachish, with Some Remarks on the Israelite Conquest." *BASOR* 87:32–38.

Albright, W. F. 1943. "A Tablet of the Amarna Age from Gezer." *BASOR* 92:28–30.

Albright, W. F. 1944. "A Prince of Taanach in the Fifteenth Century B.C." *BASOR* 94:12–27.

Albright, W. F. 1956. *Recent Discoveries in Bible Lands.* (Reprinted with additions.) Pittsburgh.

Albright, W. F. 1957. *From the Stone Age to Christianity.* (2d ed.) Baltimore.

Albright, W. F. 1961. "Abraham the Hebrew; A New Archaeological Interpretation." *BASOR* 163:36–54.

Albright, W. F. 1963. *The Archaeology of Palestine.* (Revised ed.) London.

Albright, W. F. 1964. *The Biblical Period, From Abraham to Ezra.* New York.

Albright, W. F. 1967. *Yahweh and the Gods of Canaan.* London.

Alt, A. 1953–1959. *Kleine Schriften zur Geschichte des Volkes Israel I–III.* Munich.

Amiran, Ruth. 1967. *Ancient Pottery of the Holy Land.* Tel Aviv.

Anati, E. 1963. *Palestine Before the Hebrews.* London.

Avi-Yonah, M., and Stern, E., eds. 1975–1978. *Encyclopaedia of Archaeological Excavations in the Holy Land.* Jerusalem: 4 vols.

Bar-Yoseph, O., and Tchernov, E. 1972. *On the Paleo-Ecological History of the Site of 'Ubeidiya*. (Proceedings of the Israel Academy of Sciences and Humanities.) Jerusalem.

Bright, J. 1981. *A History of Israel*. (3d ed.) Philadelphia.

Busink, T. A. 1970. *Der Tempel von Jerusalem*. Leiden.

Courtois, J. C. 1971. "Un nouveau sanctuaire de la fin de l'âge du Bronze et du début de l'âge du Fer à Enkomi dans L'île de Chypre." *Apud Alasia I.* (Mission Archéologique D'Alasia I.) Paris: 151–197.

Cross, F. M. 1962. "Yahweh and the God of the Patriarchs." *Harvard Theological Review* 55:225–259.

Desborough, V. R. d'A. 1964. *The Last Mycenaeans and Their Successors*. Oxford.

Dever, W. G. 1971. "The Peoples of Palestine in the MB I Period." *Harvard Theological Review* 64:197–226.

Dotan, T. 1967. *The Philistines and Their Material Culture*. Jerusalem. (Hebrew)

Dunayevsky, I., and Kempinski, A. 1973. "The Megiddo Temples." *Eretz-Israel* 11:8–29. (Hebrew)

Epstein, Claire. 1966. *Palestinian Bichrome Ware*. Leiden.

Ehrich, R. W., ed. 1965. *Chronologies in Old World Archaeology*. Chicago.

Franken, H. J. 1968. "Palestine in the Time of the Nineteenth Dynasty." *CAH* 67. (2d ed.) Cambridge.

Frankfort, H. 1954. *The Art and Architecture of the Ancient Orient*. Harmondsworth.

Frankfort, H. 1952. The Origin of Bit-Hilani. *Iraq* 14:120–130.

Furumark, A. 1944. "The Mycenaeans IIIC Pottery and Its Relation to Cypriote Fabrics." *Apud Opuscula Archaeologica, Acta Instituti Romani Regni Sueciae* 3:194–265.

Glueck, N. 1940. *The Other Side of the Jordan*. New Haven.

Gordon, C. H. 1958. "Abraham and the Merchants of Ur." *JNES* 17:28–31.

Grace, Virginia R. 1956. "The Canaanite Jar." *Apud* Weinberg, S. S., ed. *The Aegean and the Near East. Studies Presented to Hetty Goldman*. New York: 80–109.

Gray, J. 1964. *The Canaanites*. London.

Gurney, O. R. 1952. *The Hittites*. London.

Hallo, W. W., and Simpson, K. W. 1971. *The Ancient Near East*. New York.

Harden, D. B. 1962. *The Phoenicians*. London.

Helck, W. 1962. *Die Beziehungen Ägyptens zu Vorderasien im 3. und 2. Jahrtausend v. Chr.* Wiesbaden.

Helck, W. 1968. "Die Bedrohung Palästinas durch einwandernde Gruppen am Ende der 18. und am Anfang der 19. Dynastie." *VT* 18:472–480.

Hennessy, J. B. 1967. *The Foreign Relations of Palestine During the Early Bronze Age*. London.

Kantor, Helene. 1947. "The Aegean and the Orient in the Second Millennium B.C." *AJA* 51:1–103.

Kenyon, Kathleen M. 1957. *Digging Up Jericho*. London.

Kenyon, Kathleen M. 1979. *Archaeology in the Holy Land*. (4th ed.) New York.

Kitchen, K. A. 1964. "Some New Light on the Asiatic Wars of Ramses II." *JEA* 50:47–70.

Kitchen, K. A. 1968. "Further Notes on New Kingdom Chronology and History." *Chronique D'Égypte* 43:313–324.

Kitchen, K. A. 1973. *The Third Intermediate Period in Egypt (1100–650 B.C.)*. Warminster.

Kramer, S. N. 1963. *The Sumerians: Their History, Culture, and Character*. Chicago.

Malamat, A. 1976. "Origins and the Formative Period." *Apud* Ben Sasson, H. H., ed. *A History of the Jewish People*. Cambridge, Mass.: 3–87.

Mazar, B. 1969. "The Historical Background of the Book of Genesis." *JNES* 28:73–83.

Mazar, B. 1974. *Canaan and Israel*. Jerusalem. (Hebrew)

Mazar, B. 1975. *Cities and Districts in Eretz-Israel*. Jerusalem. (Hebrew)

Mellaart, J. 1975. *The Neolithic of the Near East*. London.

Nauman, R. 1971. *Architektur Kleinasiens*. (2d ed.) Tübingen.

Noth, M. 1960. *The History of Israel*. (2d ed.) London.

Oppenheim, A. L. 1964. *Ancient Mesopotamia*. London.

Ouellette, J. 1969. "La vestibule du Temple de Salomon était-il un Bit-Hilani?" *RB* 76:365–378.

Perrot, J. 1968. "La Prehistoire Palestinienne." *Supplément au Dictionnaire de la Bible*. Paris: 8:416–438.

Pritchard, J. B., ed. 1969. *Ancient Near Eastern Texts Relating to the Old Testament*. (3d ed. with supplement.) Princeton.

Rowley, H. H. 1950. *From Joseph to Joshua*. London.

Sasson, J. M. 1966. "Canaanite Maritime Involvement in the Second Millennium B.C." *JAOS* 86:126–138.

Schulman, A. R. 1964. "Some Remarks on the Military Background of the Amarna Period." *JARCE* 3:51–69.

Stewart, J. R. 1955. "When Did Base-Ring Ware First Occur in Palestine?" *BASOR* 138:47–49.

Stubbings, F. H. 1951. *Mycenaean Pottery from the Levant*. Cambridge.

Tadmor, H. 1976. "Period of the First Temple, the Babylonian Exile and the Restoration." *Apud* Ben Sasson, H. H., ed. *A History of the Jewish People*. Cambridge, Mass.: 91–182.

Thomas, D. W., ed. 1967. *Archaeology and Old Testament Study*. Oxford.

Van Seters, J. 1966. *The Hyksos, a New Investigation*. Yale.

de Vaux, R. 1946. "Les Patriarches Hébreux et les découvertes modernes." *RB* 53:321–348.

de Vaux, R. 1948. "Les Patriarches Hébreux et les découvertes modernes." *RB* 55:321–347.

de Vaux, R. 1949. "Les Patriarches Hébreux et les découvertes modernes." *RB* 56:5–36.

de Vaux, R. 1966. Palestine in the Early Bronze Age. *CAH* I_2. (3d ed.) Cambridge: 208–237.

de Vaux, R. 1969. "La Phénicie et les Peuples de la Mer." *Mélanges de l'Université St. Joseph* 45:481–498.

de Vaux, R. 1971. *Histoire ancienne d'Israel*. Paris.

Weippert, M. 1971. *Edom. Studien und Materialien zur Geschichte der Edomiter auf Grund schriftlicher und archäologischer Quellen*. Tübingen.

Weippert, M. 1971. "Abraham der Hebräischer." *Biblica* 52:407–432.

Woolley, Sir L. 1965. *The Kassite Period and the Period of the Assyrian Kings.* London.

Wright, G. E. 1939. "Iron: The Date of Its Introduction Into Common Use in Palestine." *AJA* 43:458–463.

Yadin, Y. 1970. "Megiddo of the Kings of Israel." *BA* 33:66–96.

PHOTOGRAPHS

1. The Tabun (Tannur) Cave. General view of the section.
Early and Middle Paleolithic

2. The el-Wad Cave

3. Beisamun in the Huleh Valley. Plastered Skulls *in situ.*
Pre-Pottery Neolithic B

4. Bone point from the Yonim Cave. Epipaleolithic

4A. Jericho. Brick with finger indentations. Neolithic

5. Munhata. Neolithic figurine

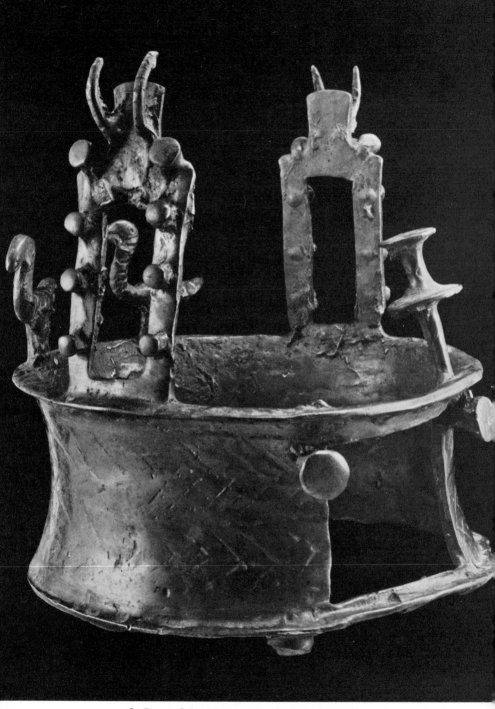

6. Cave of the Treasure in the Judean Wilderness.
Copper, crown-shaped object. Chalcolithic

7. Cave of the Treasure. Copper tubes. Chalcolithic

8. Cave of the Treasure. Hematite mace-heads. Chalcolithic

9. Azor. Ceramic ossuaries. Chalcolithic

10. Gilat. Figurine in terra-cotta of a woman seated on a stand with a churn on her head. Chalcolithic

11. Bab edh-Dhra'. Charnel house. Early Canaanite II

12. Arad. City wall and one of the towers. Early Canaanite II

13. Arad. Decorated jar. Early
    Canaanite II

14. Arad. Red burnished jar with
    dipper juglet. Early Canaanite II

14A. Arad. Ceramic house model. Early Canaanite II

15. En ha-Besor. Egyptian pottery vessels. Early Canaanite II

16. Nebi Salah. Fan-shaped scraper of flint. Early Canaanite II

17. Kefar Monash. Metal weapons and tools. Early Canaanite I–II

18. Ma'abarot. Fenestrated ax. Middle Canaanite I

19. Golan. Dolmen surrounded by stone enclosure. Middle Canaanite I

20. Tel Haror. General view of the ramparts from Middle Canaanite IIB

21. Tel Poleg. Pottery figurine of a fish with "Tell el-Yehudiyeh" decoration. Middle Canaanite IIA

22. Tel Dan. Mycenaean krater with chariot decoration. Late Canaanite

22A. Naharia. Mold for making bronze figurines. Middle Canaanite IIB

23. Lachish. Ewer with Proto-
    Canaanite inscription.
    Late Canaanite

24. Megiddo. Fragment of a
    cuneiform tablet from the
    Gilgamesh Epic.
    Late Canaanite

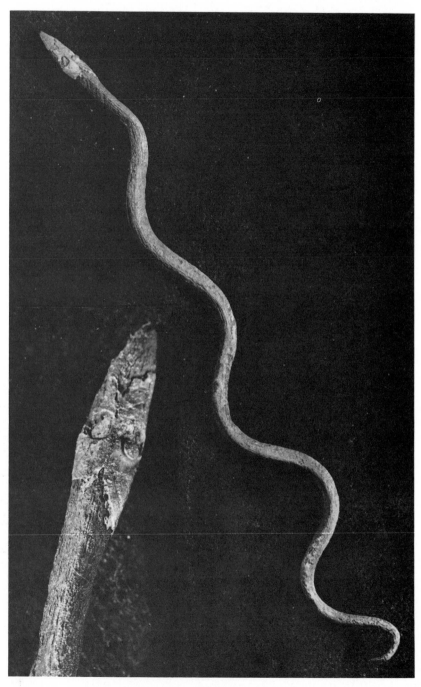

25. Timna. Copper snake from the Egyptian temple. Late Canaanite

26. The Negeb. A field of barley with Tel Arad in the background

27. Arad. The Iron Age fort under excavation

28. Arad. Wall of the Israelite fortress. Ninth century B.C.E.

29. Arad. Model of the reconstructed fortress.
Ninth-eighth centuries B.C.E.

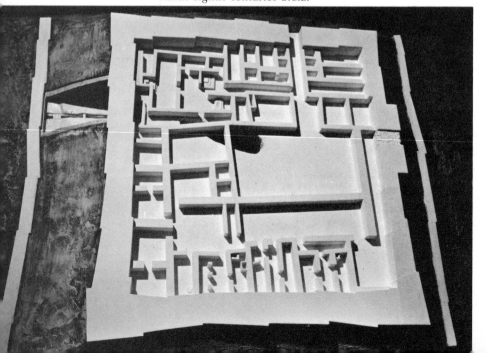

30. Arad. The holy of holies completely uncovered. Israelite period

31. Arad. Model of the reconstructed temple. Ninth century B.C.E.

32. Arad. The fortress commander's archive *in situ*

33. Arad. Hebrew ostracon "To Eliashib," commander of the fortress. Israelite period

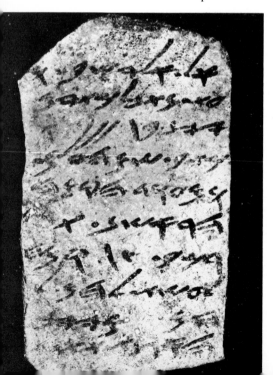

34. Arad. Stamp seal and its impr
sion, belonging to Eliashib, son
Ishiahu. Israelite period

35. Arad. Small bronze lion figurine. Israelite period

36. Arad. Implements made of bone

37. Arad. Head of Astarte figurine

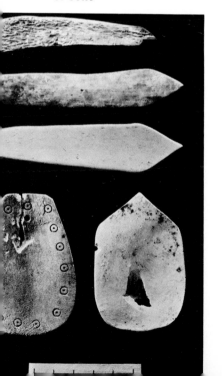

38. Arad. Fragment of an ornamented vessel made of a seashell.
Israelite period

39. Arad. Inscribed weights. Israelite period

40. Beer-sheba. General view of the excavations

41. Beer-sheba. The "governor's house," partially restored

42. Beer-sheba. The deep well just outside the city gate

43. Beer-sheba. Fertility goddess. Israelite period

44. Beer-sheba. The horned altar. Israelite period

45. Tel Qasila. Ritual bowl from the Philistine temple. Israelite period

46. Ramat Rahel. Fortress wall of ashlar masonry. Israelite period

47. Ramat Rahel. Proto-Aeolic capital from the fortress. Israelite period

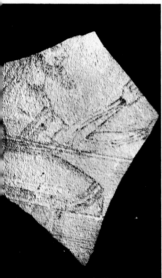

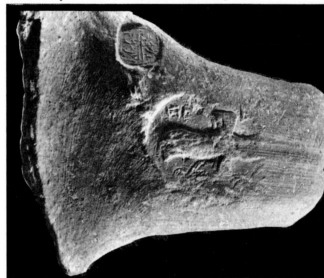

48. Ramat Rahel. Decorated sherd: a royal figure seated on his throne. Late Israelite period

49. Ramat Rahel. Jar handle bearing two seal impressions: "Nera (son of) Shibna," and "To the king—Hebron." Israelite period

50. Ramat Rahel. Reconstructed balustrade from the palace window. Israelite period

51. Samaria. Air view of the Israelite palace
(with Herodian temple at left)

52. Lachish. The temple of the Hellenistic period.
General view, 1968

53. Jerusalem. Burial cave of the Israelite period

54. Jerusalem. "Robinson's Arch" in the western wall

55. Jerusalem. View of the city from the south—"City of David"